The MEDIA Environment

The
MEDIA
Environment

MASS COMMUNICATIONS IN AMERICAN SOCIETY

by
Robert H. Stanley
and
Charles S. Steinberg

COMMUNICATION ARTS BOOKS

HASTINGS HOUSE, PUBLISHERS
New York 10016

Library of Congress Cataloging in Publication Data

Stanley, Robert H
  The media environment.

  (Communication arts books)
  Bibliography: p.
  Includes index.
  1. Mass media—United States. I. Steinberg, Charles
Side, 1913–   joint author. II. Title.
P92.U5S63   301.16′1′0973   75-43594
ISBN 0-8038-4681-9
ISBN 0-8038-4682-7 pbk.

Published simultaneously in Canada by
Saunders of Toronto, Ltd., Don Mills, Ontario

Printed in the United States of America

To Eija Ayravainen

Contents

gramming—Television News—"See It Now"—"Red
Channels"—Television Movies—Commercial Announcements—Network Entertainment Programming—Television Ratings

Preface

THE PURPOSE OF this text is to provide the reader with an informational frame of reference that will permit the formation of sound critical judgments concerning America's mass media institutions. The book examines the content, structure and control of the communications media in American society—particularly newspapers, motion pictures, and radio and television. Several pertinent questions are considered: How did the current media structure evolve? Who controls America's vast information and entertainment apparatus? In what ways does the economic posture of the media affect content? What are the legal foundations of the media's current regulatory structure? How effective are government and self-regulatory controls?

The sequence of the text is the result of the juxtaposition of literally thousands of bits of information. Very little information is presented which could be directly attributed to any one source. The authors were faced with the choice of inserting very extensive footnotes or none at all. The latter course was chosen. However, names and other details are given in the text where ideas are not part of the broad consensus in the field. Most of the published books consulted are listed at the end of the text to provide further readings. The numerous newspapers, magazines and periodicals examined include: *Advertising Age, Billboard, Box Office, Broadcasting, Columbia Journalism Re-*

view, *Editor and Publisher, Educational Broadcasting Review, Film Heritage, Fortune, Journal of Broadcasting, Journal of Communications, Journalism Quarterly, Media Decisions, Nation, Newsweek, New York Sunday News, New York Times, Playboy, Printers Ink, Public Opinion Quarterly, Publisher's Weekly, Quarterly of Film, Radio and Television* (formerly *Hollywood Quarterly*), *Television/Radio Age, Television Digest, Time, TV Guide, Variety, Wall Street Journal, Washington Post,* as well as Congressional records and Federal Communications Commission, U.S. Court of Appeals, and U.S. Supreme Court pronouncements and decisions.

Acknowledgments

The authors wish to express their appreciation to the many people, some who prefer to remain anonymous, who provided valuable source material for this book. We wish particularly to thank William Behanna, of the A.C. Nielsen Co.; James Day, former president of National Educational Television; Laurie Rich and Lesley Slocum of the Television Information Office; Sidney Schreiber, attorney for the Motion Picture Association of America; Thomas Swafford, Vice-President of Program Practices at the CBS Television Network; and James Williams of the National Urban League. We also wish to thank our colleagues James Aronson, Samuel Fleishman and Ruth Ramsay for reading parts of the manuscript and offering critical suggestions and comments.

1

Social Aspects of Mass Communication

THE TERM "MEDIACRACY" has been coined to describe the contemporary absorption in mass communication. As the Nineteenth Century has come to be known as the Industrial Revolution age, so the Twentieth Century will surely be termed the age of the Mass Communications Revolution—the era of electric technology. Mass media are pervasive and ubiquitous and their influence is obviously profound. Modern man is living in an environment permeated by communications media. Virtually every city in the United States has at least one newspaper. Most people can watch three or more television channels. Movies are available on television nightly and at the theatre as well. National magazines, despite erosion, appear regularly on the newsstands and through mail subscription. Homes and cars are equipped with one or more radios. Transistors bring the world to the peripatetic listener, wherever he may be. Paperbacks are plentiful, and available. In this age of sophisticated technology, the electronic miracles forged by science enable one continuously to discover new ways to interact with others, not only within communities, but across the horizons, under the sea and even from the great void of outer space.

The development of newspapers, radio, television and motion pictures, and the growth of information technology and instantaneous global communication by means of orbiting satellites have provided potential benefits for mankind, at least some of which have been realized. Communications technology has increased the opportunity of education for those who were intellectually disenfranchised. It has made information available quickly and cheaply to the masses. It has offered, through the instrumentality of radio and television news and public affairs programs, a unique opportunity for citizen awareness of, and participation in, the process of government. With the development of sophisticated means of communication, man was able to move out of the insularity of primitive living and to develop codes of laws, systems of epistemology and metaphysics—in short, a culture and a civilization. But this sophistication posed problems—the unfortunate discontents of urban civilization, the problems of mass education and the challenges of new ways of preserving knowledge through the techniques of automation and information storage. Because of the phenomenon of cultural lag, modern man finds it difficult to bring his sociology and psychology up to the level of the scientific achievements of the technological revolution. Technology is moving ahead so rapidly that it threatens constantly to leap far beyond man's ability to keep abreast of it. The demand for information is voracious and the techniques for information gathering are available, but the utilization and interpretation of data are still traditional from an epistemological point of view. Man is only beginning to comprehend the intricate and complex variables inherent in the process of human communication, whether it be interpersonal or mass.

The Communication Process

How does one define the complex transaction of verbal (and non-verbal) interaction which we call communication? Communication is a behavioral process which involves both verbal and non-verbal codes. Through the flow of communication, history becomes possible and meaningful. The fundamental process of human communication is deceptively simple. Basically the human communication phenomenon can be resolved into the scheme of who says what, in which channel, to whom and with what effect. This simplicity would pose no problems if all human communication were reduced to such comments as, "it will rain tomorrow" or even such denotative and verifiable statements as "that is a car." But human communication deals not only with facts, but with ideas; not only with direction or information, but with emotion. And, as one goes higher in the level of abstraction to such statements as "all college students are nonconformists," communication and meaning become a vastly more complicated affair.

If communication is to occur between two or more individuals, the participants must have some common realm of experience, or reference frame. The initiator of a message can put mental images into language, or symbols, only in terms of his own experience. The receiver can convert the symbols back into mental pictures only in terms of *his* own experience. Where their experiences have a common basis for interaction, communication will occur. Obviously, the individuals must speak the same language if verbal communication is to occur. It would be impossible for a Russian to communicate verbally with an Englishman if neither spoke the other's language. But even within the same symbol system, language difficulties may arise. For example, the use of highly specialized language may cause difficulty. Most laymen who have tried to struggle through a highly abstruse treatise have experienced this difficulty.

Colloquialisms may also cause communication breakdown to the uninitiated. Imagine the difficulty that foreigners to American shores would have with phrases such as: "My girdle is killing me," or "She's over the hill." In addition, patterns of intonation and timing affect interpretation. Take for example the sentence: "He *would have died,* doctor, if you had *not* operated?" Is the patient alive or dead? It depends on the emphasis given to the sentence.

More perplexing are the many technical and psychological impediments to clear communication. The individual, by virtue of past experiences, has developed his own frame of reference and set of values. Learning has taken place, and "communication bias" has taken hold as a result. What has been absorbed in this process of acquisition of knowledge tends not only to enlighten and to orient, but also to predispose to certain conditioned responses when stimuli occur. Positive or known experiences tend to elicit positive responses, while unfamiliar stimuli may bring about negative responses. That which gratifies the ego is accepted. That which does not bring about ego gratification tends to be rejected. Since these dispositions are formed by the triumphs and embarrassments of the past, they are not lightly discarded. Communication is interpreted by an individual basically in terms of his value system, expectancy set, and social and educational orientation. If ideas do not cohere with past experiences, they are frequently rejected out of hand as either absurd or radical. And when impasses of this kind develop, communication quickly becomes blocked and frustrated. What has been learned in the past becomes an important building block for future experience. Our social structure, to a great extent, tends to perpetuate barriers to communication which find their bases in age differences, sex differences, as well as in economic, political and religious differences. Man finds it most comforting, from an ego standpoint, to communicate with those whose experiences are similar, and with whom he can most readily relate or identify. Consequently, under certain circumstances, he employs such self protective mechanisms as selective exposure, selective perception, and selective retention. Considering all the possible breakdowns that can occur within any communication situation, it is miraculous that meaning is ever transferred from sender to receiver with any degree of accuracy or efficiency.

The likelihood of communication breakdown becomes progressively greater as the variables in the basic model increase and become more complex and abstract. For example, in a mass media situation the sender is an institution, the channel is some form of electrical energy or typography, the message is rapidly reproduced and distributed, and the receiver is a mass of people. A newspaper or a television program is the result of a multiplicity of efforts, involving creative talent, sales techniques, production facilities, advertising, promotion and electronics. And these represent only the "sending" side of the communication nexus, for communication is not complete without both a receiving audience and the transmission of content or message. In the mass media, the audience is heterogeneous. Indeed, there is not a single mass audience, but rather a multiplicity of audiences, or publics, which coalesce into the mass. The public for mass media, particularly in a democratic society, is not monolithic, but variegated and pluralistic. The mass media which direct messages to the public include radio, television, newspapers, national magazines, motion pictures and, to some extent, books—particularly paperbacks.

Media Effects

The effects of the development of communications media, beginning with print and extending through the present age of coaxial cable and satellites, are only beginning to be appraised. Controlled scientific research has, as yet, yielded little knowledge of how the media interact with society. Certain results of the revolution in mass communications are apparent. Vast economic changes were wrought by such startling technical developments as moveable type, telephony, radio and television. The techniques for gathering, storing and supplying information are miraculous and sophisticated, but one's grasp of the psychological and sociological implications of the communications revolution are still secondary to technological expertise. Once again, cultural lag persists.

The techniques of the social sciences are not as quantitatively accurate as those of the physical sciences, nor are the media themselves as amenable to empirical research. The media are volatile and changing. Society itself is in a state of becoming. Social scientists are in many ways the alchemists of the Twentieth Century. Some would contend that joining the words "social" and "science" constitutes a nonsequitur, so great—in their view—is the disparity between the social and physical sciences.

As a result, diverse, and in large part, unsubstantiated theories have been developed to encompass and explain the social implications of technological achievements in communication. The mathematicians present a structural theory in terms of integers and quantification of communications data. Communication philosophers, like Marshall McLuhan, offer speculative "probes" into the effects of communication media. Other disciplines, such as psychology, sociology and semantics, provide alternative, but related, ways of understanding the development and functions of mass communications.

Information Theory

Claude Shannon and Warren Weaver have applied the concepts of engineering and mathematics to the process of communication, with particular emphasis on linear transmission of communications data, or content, from sender to receiver. The original intent of their research, which is subsumed under the rubric of information theory, was to guide the efforts of engineers in finding the most efficient way of transmitting electrical signals from one location to another.

Information theory breaks down communication into its smallest components. The basic unit in this theory is a "bit," for binary digit. Breaking down any message into a code of just two symbols, allows information to be expressed electrically as "on" or "off." This makes it possible to consider different forms of communication—pictures, voices, telegraph signals—as using the same "language." The primary concern of information theorists is to calculate the amount of information that can be transmitted over communication channels with a minimum amount of distortion or noise.

Although this theory was designed to describe the behavior of mechanical devices, it has been adapted to countless human communication situations. Methods developed on unselective systems like telephones do not prove particularly worthwhile in studying the highly selective nature of human communication. Information theory measures communication without regard to meaning and therefore divests human communication of its significative aspects.

Precisely what relevance information theory has to understanding the process of mass communication remains to be established. It does provide an effective instrument for measuring the quantitative flow of information and allows for the diagnosis of technical breakdowns in the information flow. The difficulty with applying the information theory to communication behavior is that it tends to denigrate legitimate semantic implications in favor of an approach that is concerned basically with "transmission" of pure technology. The information theorists have provided the communications discipline with a more precise vocabulary to describe communication phenomena. Such terms as "bit," "entrophy," "noise" and "feedback" were quickly integrated into the communication nomenclature and popularized to describe a wide variety of communicative behavior. However, too frequently the use of this language is pretentious and not easily comprehended.

If communication is to be consummated successfully there must be some agreed-upon logic of language, some basic consensus as to common and accepted meaning. And for meaning to have meaning, so to speak, there must be some agreed-upon method of studying the relationship of signs to each other, to things in the external world and to other people involved in the communications chain. Communication, then, is not only mechanical or technical, but a dynamic and functional process by which individuals interact with each other and pass on their successes—and their failures—from one decade to another, from one generation to another. It is precisely because communication in a mass society is complicated that it has generated varying theories as to its function and effect in human affairs.

McLuhan: The Grand Theorist

Few communication theorists have generated as much controversy and debate as Herbert Marshall McLuhan—the grand free-for-all theorizer about media effects. His unique theory about the impact of communication media is presented in his two major works—*The Gutenberg Galaxy* (1962) and *Understanding Media* (1964). The theory states, quite simply, that the medium itself is the message—media, in and of themselves and regardless of the messages they communicate, exert a compelling influence on man and society. His theory anchors societal change in the transformations of communications media.

McLuhan advances the notion that communication media dramatically alter sensory organization and thought; thereby altering society. To understand the impact of media, certain basic assumptions must be accepted, chief among which is the idea that media alter sense ratios or patterns of perception. Media are seen as extensions of human abilities and senses that affect sensory balance. They are, in effect, extensions of our nervous system. Print, states McLuhan, jolted man out of the cohesiveness of tribal society into a period of social fragmentation. Tribal man existed in a harmonious balance of the senses, perceiving the world through hearing, smell, touch, sight and taste equally. The alphabet gave dominance to the eye. Moveable type accelerated this process and society was inexorably reshaped. The invention of the telegraph heralded the coming of the electronics revolution (radio, films, television, telephone, computer) which will eventually "retribalize" man by restoring his sensory balance. Through a kind of Hegelian thesis and antithesis, man will achieve a "synesthesia" of all his senses.

Media, according to McLuhan, are either "hot" or "cool." A hot medium (print, radio, film, photography) is one that extends a single sense with high definition—a complete filling in of data by the medium. Hot media are low participation, or completion by the audience. Radio is a hot medium because it provides a large amount of high-definition auditory information. In a cool medium, the audience is an active constituent of the viewing or listening experience. Cool media are high in participation. Television is a cool medium because it is visually low in data, thus insuring a high degree of audience involvement. (The television image offers some three million dots per second to the receiver from which he perceives only a few dozen each instant.)

McLuhan's theory of the media generates some perplexing problems for the conventional wisdom. The classic concepts of communication do not apply. Since content is consigned to limbo in favor of the medium as message, it makes little difference whether television carries Shakespeare or situation comedy, whether programs are deemed benign or violent. One book is not discernibly different from another in its impact. Tolstoy and popular novelist Harold Robbins are simply "typography." One McLuhan critic is reminded of the late Jean Harlow's quip when asked what she wanted for her birthday: "Don't buy me a book; I got a book."

Since the medium, rather than content, comprises the message, problems of effect and feedback are equally insignificant. By a "technological extension of consciousness" man would have no moral values with which to concern himself, for he would develop a "servo-mechanism" toward a computerized society. Man is then confronted with what the distinguished scientist-humanist René Dubos called "undisciplined technology." The new, non-print world can do without literature or the press, for man "does not need words any more than the digital computer needs numbers." Literature and language—the basic stuff of art and of communication—will be transcended by a "general cosmic consciousness."

Paradoxically, however, McLuhan has expressed the conviction that a medium like television demands a "creative participant response." But this response must be to the medium itself and not to what it conveys for, seemingly, man need no longer concern himself with the creative or moral implications of mass media or with value judgments about them. Unfortunately, this separation of form from content is artificial; in communication form and substance are inseparable. Furthermore, a philosophy which resigns itself and consigns man to become a "servo-mechanism" of electric technology is spurious and self-defeating, for it truly ignores the social and ethical implications of mass communications. The effect of mass media is irrelevant if the medium, rather than communication content, is the message. It is not only the media which have revolutionized the ways in which media are used. Who says what to whom under what circumstances and with what effect cannot be delegated to the computer alone to determine. The ethical alternatives and the value judgments inhere in man.

McLuhan's theory, however provocative, is more significant for what it omits than for what it includes. The medium is not the message, although there is little doubt that the mass media, by the very act of transmission, do have considerable effect on the message, and consequently on society. We live in a constant flow of communications stimuli, for the mass media impinge on every aspect of our existence. There is something to be said for McLuhan's basic thesis, if one doesn't push it too far. Many are convinced that he does.

An Eclectic Approach

No one theory can encompass or fully clarify the extraordinarily complicated process of mass communication. The effects of mass media are difficult to explain or predict for several reasons. The media function through a complex nexus of mediating influences. There is no direct communication-response link. Other stimuli intervene, and there is a time lapse between the origination of the message and the receiver's response. An individual responds to media content in terms of many factors. He brings his training, orientation and judgment to the communication. The personality of the communicator and communicant, the nature of the communication content, the particular medium through which the message flows and the reaction of the communicant's reference group all affect communication. In the balance between media and environment, each communicant will respond in terms of his own value system, his orientation and his status in the peer group. In mass communication, too, no man is an island.

Despite the thrust and reach of mass media, interpersonal communication still tends to play an ultimate and powerful role in influencing opinion and behavior. Mass media messages are mediated by personal discussion before decisions are made and courses of action taken. The impact of media is buttressed by the influence of home, school, church and the peer group. The media entertain and inform and sell products and even ideas. But each of these messages must filter through interpersonal networks of communication.

The interrelationships between interpersonal and mass communication can be seen by examining the mass hysteria inadvertently precipitated by the Mercury Theatre on the Air's radio adaptation of H. G. Wells' *War of the Worlds*. The radio play, which was broadcast on the Columbia Broadcasting System's coast-to-coast network from 8 to 9 o'clock on the evening of October 30, 1938, simulated a music program with periodic interruptions for "news bulletins." The first news bulletin noted that a series of gas explosions had erupted on the planet Mars and subsequent news reports and "on-the-scene" broadcasts described the landing of a cylindrical shaped object at Grovers Mill, New Jersey, and the emergence from the cylinder of strange creatures armed with "death rays."

The broadcast caused widespread panic, disrupting households, interrupting religious services and creating traffic jams. Dozens of adults required medical treatment for shock and hysteria. Thousands of people called the police, and newspapers and radio stations were overwhelmed with telephone calls. *The New York Times* received a total of 875, while at the *Daily News* 1,100 calls flooded the switch board. Priests were deluged with requests to hear final confessions from panic stricken transgressors. Ministers were sought by parishioners desiring spiritual consolation. An electrical blackout near Seattle, Washington, occurred almost simultaneously with the arrival of the Martians on the CBS broadcast. Women fainted and men prepared to take their families into the mountains for security. In the days following the broadcast, an enterprising farmer in Grovers Mill charged 50¢ per parking space for the hundreds of cars that descended on his farm bringing people who wanted to see the location "where the Martians landed." Individuals who claimed they were injured because of the broadcast filed damage suits totaling $750,000, none of which stood up in court.

Why did the broadcast have such an incredible effect? Why had people failed to associate the presentation with the newspaper listing of the program? Why did they ignore the three announcements made during the program emphasizing its fictional nature?

An examination of some of the factors operating during the broadcast may help to explain its impact. The economic depression of the early 1930s was still vivid in the minds of many adults. The shadow of war was moving toward America in 1938—the broadcast occurred soon after the Munich crises and fear about impending war was prevalent throughout the United States. As a result of the war scare, people were accustomed to frequent interruptions in the regularly scheduled programs for reports about the potential crisis. Apparently, *previous experience* had *conditioned* people to interpret the Martian invasion as a legitimate news bulletin.

A large portion of the American public, particularly those in lower income brackets, relied more on the radio than on newspapers for their news. Radio was shown to have a higher degree of credibility for many listeners. People *expected* to hear the truth on radio newscasts. Many people telephoned their friends and neighbors seeking verification of the invasion, or to warn them of the threat. *Interpersonal networks* of communication reinforced the mass media message. There were many contributory causes which induced the widespread panic.

Although the impact of media is formidable, it is tempered by psychological set, previous experience, conditioned behavior, and by group customs and value judgments. In other words, the content of mass communications goes through the crucible of experience, discussion and interaction. Media influence behavior but are neither the sole, nor the strongest, determinant of that behavior.

Violence and the Media

The lack of an all-encompassing theory of media effects helps to explain why scientific research has yielded no demonstrable cause-and-effect relationship between violence on media and violence in society. There is hardly likely to be a clear statement of any correlation until much more sophisticated parameters of judgment are established than now exist. Only short-term effects of the mass media in experiments conducted under artifically controlled circumstances can be subjected to rigorous empirical analyses at this time. Even under the most carefully structured and promulgated research conditions, it is extremely difficult to show by empirical evidence that there is a direct correlation between media violence and violence in society. It can only be assumed, if not proved, that violence in the media may trigger violence in individuals psychologically predisposed to commit violence; or that depictions of violence may inure the public to the many violent acts which occur in society.

The lack of irrefutable evidence should not absolve the press, motion pictures and television from their respective obligations to see to it that violence, when portrayed, is not only integral to the content, but that it is also portrayed with literary taste and moral decency. Violence which does affect and involve the viewer both morally and emotionally, violence which is integral to the portrayal of character and events, which is drawn from aesthetic and creative resources may, conceivably, have a salutary effect, as critics believe it has in the Greek or Shakespearian tragedies. Popular art need not aspire to high culture in order to conform to the Aristotelian concept of violent tragedy as a catharsis that purges the emotions of fear and pity. Violence, as well as sex, must be recognized as very much part of the human condition. In terms of this recognition, violence presented on the media should be condemned only when it is presented for its own sake, when it exploits its audience and when its consequences are morally and socially indefensible. In the last analysis, the media cannot pretend that violence does not exist. Those who would prefer to avoid exposure to media portrayal of violence have the option to turn off the set or close the book.

Media Content

The inclination to turn off the set, however, is probably more a consequence of boredom than an aversion to brutality. A sense of eventlessness and sameness too frequently prevails in the media. Media content, particularly in television, tends to be bland and irrelevant. Even news programming glosses over critical issues. What passes for in-depth analysis of urban crises, government surveillance, military insurgency, corporate expansion, and other social, political and economic problems is fundamentally superficial.

The superficiality and irrelevance of certain media content may be attributed, at least in part, to the communication industry's consumer-pleasing economic posture which reflects a fear of offending or upsetting audiences with controversial material. Certainly some of the limitations of television and, to a lesser extent, motion pictures stem from the enormous cost of production and the resultant need to reach and attempt to please the largest possible audience. As a rule of thumb, the evaluation of the worth of a program or movie is not by an aesthetic poll or a determination of public enlightment, but by the sheer "tonnage" or numbers who are watching. Size of movie attendance or of the television audience are the determinants of success, even though the critical reaction may be negative. Paradoxically, the goal and the dilemma of the mass media is to attract the greatest number of people and give some degree of pleasure to most of them. It is a formidable and frequently an impossible task.

The media can claim, with some truth, that what is presented does conform to what the public wants, for the public can always express its opinions and exercise its options by turning to other activities. Achieving a balanced effort, whereby the majority of the public gets not only what it appears to want, but also receives exposure to ideas and information which may ultimately prove beneficial and rewarding, is no easy task. By programming for majority interests and needs and, at the same time, considering the legitimate needs of minority publics American television and motion pictures have occasionally accomplished this goal. But many critics believe that "occasionally" is not enough.

Other communication media also have limitations attributable in part to economics. The number of national magazines in publication has dwindled through a slow process of erosion over the past 15 years. There are, however, several thousand publications designed for circulation to large minority audiences. Some of the prestige business and news magazines show an unfortunate inclination to reflect, and to strive to maintain, the status quo, rather than the keen spirit of inquiry which should be the goal of all good journalism. The newspaper field has also grown smaller. Competition for circulation has forced many papers to fight the competitive battle, not on journalistic grounds, but through the device of adding comics and popular syndicated features, with an unfortunate paucity of reportorial coverage in such areas as international news and foreign affairs, science and medicine, art or book reviews.

The medium which offers the consumer the greatest choice is the book, paradoxically the form with the least mass circulation. Particularly since the inexpensive paperback has become available, the public does not lack a wide choice of titles—in both fiction and non-fiction. Even though the distribution through newsstands and drug counters has, in the opinion of some critics, cheapened the book business because of the plethora of lurid titles on display, there is still a variety of good literature to be found and purchased cheaply. The paperback revolution has made literature available to greater numbers of readers than ever before, but increase in readers has not been paralleled by a necessary increase in good bookstores or public libraries. In an age of literacy, it is a profoundly discouraging sign that some of America's large urban library systems have to curtail services and hours because of a shortage of funds for necessary maintenance.

Although the proliferation of communication media has reached a point where it would seem improbable for an individual to be without access to some medium, there are still sectors within the society which remain virtually without information, or where what little information is conveyed is simply inadequate and non-meaningful. There is a pressing need for the media to engage in a dynamic spirit of inquiry which will stimulate the imagination and prod the intelligence of all those who will read, listen and view. Although at least some segments of the public, owing to mass media, are more informed about political and economic issues than ever before, it does not follow that they have developed greater *comprehension* or better understanding of the *meaning* of social and political phenomena. There is little evidence to show that inundating the public with the stimuli from many media increases the ability to grasp concepts, make distinctions, and, above all, arrive at intelligent and useful decisions on the major problems in the world community.

It may be premature to attempt to assess the effects of mass communications on contemporary civilization. And yet, if man is to survive the travail of the Twentieth Century he must strive to understand the character, structure and impact of the communications media. The technology of mass communication provides the one best hope for understanding and cooperation throughout the world. Indeed, it may be the last hope for the successful survival of man in the age of the missile and the hydrogen bomb. What is now needed is to match superb hardware with equally superb dedication to intelligent inquiry, high standards of performance and informed judgment.

2

The Phenomenon of Print

THE DEVELOPMENT OF PRINTING revolutionized the entire fabric of civilization, making literacy and education available to the masses and ultimately opening the way to mass communication. The book was the first dividend of print, and it is still the most culturally significant. Despite the gloom of pessimists who assert that the electronic media have stifled the desire to read, the amazing growth of book publishing continues each year.

Not only are there an unprecedented number of hardcover books being published, but the paperback has radically altered publishing by bringing the classics, educational volumes, and reprints of popular fiction and non-fiction to more readers than ever before in history. Books which heretofore were available only in bookstores are now also sold in drug and department stores, airline and railroad terminals, supermarkets and other popular consumer locations. The millions of paperbacks in circulation literally have made the book a medium of mass communication.

The Invention of Print

The book, as we know it today, could not have become the indispensable means of communication it is if it had not been for the invention of printing, perhaps the most notable process ever devised by man. Certainly the invention of printing by means of moveable metal type changed the face of civilization in a way accomplished by few other developments, and many scholars consider the advent of print

15

the most important cultural explosion in world history. Without print, the Industrial Revolution of the Nineteenth Century and the contemporary electronic revolution would never have occurred. The concept of moveable type entails the use of individual pieces of metal cast for each letter of the alphabet. Originally, the metal letters were wedged together into a wooden form to make up a single page. After a sufficient number of copies had been made, the letters were reorganized into words for the second page, and so forth.

The invention of this revolutionary process is generally attributed to Johannes Gutenberg. Born in Mainz, Gutenberg is known to have moved to Strasbourg where, in the middle of the Fifteenth Century, with two associates, he began experimenting with a device which was to become a printing press. His famous Gutenberg Bible is considered historically the first book produced by moveable type in Europe. The production of printed books, therefore, began in Mainz, Germany.

The military and political upheavals which shook Europe in the Fifteenth Century caused many of the German printers to migrate to other countries. In this way, the art of printing spread successfully to France, Switzerland, Spain and Italy. Such craftsmen as Nicolas Jensen, a Frenchman, and the famous Aldus Manutius produced books of brilliant type design and went far beyond the primitive typographical efforts of Gutenberg. Manutius, in particular, combined fine typography with an excellent selection of books, including editions of the works of Aristotle. Thus did the book publishing industry contribute to the remarkable revival of classical learning which characterized the Renaissance.

Historical evidence reveals that the first volume in the English language, brought out by William Caxton, was printed not in England but in Belgium. Caxton, a name not unfamiliar to students of English literature, went from London to Belgium and eventually entered the service of the Duchess of Burgundy. At that time, and under the encouragement of the Duchess, he translated into English a volume entitled *Recuyell of the Hystroyes of Troye*. Caxton then undertook to publish copies of the translation and, as a result, he became the first to publish in the English language. Returning to England in 1476, Caxton set up his own print shop where he brought out, among other books, an historic and famous landmark in English printing, the Caxton edition of Chaucer's *Canterbury Tales*. Caxton's contribution, when compared to the typography that was being accomplished on the continent, was not aesthetic but historical in significance. His books were not fine printing, but he did publish some of the major literary works of the period, such as the Chaucer edition. This is his claim to fame in the history of both literature and bookmaking in England.

Throughout Europe, however, the intellectual quickening engendered by the Renaissance, along with the fact that printing was available and books could now be produced, resulted in an outpouring of volumes, particularly of the Bible. The publication of books became an integral part of the excitement of the revival of learning in an age of discovery and of intrepid exploration. Printing helped bring about the transition from the philosophy of the medieval era to the new and exciting cultural perspectives of the Renaissance. Printing flourished, particularly on the European continent where some of the most beautiful books, such as the illustrated *Book of the Hours,* were produced. These volumes were for the most part superb examples of fine typography, as were the many notable reproductions of the classics of Greece and Rome which were printed at that time.

The works of certain bookmakers stand out as landmarks at a period when the whole spectrum of the arts was flourishing. Christopher Plantin on the continent and John Baskerville in England are notable examples, although removed from each other both in location and in time of production. Plantin was French, but worked in Antwerp to escape religious persecution. He started a publishing business in the Sixteenth Century, bringing out editions of the classics and engaging in printing books as well as in publishing them. Because a prayer book which he published did not adhere to the religious and political convictions of the authorities, Plantin went to Paris where he published many magnificent examples of fine printing. His plant became the greatest and most productive in all of Europe, publishing among many volumes the famous Polyglot Bible which could be read simultaneously in Greek and Latin. Its ornamental title page announced that it was a publication of the sacred Bible in "Hebraice, Chaldean, Graece and Latine." Plantin was one of the great contributors to the development of the printed book.

In England, the great name in printing was John Baskerville who worked in the Eighteenth Century. Beginning as clergyman and teacher, Baskerville eventually turned to printing as a hobby. Since he was amply provided for and needed no sponsor, Baskerville was able to experiment painstakingly at perfecting the art of printing fine books on fine paper. He succeeded in developing a new kind of paper and a printing process never before used either on the continent or in England, finally bringing out an edition of the works of the Latin poet, Virgil. Successful with this effort, he then turned to an edition of Milton's *Paradise Lost* which was, again, beautiful in terms of lettering, color and print. Baskerville's work is not flamboyant, for his objective was clarity and beauty of line. He paid great attention to layout and spacing; and the type face he invented became famous and is still used widely today.

Baskerville's work produced what was probably the finest and clearest bookmaking of any printer in Europe. His style and typography were adopted by the famous Didot printers in France, and Baskerville also influenced another famous originator of type face, Giambattista Bodoni, an Italian printer whose typography is also widely used in contemporary book design and printing. Bodoni's work, however, was also influenced stylistically by the Far East. Most Eighteenth Century printing on the continent was. both ornamental and flamboyant, but Bodoni's work reflected a more classical approach to the art.

Print in Colonial Times

The first printing presses in the American colonies were established in the Seventeenth Century in Massachusetts Bay Colony. In the early American colonies, Jose Glover, an English curate, sparked the setting up of a college and printing establishment with a press he had brought from England with the assistance of Matthew Day. It was Day who established a printing press at Harvard College and who issued the Book of Psalms in 1640. Day's work was carried on by Samuel Green who brought out several books printed in Indian languages, which were designed to convert the natives to Christianity. Green also published the first American edition of the Holy Bible, in Indian languages and English, encompassing both Old and New Testament.

The Emergence of the American Newspaper

Most of the presses in the New World produced both books and newspapers. The first American newspaper was published by a man of questionable integrity named Benjamin Harris, who had fled England because what he printed there created such difficulty with the authorities that he was forced to leave and come to the colonies. He was to fare no better in America. In 1690 he published *Publick Occurrences Both Foreign and Domestik* in Boston. The paper had three pages with two columns on each page. A fourth page was blank, except for a dedication to "Memorable Occurrences of Divine Providence," and provided an opportunity for readers to add their own news before sending the paper to friends who lived elsewhere. Harris ran true to form in the colonies. The press was licensed; no printing was permitted without official sanction. Since Harris had no official license to publish, and particularly because he presented information certain to offend allies of the colonial government, he was put out of business after the first issue. Among his other derelictions, he impugned the morals of the King of France.

The second newspaper in the colonies was the *Boston News-Letter,* published in 1704, 14 years after Harris' abortive attempt, by the Boston postmaster, John Campbell, and printed in the shop of Bartholomew Green. This sheet created no problem, because Campbell, as postmaster, operated under the official license and took pains to state in print that the *Boston News-Letter* was published by permission of the government authorities. Campbell's newspaper eventually ran into competition when, in 1719, William Brooker started the *Boston Gazette.* Brooker had succeeded Campbell as postmaster and he, too, published under authority. Campbell, having prospered in business affairs, lost interest in his newspaper and it was inherited by Bartholomew Green. With this succession, a pattern of printer as publisher, editor and seller became established.

The style of early colonial journalism was crude, as might be expected. Literacy was not widespread, and printers were neither men of learning nor journalists in anything resembling the contemporary meaning of the term. It was not until the journeyman printer as publisher was succeeded by genuinely independent newspaper editors that a style which can be called truly journalistic developed.

One of the early editors who revealed a talent for writing was James Franklin, who published the *New England Courant* in 1721. This newspaper was a cut above its contemporaries in that it was literate, flavorsome and carried articles of genuine human interest to its readers. It was also outspoken. This was, by far, the most literate paper to appear to that point. It came about because Franklin, a printer, had lost the contract to print the *Boston Gazette* after it was taken over by Philip Musgrave, who then decided to publish his own newspaper. The *Courant* thereafter became the third newspaper to appear, in competition with the *Boston Gazette* and the *Boston News-Letter*. It was Franklin's *New England Courant* which showed the first spirit of independence against the rigid authoritarianism of the licensing system and which printed material critical of colonial rule. Ostensibly, Franklin undertook a campaign in print against research that was underway to develop a vaccine for smallpox, a disease that was epidemic at the time. Actually, the campaign fulminated against the pompous and insufferably disciplinarian attitude of Cotton Mather, a clergyman who demanded unquestioning obedience to authority, both in his addresses and his pamphlets. Mather fought back through the instrument of rival newspapers, but Franklin's editorial crusade had established for the first time that a newspaper was not a passive journal, but a genuine medium of communications with a powerful ability to reflect and influence public opinion. James Franklin was an editor with a point of view, a tough-fibered journalist who did not succumb easily to authority and whose strong position contributed significantly toward freeing the press from the shackles of censorship. It was in the *New England Courant* that Benjamin Franklin's felicitous articles signed by "Silence Dogood" first appeared.

When James Franklin was temporarily imprisoned because of his criticism of the administration, Benjamin Franklin (James' younger brother) through a legal maneuver, was able to assume the position of editor of the *New England Courant*. In actuality, he was a titular head and still served as apprentice to his imprisoned brother. Benjamin Franklin was America's Renaissance man, the true "man for all seasons." After taking over the paper, he wrote urbane and entertaining pieces which prodded without inviting trouble. Ben's success caused James to become jealous of him and, after several quarrels, Ben fled to New York.

In 1729, Ben established the *Pennsylvania Gazette* in Philadelphia which almost at once became the best newspaper to appear in the colonies. This publication and Andrew Bradford's *The American Weekly Mercury*, a rival to the *Gazette*, were the first newspapers to appear outside New England, and the *Pennsylvania Gazette* proved, under Franklin's direction, to be one of America's fine early newspapers. Since it was almost entirely written and edited by Ben, it was, as might be expected, literate, pointed and sophisticated in character—a distinct improvement over the perfunctory journalism of the period. Although the paper was conservative, it was never subservient to the authorities. In 1725, William Bradford published the *New York Gazette,* the state's first newspaper. In 1733, the *New York Weekly Journal* appeared and became one of the first colonial newspapers to defy the authority of the British Crown and to take an editorial position in favor of the demands and dissatisfactions of the colonial people.

The *New York Weekly Journal* was edited by Bradford's former apprentice, John Peter Zenger, whose name today is synonymous with the battle for freedom of the press in America. History has credited Zenger with greater glory than he merited, for his case was more a symbol of press freedom than a concrete accomplishment. Zenger himself was not an outstanding figure. A combination of circumstances, including Zenger's criticism of Governor Cosby for allowing units of the French navy to move into New York Harbor, prompted Cosby to request that his Chief Justice, James Delancy, institute proceedings against Zenger. Finally, in 1734, Zenger was arrested and charged with criminal libel. When the case came to trial in 1735, Andrew Hamilton, the famed Philadelphia lawyer, offered his services in behalf of the accused.

Much of the importance of the case is derived from Hamilton's eloquent address to the jury. Hamilton, who was then in his 80s and had shoulder-length white hair, decided not to deny what Zenger had published, but to base his defense on the fundamental issues of free press. Zenger, argued Hamilton, could not be guilty unless what he printed was indeed libelous. To be libelous, said Hamilton, the words themselves must include seditious and malicious falsehoods. The jury found Zenger not guilty, and the Chief Justice did not set aside the verdict, although it was certainly within his power to do so. The idea of a free press was established philosophically, if not operationally. Hamilton won a moral victory. Libel laws were not changed for the next half century, but at least truth as the best defense against libel was finally enunciated in America.

By the middle of the century there were approximately 30 newspapers published regularly, five in Boston alone. Although there was the beginning of a trend toward bona fide editors, most newsmen were still publishers or booksellers. William Parks, with his publication of *The Maryland Gazette* in 1727, offered a far superior newspaper than had heretofore been published. Parks also established *The Virginia Gazette* in 1736 at Williamsburg, where his quaint print shop still stands as a permanent exhibit of the typical printing establishment of the period. The news in most publications contained information of political developments abroad, with particular reference to the impact on the colonies. Strong positions of pressure were taken by newspapers which inveighed against the colonies or against England. The press, however, was still cautious not to offend political authority. It was the passing of the Stamp Act in 1765, considered highly inimical to the functioning of a free press, which evoked the wrath of many newspapers against England. The Act placed a heavy tax on paper used in publishing newspapers and on all legal documents. Thus, the law alienated both journalists and lawyers. Newspapers began vehemently to argue the revolutionary philosophy.

Typical of the militant newspapers was the *Boston Gazette and Country Journal,* descendant of the second newspaper published in the colonies. A frequent contributor to the *Gazette* was Samuel Adams, one of the most prolific journalists of his time. He was a master propagandist and instilled in his readers fierce hatred against the British. His quill was dipped in the venom of vituperation. He gave lurid descriptions of British soldiers beating small boys, violating matrons and raping young girls. English officials indignantly denied these charges but Bostonians, nevertheless, began to resent bitterly the presence of the soldiers. Adams, many historians believe, instigated the attack of British soldiers which led to the Boston Massacre in March 1770. Although the soldiers were acquitted by a jury of Massachusetts citizens, the "massacre" became a *cause célèbre* for colonial newspapers providing an unparalleled opportunity to inflame the already outraged colonists.

There were some moderates among the colonial journalists; others staunchly took up the defense of the Crown. John Dickinson believed in the sanctity of property rights and free enterprise. His capitalist philosophy appeared in a series of articles entitled "Letters From a Farmer in Pennsylvania" which were printed in the *Pennsylvania Chronicle* and reprinted in other newspapers throughout the colonies.

Dickinson was unalterably opposed to revolution. However, he strongly favored "home rule" for the colonies, and resented English control over American foreign trade. Although Dickinson was contemptuous of the radicals, he did more than any other writer, except Sam Adams, to foment the spirit of revolution.

By 1775 war was inevitable and the press became increasingly partisan. In New York, James "Jemmy" Rivington's *New York Gazetteer* ceased to be objective after the battles of Lexington and Concord. Rivington, a man of keen literary talent, presented the cause of the British with skill and force, although his charges against the American leaders were often unfounded. In May of 1775, he was attacked and in November of the same year his print shop was destroyed—one of the first casualties of any war is free expression.

The Post-Revolution Press

The changes that occurred after the revolution were not quite as great as they first appeared. Economic interests and political ambitions took over as insurrectionary fervor diminished. The new order soon began to acquire disturbing similarities with the *ancien régime* that it had overthrown with so much violence.

The war had united large property owners, merchants, bankers, and manufacturers along with small farmers and wage earners in a common cause. With the end of the war, came an end to unity. The noble ideas that invariably form and nurture revolution rarely become realities.

In the interim period immediately after the war American journalism was most undistinguished. The quality of editorship improved but overt propaganda and partisanship were very much in evidence. The partisan press engaged in extreme vilification and outright lies. The target of their abuses was men of high station such as Washington, John Adams, Jefferson and Hamilton. George Washington, unlike Jefferson, had deep reservations about the nature and function of the press. Like many of his successors as President, he complained bitterly about those journalists who attacked him in print. The relationship of Washington with the press serves as a reminder to those who speak of a contemporary "credibility gap" that officialdom and the press have always had their antagonisms. Washington had about as difficult a time with the journalists as any President in American history with the exception, of course, of Richard M. Nixon.

There was bitter schism between Federalists and Democratic-Republicans, between the advocacy of states rights as against a strong central government. Alexander Hamilton established the *Gazette of the United States,* a Federalist newspaper edited by John Fenno, while Thomas Jefferson appeared to be the motivating spirit behind the *National Gazette.* The paper was edited by Philip Freneau, the "poet of the Revolution," who articulated the Jeffersonian philosophy. Freneau, writing under the name of "Brutus," attacked Hamilton vigorously and engaged in a series of journalistic jousts with Fenno.

One of the most vitriolic journals of the period was the *Philadelphia General Advertiser,* sometimes called the *Aurora.* Published by Benjamin Franklin Bache, grandson of Benjamin Franklin, it was viciously anti-Federalist. Bache was only 21 when he started his paper in 1790. Much of the newspaper's content was devoted to a virulent campaign against Washington and the Federalists. Bache went so far as to say that the nation had been debauched by Washington.

Although Jefferson pleaded for journalistic responsibility, the press was neither free nor responsible. Despite Jefferson's articulated idealism, the press was poisonous, malicious and irresponsible. But Jefferson's oft-quoted statement still exemplified the basic need and principle of a free and responsible press: "Were it left to me to decide whether we should have a government without newspapers, or newspapers without a government, I should not hesitate to prefer the latter." The public—and eventually journalists—evidently agreed, for in the long run America developed one of the freest and most responsible systems of journalism in the world.

At the close of the first quarter of the Nineteenth Century, there were several hundred newspapers in the United States. Most were distributed by subscription which cost from $6 to $10 a year in advance. They obviously were intended for people of means, since the average worker could not afford that much in a lump sum. There were about 20 daily newspapers throughout the colonies which sold for about 6¢ an issue. But most papers were still published on a weekly basis, and most were in the East where the ups and downs of politics were reflected in a predominantly party press.

But factionalism was receding before a more colorful kind of journalism. The beginnings of the editorial appeared, and newspapers were now published by editors rather than by the old printer-journalist. The so-called "penny dreadfuls," because they began to include a more sensational kind of copy which highlighted police news, murders, rapes and suicides, also appeared. Paradoxically, the editorials stressed ethical principles and espoused a stringent morality. Subscription sales gave way to newsstand circulation, the newsboy became a popular figure on the American scene, and the press began to carry much more advertising. As much as half of a successful weekly newspaper might consist of advertising.

Newspapers for the Masses

In 1833 Benjamin Day launched the first successful penny newspaper, the *New York Sun*. The *Sun* represented a revolutionary idea in the newspaper industry—a press intended to tap the large reservoir of potential readers collectively designated as "the common man." The emphasis of the *Sun* was on local occurrences, particularly those of a sensational nature. The paper was an almost instantaneous success.

Day hired George Wisner to write a column entitled "Police Office" which presented news from the police stations and the courts. His stories were well written, blending crime with pathos and humor and were so successful that within a year Wisner became co-owner of the paper.

Day was not above fabricating the news to increase circulation. One of his reporters, Richard Adam Locke, a descendant of political philosopher John Locke, wrote a series of articles purporting to describe life on the moon.

The most important ingredient to Day's financial success was marketing. His was the first newspaper to be hawked in the streets by newsboys. The papers were sold to the newsboys for 67¢ a hundred. The public was able to read stories of murder, sex crimes, violence—all purchased for only a penny. By 1835 the *New York Sun* had nearly tripled its circulation.

Day's determination to publish a penny newspaper marked the beginning of a period of colorful and flamboyant figures in American journalism—James Gordon Bennett, Horace Greeley, and eventually Joseph Pulitzer, William Randolph Hearst and the Scripps family. Journalism also developed distinguished and more sober figures such as Henry J. Raymond and Adolph S. Ochs. In succession, a series of successful newspapers was founded. The *New York Herald* began publication in 1835, and the *New York Tribune* went into publication in 1841. The greatest of newspapers, the *New York Times,* came upon the journalistic scene in 1851.

These newspapers and others, some of which became the flagships of great publishing empires, established an age of mass communication for the American press. They became, in a sense, the first of the mass media—journalistic ventures whose goal was to attain the largest possible circulation. In order to do so, they were obliged to depend upon advertising, to engage in promotional and editorial gimmicks and exploitations, and to expand their content from sheer information to more provocative areas of human interest and entertainment. Above all, however, the press as a mass medium needed galvanic and dynamic figures to provide the impetus that made journalism a tremendously powerful force in informing and reflecting public opinion, a mass communicator in every sense of the term.

James Gordon Bennett

The first of these larger-than-life figures was James Gordon Bennett, one of the most vigorous and colorful in American journalism. Bennett was the prototype of the new publisher. He was strictly an editor and reporter, in contrast to the printer-journalists who preceded him. A Scotsman of French ancestry, he learned the newspaper business while working as the Washington correspondent for the *New York Courier*. Twice he had tried to start a paper of his own, and twice he failed. Penniless and disillusioned, Bennett, at 40 years of age, made another attempt.

In 1835, spurred on by the success of Benjamin Day's *Sun,* Bennett founded a penny newspaper entitled the *New York Herald*. Although clearly an imitator of the *Sun* in form and content, the *Herald* soon demonstrated its own special flair for sensationalized news. Bennett went further than Day in the exploitation of sex. In one instance, he devoted the whole front page to the murder of a prostitute in a brothel. He vividly described how the murderer killed her, and then set fire to her bed. Interest in the case was high and the *Herald* grew in advertising and in circulation.

Bennett displayed a talent for news, a penchant for timely and human interest stories. He established coverage of finance and religion, of society and the theatre. Journalism became more sensational, but also more sophisticated. Bennett, above all, realized that competitive conditions necessitated beating the opposition to the news with what became known as "scoops." He utilized new technology, developed and trained foreign correspondents and, in general, opened new horizons for journalism as a mass medium. Although he exploited the news and sensationalized it, he was one of the first bona fide journalists, one of the truly forceful editorial personalities. His thrust was toward the mass audience, the new and growing public of immigrants who crowded the cities and were hungry for news.

By 1860, the *Herald* was the world's largest newspaper with a readership of over 77,000. Bennett's *Herald* covered the teeming life of a growing city and, if his brand of journalism was frequently trenchant and distasteful, it displayed a pragmatism that resulted in success. He was succeeded by his son, James Gordon Bennett, Jr., in 1872 who, while able, was also unreliable. His claim to distinction was the adventure of one of his correspondents, Henry M. Stanley, who went to Africa to find the missing Dr. Livingstone.

Horace Greeley

The elder Bennett's chief competition came from Horace Greeley, one of America's distinguished figures. Greeley, who founded the *New York Tribune* in 1841, has been called "the father of American journalism." His distinction rests basically on the concept that the editorial was an important part of journalism as a communications medium, that the editor ought to take a stand and espouse causes with conviction. Greeley was what many of his peers were not—a journalist of integrity. He took a position in support of anti-slavery and his views were essentially liberal and humanitarian. Greeley gathered about him a corps of excellent journalists and established a first-rate newspaper. While the *Herald* was colorful and sensational, the *Tribune* had journalistic candor and a distinct editorial point of view.

Greeley proved that a newspaper could appeal to the masses without resorting to sensationalism—that the common man could be attracted by reason as well as emotionalism. By the turn of the century, even the *Sun* and the *Herald* were offering their readers more substantive material.

The New York Times

The trend toward responsible journalism was accelerated with the establishment of the *New York Times* in 1851 by Henry Jarvis Raymond and George Jones. They began the paper with $100,000 capitalization. Only 10 years before, Greeley had founded the Tribune with $2,000, Bennett's capital 16 years before was only $500. The economics of the newspaper business were changing rapidly.

The *Times* presented a conservative economic, political, and social policy and offered a wider range of news than most of its contemporaries. Raymond, who became its editor, established a reputation for being reasonable and objective. The distinction of the *Times* from its inception was sobriety, balance and moderation. It presented contrasting points of view thoughtfully and soberly, without invective or partisanship. Misleading advertising was not accepted and scandal was rejected in the pages of the *Times*. After Raymond's passing, the *Times* lost circulation steadily until it was taken over in 1896 by Adolph Ochs who had been successful as publisher of the *Chattanooga* (Tenn.) *Times*. Ochs bought a shaky enterprise and made it eminently successful. Circulation increased as the *New York Times* became the leading newspaper of the country with its editorial criterion of "all the news that's fit to print."

The *Times* covered the news—national and international, cultural, political and economic—with a thoroughness and integrity matched by few other newspapers in the country. This spirit of fairness, thoroughness and probity continued under the direction of family publishers. When Ochs died in 1935, his son-in-law, Arthur Hays Sulzberger was named publisher. In 1961, he was succeeded by his son-in-law, Orvil E. Dryfoos, who died unexpectedly in 1963. The current president and publisher is Arthur's son, Arthur Ochs Sulzberger.

In the past few years the administrative, as well as the journalistic, policies of the *New York Times* have come under criticism. Gay Talese, a former *Times* writer, and others have written pointedly of internal jockeying for control, of office politics, of a growing deterioration in what had once been an enviable relationship between management and employees. The *Times* has been experimenting with cultural news departments, with eye-catching features, with greater use of photographs. The *"Times* style" has undergone subtle changes, too, in an apparent effort to liven up the paper. In September 1970, the *Times* inaugurated an Op. Ed. page (Opposite Editorial) which presents the views of government officials, scholars, and others, as well as those of the *Times* regular public affairs commentators—James Reston, Tom Wicker, and Anthony Lewis. In 1973, former Nixon speech writer, William Safire, was added to the staff to provide a more conservative viewpoint. Since the retirement of Harrison Salisbury in December 1973, the Op. Ed. page has been edited by Charlotte Curtis.

The paper remains a great journalistic enterprise, but there are those who feel that some of its aura has dimmed, largely owing to the more impersonal "computerized" approach both to its employee relations and to its coverage of the news. During the early 1970s the New York Times Company underwent extensive expansion. In 1971, in exchange for *Times* stock, it acquired many interests of Cowles Communications, Inc., including *Family Circle* magazine and several Florida newspapers.

The Establishment of Press Associations

As newspapers expanded their coverage and became reflectors of the national scene, it was obvious that no one paper could continue indefinitely to meet the multiplying problems of individual news collection. The need for a cooperative effort to gather and transmit news became apparent. In 1848, six New York newspapers joined together to share the expense of procuring national and international news under the name of Associated Press of New York. This group was the forerunner of the modern-day press association. The New York organization merged with a Western Press Association in the 1860s and extended its franchise to provide service to newspapers throughout the country. Since the member papers represented a variety of editorial viewpoints, the Associated Press provided impartial collection and dissemination of news. By 1900, the Associated Press (AP) had become a cooperative organization—each paper made its stories available to other members. Members shared the cost of exchanging news, and paid for the association's news staff which collated the news and augmented it with additional coverage. The organization operates in essentially the same manner today.

Various wire services emerged to compete with Associated Press, but the most formidable was the United Press (UP) association—

actually a merger of two smaller services—which was formed by E. W. Scripps in 1907. In addition to supplying the Scripps' papers with news, it provided service for those papers not admitted to the Associated Press. Besides its own correspondents, United Press established connections with foreign news agencies and newspapers. In 1909, William Randolph Hearst developed a third major news service, the International News Service (INS). Although it was smaller than its rivals, the INS distinguished itself in providing comprehensive coverage of the news by well-known writers. United Press and the International News Service merged in 1958, forming the United Press International (UPI).

An important collective news organization during the American Civil War was the Press Association of the Confederate States of America which consisted of all the South's 43 wartime daily newspapers. Despite the raging war, its reports of the conflict were remarkably objective.

The American Civil War

The Civil War deeply affected all aspects of American life. The war was essentially a dispute between conflicting ideologies—the emerging industrial capitalism of the North vs. the agrarianism of the Southern states. Contrary to popular myth, slavery was not a primary cause of the conflict. Sectional strife would have existed with or without slavery. Indeed, the North had its own form of slavery manifested in its industrial exploitation of the defenseless working class. Nevertheless, slavery became a rallying cry which united those of diverse background and interest.

The war, in large part due to news coverage, aroused unprecedented hate and bigotry in the country, nearly obliterating the sense of unity which had prevailed since the Revolution. As in colonial days, the tensions produced by the struggle once again developed a partisan press which frequently became vicious and slanderous. Joseph Medill, publisher of the *Chicago Tribune,* was even accused by President Lincoln of helping to foment the Civil War. The impact of the war on journalism was to increase newspaper circulation, develop the importance of the war correspondent and reveal the usefulness of the newly established press associations. In the aftermath of the war, Bennett, Greeley and Raymond survived as successful publishers with fairly strong and established newspapers.

The Press After the War

Several important newspapers emerged in the decades following the Civil War. In 1882, Charles H. Dow and Edward T. Jones founded a financial news service for private clients which evolved into the prestigious *Wall Street Journal*. Under the direction of Clarence W. Barron, who acquired Dow Jones and Co. in 1902, the newspaper specialized in the coverage of business and finance. In 1940 the paper broadened its concept of business news to include all news of national and international importance that affects the business community. As the first half of the 1970s came to a close, the *Wall Street Journal* was second only to the *New York Daily News* in circulation. Ten different plants around the country print its four editions—East, Midwest, South and Pacific Coast. Dow Jones and Company started a general interest weekly newspaper in 1962, titled the *National Observer,* which provides in-depth reports on national and international news as well as comprehensive studies on problems such as health, education and employment.

The early Twentieth Century saw the emergence of another nationally read newspaper of distinction, the *Christian Science Monitor*. The *Monitor* was started by the Christian Science Church in Boston in 1908, at the urging of the church's founder, Mrs. Mary Baker Eddy, in protest against the sensationalism that characterized many newspapers of the day. The paper pioneered an interpretative approach to problems and trends in regional, national and international affairs. The *Monitor* utilizes a facsimile system to transmit page proofs to its offset printing facilities in New Jersey, Chicago and Los Angeles. In early 1972, the *Monitor* made its news and features available to other newspapers through the Christian Science Monitor News Service.

The major newspaper in the midwest was Medill's *Chicago Tribune,* a paper which challenged the *New York Herald* in flamboyant, personal journalism. It was a vitriolic publication which, despite its overt emphasis on ideal values, did not hesitate to use its power as a mass medium to pour invective on those with whom it was in disagreement. But circulation soared, and then, as now, the *Chicago Tribune* was considered a newspaper with a strong conservative —its critics call it reactionary—point of view. It was anti-labor and defended the status quo with vigor and stobbornness.

Robert McCormick and Joseph Patterson assumed control of the

Tribune in 1914. Under McCormick's direction, until his death in 1955, it became one of the best-written newspapers in the country with a large circulation and substantial advertising revenue. Despite the criticism of its editorial viewpoint, it has become one of America's most forceful newspapers. It was included in *Time* magazine's top-10 rankings for 1975. The Tribune Company (which includes the *New York Daily News*) is the current leader in total circulation.

There were papers of distinction in other areas outside of New York and the Eastern seaboard. William Rockhill Nelson established a superb publication in the *Kansas City Star* and showed what a medium of mass communication can accomplish when it determines to drive corruption out of a city by exposing it to public view through the instrumentality of the press. The *Kansas City Star* remains one of the great independent newspapers in the United States. In general, however, the newer papers which sprang up in the South and West after the war were not particularly impressive. Chicago's papers, in addition to the *Tribune,* were the *Daily News* and the *Chicago Times.* The latter, highly sensational in content, merged with the *Sun* in 1948, forming the *Sun-Times.* The *Denver Post,* a sober publication today, was launched on sensationalism and a series of wild exploitations and promotional gimmicks by Harry H. Tammen and Fred G. Bonfils. The *Denver Post* did not stand out as one of the proud examples of fine journalism. In San Francisco, the *Chronicle* was an enterprising and exemplary journalistic endeavor until challenged by the emergence of William Randolph Hearst and the *San Francisco Examiner,* a classical example of lurid journalism, replete with roaring headlines and other circulation-building devices. The third San Francisco paper was *The Bulletin* until Hearst merged it into the *San Francisco Call-Bulletin.*

In the South, journalism was undistinguished with the exception of Henry W. Grady's *Atlanta Constitution* which reflected the blunt and enterprising disposition of its publisher and became one of the great newspapers of the country. The University of Georgia's School of Journalism, which offers the annual television Peabody Awards, is named after Grady. One other fine newspaper in a generally lackluster area was Henry Watterson's *Louisville Courier-Journal,* a paper which, like the *Atlanta Constitution,* looked forward to the rehabilitation and development of a vigorous South.

3

The Press in Transition

BETWEEN THE END of the Civil War and the beginning of the Twentieth Century, America experienced dramatic changes characterized by industrialization, immigration and urbanization.

The industrial expansion which occurred in the United States during the last third of the Nineteenth Century was attributable in large part to the exploitation and utilization of America's natural resources—coal, oil, iron, lumber, and electricity. This was the age of steel mills, oil refineries, railroad interconnections, expanding factories and a growing labor force.

Factories needed workers and people were immigrating to America by the millions. Between 1870 and 1900, the population almost doubled. The influx of people tended to concentrate in the industrial northeastern states. New York was fast approaching a population of four million by the beginning of the Twentieth Century. There were 58 cities with a population of more than a half million by 1890.

Communications Technology

With industrialization came enormous advances in communications technology. The use of the telegraph, which had been invented in the 1830s by a painter-turned-scientist, Samuel Morse, was greatly increased. Telegraph lines were extended into remote sections of the country, stretching from the Atlantic to the Pacific Coast. The telegraph, which revolutionized information transmission, is remarkably simple in concept. In 1856 the Western Union Company was organized to exploit the invention. The advent of electrical telegraphy portended the electronic marvels of the Twentieth Century. Stemming from Morse's invention came the whole concept of transmission of communication content by electrical energy.

In 1866 the first successful transatlantic cable was uncoiled. It stretched from Newfoundland to Ireland and permitted up-to-the-minute news to be transmitted beneath the ocean via telegraphy. Mechanical advances in the print industry greatly accelerated and improved the production of newspapers. Typesetting machines, electrical presses, improved paper-making techniques, typewriters, and photoengraving were all developed by the beginning of the Twentieth Century.

In 1876 a Scottish immigrant, Alexander Graham Bell, patented a telephone instrument which greatly speeded the flow of information. Interestingly, the importance of this invention was not immediately recognized. The Bell Telephone Company, launched in 1877, experienced serious financial blows and offered to sell its entire assets including the telephone patent for $100,000 to Western Union. The telegraph company, much to its later chagrin, refused the offer. Western Union soon realized its mistake and attempted to gain dominance over telephony through the acquisition of some pre-telephony patents of Thomas Edison. A bitter fight ensued and the Bell Company emerged victorious. Less than a quarter of a century later, the American Telephone and Telegraph Company was incorporated with a capitalization of a quarter of a billion dollars. Ironically, by 1909 Ma Bell, as AT&T has come to be called, purchased control of Western Union with a check for $30 million. Antitrust action forced separation of the two companies. Today AT&T is an enormous enterprise whose assets are three times those of General Motors and are larger than the annual gross national product of most nations.

Electricity, so important to the communications industry, was developed by Thomas Edison in the 1880s. In 1882, Edison constructed a generating distributing plant in New York. Within a few years, franchises were obtained which provided electric light to cities throughout the nation. Edison's incandescent lamp also stimulated the publication and sale of evening newspapers.

Communications Empires

Advances in communications technology required enormous capital, and the press changed from a political and factional entity to a vast and impersonal institution—a medium of mass communication which distilled in its coverage the rise of urban America and the far-reaching consequences of the Industrial Revolution. Advertising became an essential ingredient of newspaper publishing, circulation became essential for success in attracting advertisers. The press not only became a national institution, it became institutionalized. Newspapers began to become part of large business enterprises. But journalism also became more far-reaching and informative, and editorials were written cogently, rather than out of fierce partisanship. The end of the Nineteenth and the beginning of the Twentieth Century witnessed the appearance of such titans of journalism as Pulitzer and Hearst and the development of powerful—some believed too powerful—communications empires.

Joseph Pulitzer

Joseph Pulitzer purchased the *New York World* in 1883. The paper immediately established a reputation for combining sensationalism with crusading journalism. Indeed, a cynical appraisal might conclude that the Pulitzer technique of revealing abuses had no objective other than to provide a vantage point for the publication of sensationalized news. Pulitzer himself was one of the more interesting phenomena of American journalism. An immigrant from Hungary, Pulitzer originally acquired a German language paper, the *Staats-Zeitung,* which he promptly sold. He then turned to the law, but ultimately gravitated back to journalism. His combining of the *St. Louis Dispatch* with the *St. Louis Post* became an immediate success and was followed by the acquisition of the *New York World.* This undertaking began auspiciously. It was to be a people's paper, devoted to journalistic integrity, and it did not hesitate to challenge authority and privilege in its editorial crusade. Pulitzer wholeheartedly championed the cause of workers and small businessmen. But, paradoxically, while the editorials were marked by a tone of journalistic idealism, the news emphasized sex and violence and the sensational exposé of corruption in high places. Unfortunately, a nervous disorder kept Pulitzer from his business a great deal of the time and forced him to edit his paper in absentia. Pulitzer was going blind and his nervous affliction had almost crippled him. Nevertheless, he remained active in the operation of his newspapers.

Pulitzer instituted the editorial cartoon. The first cartoon was entitled "The Yellow Kid." It was drawn by Richard Outcault with a yellow tint overlay. The cartoon was enormously successful and circulation soared. By 1887, *The World* had the largest circulation in the country, about a quarter of a million. At this juncture, the imposing figure of William Randolph Hearst entered the field of journalism.

William Randolph Hearst

By far the most controversial figure in modern journalism was William Randolph Hearst. He came from a background of enormous wealth. His father, George, had amassed a fortune in the silver mines of the Comstock Lode and made additional millions from copper and ranching interests.

In 1880, George Hearst acquired the *San Francisco Examiner* in an effort to further his political career. William showed an interest in the paper, and his father, who thought little of newspaper people, sent him off to Harvard in 1882. William's career at Harvard may not have been distinguished but it was certainly colorful. Prone to excessive beer drinking and wild pranks, he was suspended in his sophomore year and finally expelled in 1885.

While at Harvard, William Randolph Hearst had spent a summer vacation working as a cub reporter for Pulitzer's *World*. Fascinated by the paper's sensational techniques he became determined to enter journalism. When his father became a U.S. Senator from California in 1887, 24-year-old William was given control of the *San Francisco Examiner*. Almost immediately, young Hearst patterned the paper after Pulitzer's *World*. With his enormous funds Hearst purchased a first-rate staff of writers and artists. The *Examiner* soon became one of the most profitable papers in the United States.

In the fall of 1895, Hearst entered the New York City market through his purchase of the *Morning Journal* which, ironically, had once been owned by Joseph Pulitzer's brother Albert. In the first few months of his ownership, Hearst conducted a series of raids on Pulitzer's news staff. The competition between the papers thus began. The "Yellow Kid" played a key role in the fight for popularity and circulation supremacy between Pulitzer and Hearst. Hearst quickly seized upon Pulitzer's use of color and, as he was able to do in the case of many of Pulitzer's staff, he succeeded in persuading Outcault to leave the *World* in what was probably the greatest journalistic coup of the period. Both newspapers carried the "Yellow Kid" and the competition over the cartoon came to symbolize the circulation battle between the *Journal* and the *World*. Highly emotional, cheaply sensational news became characterized as "yellow journalism."

Hearst outdid Pulitzer in sensational news. Violent crimes, preferably sexual, were prominently featured on the front page of the *Journal*. Typical headlines included: "The Mysterious Murder of Bessie Little," and "One Mad Blow Kills Child." Hearst, like Pulitzer, also championed the causes of the disenfranchised. He advocated an eight-hour work day, women's suffrage, and embarked on many crusades against corruption in government.

By the Spring of 1897, both the *World* and the *Journal* published morning, evening and Sunday editions. Hearst's Sunday edition was 80 pages and included three supplements—*American Magazine, American Women's Home Journal* and the *American Humorist.*

Both the *World* and the *Journal* played an important role in inflaming the American public against Spain. Hearst was a particularly powerful advocate of Cuban independence from Spain. He was, in fact, with good reason accused of helping to foment the Spanish-American War.

Hearst's journalism was overwrought, shocking and frequently lurid. The editorial page was the antithesis of sobriety and rationality. His was a journalism of color comics, editorials of a no-holds-barred nature, and news pages of unadulterated "front page" variety. Like Pulitzer, Hearst's empire flourished, and circulation bounded to unprecedented levels. At the height of his power, Hearst controlled 29 daily newspapers in 18 large cities.

In their own flamboyant way, both Pulitzer and Hearst contributed importantly toward the growth of American journalism. They fought for public service causes and were champions of the working class. Newspaper circulation soared. The demand for news was voracious. And, to the oblique credit of Pulitzer, he did endow the Columbia University School of Journalism in 1912. Today the Pulitzer Prize is the most prestigious award in journalism.

Hearst's success ultimately forced the sale of the *New York Herald* to that most utilitarian of journalistic dealers, Frank Munsey, who sold it, in turn, to the *Tribune* in 1923, establishing the respected *New York Herald Tribune*. But not even this distinguished paper has survived, for in the retrenchment of the 1960s it was swallowed into the *World Journal Tribune* which went out of business in 1967.

Canons of Journalism

The American Society of Newspaper Editors (ASNE), which was organized under the leadership of Casper S. Yost of the *St. Louis Globe-Democrat* in 1922, adopted a code of ethics at its first annual meeting in April 1923 called the "Canons of Journalism." The seven "canons," which were principally the work of H. J. Wright, founder of the *New York Globe,* are entitled: Responsibility; Freedom of the Press; Independence; Sincerity, Truthfulness, Accuracy; Impartiality; Fair Play; and Decency. Their basic tenets are no more specific than their titles.

The ASNE code of ethics does not provide an adequate enforcement mechanism, and subscription is on a voluntary basis. A revised version of the code was proposed at the April 1975 meeting of the ASNE which is just as vague and abstract as its 1923 counterpart.

Concentration and Consolidation

The Twentieth Century has been an era of concentration and consolidation for American journalism. The trend toward mergers has been inevitable as newspapers were forced to join together in order to survive. Multiple ownership of newspapers became a major characteristic of the American system. Hearst added newspapers in Chicago and Boston. One of the largest newspaper chains was developed by Edward W., George H., and James E. Scripps. The Scripps empire began in the Middle West with such papers as the *St. Louis Chronicle,* the *Cleveland Press* and the *Cincinnati Post.* By the end of World War I the Scripps chain had expanded to include an interest in more than 30 newspapers in 15 states. In 1920, Roy W. Howard and Robert Scripps (son of Edward) joined forces and the chain became known as Scripps-Howard. In the 1970s the organization remains among the leaders in total circulation.

By the 1930s newpaper chains were becoming increasingly prominent. John S. Knight developed formidable papers in Miami, Chicago and other cities to which he contributed his own signed personal column. In 1937 he merged the *Miami Herald* and *Tribune,* and acquired the *Detroit Free Press* in 1940. In 1954 and 1959, respectively, he added the *Charlotte Observer* and the *Charlotte News* to his chain, and in 1969, he acquired the *Philadelphia Inquirer* and the *Philadelphia Daily News.* In September 1974, Knight Newspapers, Inc. merged with Ridder Publications, Inc., making the new chain, Knight-Ridder Newspapers, Inc., a potential new leader in total circulation. The Knight-Ridder enterprise now controls a national network of 35 newspapers in 26 cities with an aggregate circulation approaching 30 million copies a week.

In New York State, Frank E. Gannett built a chain of 15 major newspapers during the 1930s and 1940s. By early 1974, the Gannett chain controlled 56 newspapers, the largest number of any group. Gannett's board is comprised of several members of the government-military-industrial hierarchy, including President Nixon's Secretary of State, William P. Rogers.

Although a number of newspapers in the Hearst chain have been liquidated and consolidated over the past several decades, the organization still exerts influence through its large circulation. William Randolph Hearst died in 1951 leaving an estate of almost $60 million. His family continues to maintain control of the newspapers which include the *Los Angeles Herald-Examiner,* the *San Francisco Examiner* and the *Baltimore News-American.* The second generation of Hearsts have none of the style and grandeur of the late William Randolph Hearst. However, granddaughter Patty appears to have inherited some of her grandfather's flair for creating sensational news.

The Press in the Middle 1970s

The trend toward greater concentration of ownership is expected to continue throughout the 1970s. The number of newspapers owned by groups has doubled since the close of World War II and together the group-owned newspapers account for 63 per cent of the total weekday circulation. Cross-media owners—those who own more than one type of communications medium—control more than a third of the daily newspapers. Less than 4 per cent of the nation's cities have competing newspapers. New York City which once boasted 14 papers, is down to three. Similar attrition has taken place in Boston, Philadelphia, Chicago, San Francisco and Los Angeles. The main theoretical danger of such media monopolies is that they constrict the range of opinions to which the public has access. There is, however, little concrete evidence to demonstrate that multiple ownership necessarily inhibits the free flow of information. Certainly there have been abuses, but media monopoly does not appear to be inherently either good or bad.

The quality of several group-owned papers has improved considerably in recent years. The *Los Angeles Times,* owned by the Times-Mirror Company, has become a relatively independent and responsible source of news with earned recognition as one of the nation's ranking newspapers. Under the guidance of James L. Knight the *Charlotte News* and *Observer* have improved dramatically. Another Knight newspaper, the *Miami Herald,* has won numerous awards for excellence in journalism. A third generation Pulitzer, grandson Joseph Pulitzer III, maintains the high journalistic standards of the *St. Louis Post-Dispatch.*

Cross-media ownership does not appear to have deterred the journalistic excellence of the *Washington Post.* Under the direction of Philip Graham, the *Post* acquired radio and television interests in the late 1940s and early '50s, and in 1961, *Newsweek* magazine came under its domain. After her husband's death, in 1963, Katherine Graham took control of both the newspaper and the parent corporation. In recent years, the newspaper has achieved national acclaim for its investigative reporting. The *Post's* most notable achievement, of course, was its exposure of the Watergate scandal. *Post* reporters Bob Woodward and Carl Bernstein have won numerous awards for their extraordinary work, and the dubious distinction of being portrayed by Dustin Hoffman and Robert Redford in the movies. In 1973 the *Washington Post* was awarded a Pulitzer Prize for distinguished public service.

Despite the trend toward multiple ownership, the threat of a national monopoly seems remote. Where the danger of local monopoly appears imminent, the Justice Department can proceed to alleviate the problems under existing legislation. Local newspaper competition has supposedly been bolstered by the passage of the Newspaper Preservation Act of 1970. This act grants limited immunity from antitrust laws by allowing an ailing newspaper to share the facilities and commercial operations of another newspaper, but requires that separate and competing news and editorial departments be maintained. The act, which sanctioned all existing joint operating agreements, also requires that new proposals for sharing be submitted to the Attorney General for approval. Some critics contend that the Newspaper Preservation Act in fact hinders competition because a new newspaper could not compete against existing papers that share operating expenses.

A non-legislative step to insure the maintenance of a free and responsible press was taken with the establishment of the National News Council in 1973. The primary function of the Council, which is financed by the Twentieth Century Fund as well as other foundations, is to encourage accuracy and fairness in the dissemination of news. Although the Council has no enforcement power, it can exert influence through the public reporting of decisions. The Council's membership is comprised of distinguished individuals from the general public along with some media representatives. Thus far, the reaction to the National News Council has been mixed. It is too soon to determine the Council's overall effectiveness.

In the final analysis, the most serious problem confronting American journalism concerns the nature of the newspaper industry itself. In the United States, newspapers function primarily as economic enterprises—they are in the business of making money and maximizing profits. Advertisements occupy roughly 60 per cent of the available space in the average newspaper. A business corporation, by its very nature, is organized and conducted primarily for the financial benefit of its owners and stockholders. Corporate interest, not the public, will be favored whenever profits are affected. The newspaper industry, like any business concern, heeds the imperative of profit maximization.

Magazines

The magazine is not only one of the oldest of the mass media, dating back almost—but not quite—to the invention of printing, but is also one of the most interesting and varied. These publications are not newspapers, nor are they syndicated material. The magazine is print, of course, but it is a distinct medium of communication with its own unique character, style and substance.

Magazines derive their name from the original French term, "magazin," which means storehouse. And this is precisely what such publications are—storehouses of entertainment, comment and information on an amazing and often challenging variety of subjects. Indeed, any subject on earth would be relevant for magazine coverage, and most of them have been. A mere listing of a few diverse magazines will indicate the breadth, scope and variety of this medium: *The New Yorker, Journal of the American Medical Association, Playboy, New Leader, Popular Science, Ebony, Vogue, Screw, The Nation, Harvard Business Review, Rolling Stone, Foreign Affairs, Harpers, Think.* And these are only a few of the thousands of such publications which readers receive by subscription, through institutional membership and by newsstand sales.

A magazine, then, is an all-encompassing concept, running an enormous gamut and range from popular entertainment and fashion to erudite scholarship and complex technology. It is almost impossible to determine, at any given time, the precise number of such publications in print, for new magazines are being produced and discontinued constantly. One of the reasons for this lack of consistency is that it is still possible to start a modest publication with a relatively small investment. By contrast, it is all but impossible to establish a newspaper or television station without millions of dollars in investment—assuming, of course, that printing and union problems do not make such enterprises impossible; and that the FCC is convinced that it is sound and feasible to issue a construction permit for a broadcast station. Many magazines can be published modestly. They do not require glossy stock, *National Geographic* quality photography and fine printing. Many special-interest publications are simple, indeed, but the message they want to purvey reaches its target audience without either expensive outlay or demanding middlemen. In addition—despite some raises in postal rates—magazines enjoy a form of government subsidy which traditionally has given them preferential mailing privileges, without which many fine cultural publications simply could not manage to survive.

Survival, however, has been a major problem since 1950 for many of this country's once most prestigious and economically successful magazines. Had anyone predicted, in 1940 for example, that by the early 1970s such magazines as *Life, Look, The Saturday Evening Post* and *Collier's,* among others, would be defunct, such a prediction would surely have been dismissed as absurd. Yet, these once fabulously successful publications no longer exist—the victims of high production costs, erosion of advertising dollars to television, loss of readers to TV and a generally changing environment in audience taste. With the picture tube and color TV, could *Life* any longer be the weekly phenomenon it once actually was? With anthology, drama and public affairs programs on television, was there any longer a feeling on the part of Middle America that *The Saturday Evening Post* was essential weekly reading?

Magazines, however, still flourish, although after the advent of television they became more specialized and, in many cases, more daring and permissive in pictures and editorial content. Of the traditional periodicals, *The Reader's Digest,* established by the redoubtable DeWitt Wallace as a voice of conservatism, still maintains high circulation, although it has succumbed to the lure of the advertiser. Only *TV Guide,* significantly a magazine which covers the TV scene weekly with a circulation of about 19 million, and which carries program listings in a number of regional editions, matches the *Digest* in numbers.

The weekly news magazines—*Time, Newsweek* and, to a lesser degree *U.S. News and World Report*—also survived television, although the motion picture newsreel did not. But neither *Time* nor *Newsweek* had an easy road, managing only recently to regain their former reach. To many, however, these news magazines are utterly indispensable. They expand on data that has already been covered by the newspaper. They have their own unique style of reporting and investigation—particularly in the case of *Time,* and more so when its founder, Henry R. Luce was in charge. The hallmark of this style is a patina of editorial opinion and comment. The news magazines cover the world scene. The so-called "front of the book" carries weekly major stories and issues, interspersed with pictures, while the back of the book includes sections on medicine, television, books, theatres, art, education, business, religion, and sports. Frequently, the news magazine will seize upon a news item and expand it into a full-fledged feature.

In essence, there are magazines for everyone, and this is the fundamental importance of the medium. Institutions and organizations produce magazines for their members and for the public. Industry distributes magazines in the form of company publications. Trade associations and unions print special-interest magazines. Professional associations offer publications which carry not only essential scientific news, but also political and economic data of interest to the membership. Educational and scholarly publications reach professors and students in a wide range of disciplines, such as psychology, sociology, biology—and even mass communications. In the area of the media, for example, there are several publications including the *Journal of Communication, Journal of Broadcasting, Educational Broadcasting Review* and *Columbia Journalism Review*—the last a magazine that reaches readers who are broadly concerned in matters affecting the press. Magazines, in short, are—to cite the title of a magazine once very popular—Everyman's medium. They are the one mass medium which—apart from a 16mm film—an enterprising and inventive individual or group can establish with some hope (however tenuous) of possible success.

4

Early Motion Picture History

ALMOST FROM ITS inception the motion picture was an ambivalent medium, torn between the demands of the box office and its obvious potential as a genuine art form. Consequently, the development of the motion picture is both the history of a new art form and the emergence of a major industry with enormous power, reach and appeal.

The Illusion of Movement

The technique of motion pictures combines photography, projection and the singular function of the human eye. There is, of course, no motion in a "motion picture." Still pictures printed on celluloid are projected on a screen at a determined rate of speed to give the illusion of movement. A minimum of 16 pictures, or frames, per second was established to create the illusion. The basic principle involved, discovered by Peter Mark Roget, of Thesaurus fame, around 1824, is that the brain retains an image briefly after the picture is gone. This can be demonstrated quite simply by rotating a flashlight in a circle in a darkened room. The individual points of light are blurred by the brain and the illusion created is that of a continuous circle of light. This optical phenomenon is known as persistence of vision. In silent motion pictures each successive picture was held on the screen for about $^1/_{16}$th of a second, which gave the illusion that the flow of movement was continuous. When sound films were introduced, the speed was increased to 24 pictures per second to allow higher sound frequencies to be recorded and reproduced.

Early Attempts at Motion Pictures

Eadweard Muybridge, an English photographer working in San Francisco, first demonstrated that motion could be photographed in 1878. He arranged a series of 24 cameras in sequence along a race track to photograph the action of a galloping horse in order to settle a bet of $25,000. By attaching a string to each camera and stretching it across the track the cameras were set off in rapid succession as the horse ran by. Thus, he was able to prove that a horse at full gallop lifts all four feet from the ground.

The genesis of the motion picture as we know it today occurred near the end of the Nineteenth Century. At that time, there were simultaneous efforts to produce motion pictures in France, Germany, Russia and England, but it was Thomas Alva Edison's conception and development of the basic technique which stimulated the growth of the motion picture industry in the United States and throughout the world.

By the early 1890s, Edison and his enormously gifted assistant, William Dickson, perfected the Kinetoscope—a cabinet in which electric light was flashed on celluloid film. Since Edison's cameras and viewers ran at 48 frames per second, the original presentation lasted less than a half-minute. The film contained perforated holes along the margin of the strip so that it could revolve on sprocketed spools moved by a tiny motor. The films did not present stories. The subjects included a boxing-match, a man sneezing, and other such events. The viewer looked through a peep hole at the moving pictures—thus, the name "peep show" came in use.

Edison also constructed the first movie studio, which was called the "Black Maria" because the outside of the studio was protected with black metal plates. Within the studio a bulky indoor camera, which Edison called the Kinetograph, was built on a trolley to allow it to move closer to or further away from the subject. The Kinetograph could expose a series of some 600 pictures on a strip of film about 50 feet in length. The Black Maria's roof opened in order to light the studio for shooting. The entire studio could be rotated in order to provide sufficient light from the sun throughout the day.

Edison did not devote very much time to the development of motion pictures, since he regarded them as an unimportant plaything designed primarily to enhance the phonograph, which he patented in

1887. He patented the Kinetograph and the Kinetoscope in the United States, but didn't bother to spend the few hundred dollars necessary to secure European patents. Consequently, Europeans were allowed to utilize his work without paying royalties. Robert Paul in England and the Lumière brothers in France, among others, proceeded to make peep show cabinets and cameras.

The Lumière brothers, Auguste and Louis, owners of a photographic factory in Lyons, France, substantially improved upon Edison's basic invention. They built a lighter portable camera which could be used outdoors and made many other significant and enduring contributions, including the standardization of film width at 35mm, the movement of film at the speed of 16 frames per second, and the establishment of the concept that film movement must be intermittent to permit the projection of a clear, sharp image on to a screen. Expanding on the work of Edison, the Lumière brothers invented a combined camera and projector in 1894, which they named Cinématographe. Early in 1895, the Lumières shot their first film, ''Workers Leaving the Lumière Factory.'' By the end of the year, public presentations of projected films were given in the basement of a Paris Café to paying audiences.

In the United States, Thomas Armant, working with Francis Jenkins, also developed a projector using intermittent movement of film. Armant employed a small loop before and after the film gate to relax film tension, which all projectors still use today. Edison entered into a business agreement with Armant to sell his projector under the Edison trade name. The result was the Edison Vitascope, a projection version of the Kinetoscope. In April, 1896 the Edison Vitascope gave its first official public exhibition in America at Koster and Bial's Music Hall, a leading vaudeville theatre in New York City.

Early attempts at motion picture projection were plagued by fire. When Jenkins and Armant demonstrated motion pictures at the Cotton States Exposition at Atlanta in 1895, their projector caught fire and was completely destroyed. Flames from a motion picture projector exhibited at a bazaar for the underprivileged of Paris in 1887, ignited the barnlike exhibition hall and 180 people lost their lives. Nevertheless, the public's enthusiasm for motion pictures did not diminish.

The early tentative efforts to reproduce reality were truly literal in conception. They concentrated on such details as trains roaring down tracks. Soon these isolated instances of sheer realism were transmuted into stories which distilled reality and combined it with fantasy. One of the first American films with a plot was Edwin S. Porter's "The Great Train Robbery," a melodramatic story about eight minutes in length. The film is distinguished because of the flow and careful detail of the narrative sequences. Porter employed close-ups, cuts, and other techniques which soon became conventional. The one-reel film was shot on location and exhibited to the public in 1903. It proved immediately successful, and it was inevitable that the American businessman would seize the opportunity to venture into the promising new field. Motion picture houses proliferated around the country. The early theatres were no more than stores. By 1905, film showings were accompanied by piano music. The admission price was 5¢, hence the term "nickelodeon."

Many companies, sensing an opportunity, entered the motion picture production and exhibition business. By 1909, after many patent disputes, nine companies, calling themselves the Motion Picture Patents Company (MPPC), combined and agreed to share their various patents for the photographing, developing, and printing of motion pictures to the exclusion of all other competitors. By this time a middleman emerged to function between the producer and the exhibitor. He was called the distributor and worked out of a "film exchange," buying or leasing films from the producer and renting them to the exhibitor. Thus, the tripartite structure of the American film industry evolved—producer-distributor-exhibitor. The MPPC agreed not to provide film to any distributor who dealt with companies outside the combine. The MPPC also made an exclusive contract with George Eastman's company for raw film stock. The film distributors who accepted the MPPC terms eventually became amalgamated as the General Film Company and these two organizations dominated the film industry for several years.

The Rise of the Independents

Independent distributors and exhibitors thus were compelled to produce their own films. Carl Laemmle, a distributor, entered the arena of film production and the company he formed, the Independent Moving Pictures Company, eventually became Universal-International. Another distributor who also exhibited films, William Fox, began producing films and his company evolved into 20th Century-Fox. In 1912, an independent distributor, Adolph Zukor, imported the first full-length film to be shown in America, a French production entitled "Queen Elizabeth" which featured Sarah Bernhardt and members of the Comédie Française. Zukor's Famous Players Company was the progenitor of Paramount Pictures.

Most of the MPPC members were unalterably opposed to the full-length film. The General Film Company would not distribute any films longer than two reels. They were convinced that the interest in the feature-length film was a passing fancy. This, in part, led to the demise of the MPPC and its distributing arm. The final downfall of the MPPC came in 1917 as the result of an antitrust action by William Fox, which required the combine to discontinue all unlawful practices and dissolve back into separate units. However, inefficiency and resistance to change had already made the MPPC wholly ineffectual by 1914.

The battle waged by the patents company against the attempts of independent entrepreneurs to establish productions of their own, accompanied by the inducement of a favorable climate, caused the independents to move to California. There Hollywood, in all its glamour and glitter, eventually became the film capital of the world.

D. W. Griffith

One of the most distinguished directors in the early development of films was David Wark Griffith. He firmly established that the motion picture was more than just a reproduction of reality, more than a static medium. After a career in acting he turned to directing at the Biograph Studios in New York. He worked with the conviction that film had an artistic purpose and integrity of its own, a unique character which could be found in no medium other than motion pictures. If film art has a form and rule of its own, Griffith discovered and developed that art form. He struck out in fresh ways in the use of camera, in the development of long shots, close-ups, angle shots, and other techniques. He introduced the practice of rehearsing before shooting a scene, and developed a company of performers including Mary Pickford and Mack Sennett. He directed with both discipline and a desire to explore new ways of film presentation.

Griffith was determined to move from the one-reel film to a longer film, for he saw in the full-length feature the genuine creative potential of the motion picture as an art form. From a novel entitled *The Clansman* he produced one of America's classic films, "The Birth of a Nation." The dramatic power, eloquence, vigor and beauty of this classic of 1915 remains unchallenged. Unfortunately, the film's presentation of a negative Black stereotype and its glorification of the Ku Klux Klan is tragically antithetical to every principle of contemporary civil rights philosophy. But the revolutionary cinematic techniques of the picture are unquestioned. It remains a towering achievement and, above all, a motion picture from which innumerable directors have learned the art of film-making.

Early Screen Stars

Griffith, along with Thomas Ince and Mack Sennett, launched the Triangle Film Corporation. In addition to the comedy of Sennett, Triangle could boast also of the histrionics of Douglas Fairbanks and the emoting of the first great granite-visaged western hero, William S. Hart. Mack Sennett's experience in burlesque provided the necessary training for his marvelously comic screen improvisations—the mad, scrambling, hilarious and fast-moving antics of the classic Keystone Komedy Kops. Sennett was the true forerunner of the immortal Charlie Chaplin, America's greatest screen comedian. Chaplin is perhaps too well known over the past two decades for his political alienation and his disenchantment with the values and virtues treasured by middle class America. His contribution, however, was not political, but artistic. In the realm of cinema art he had few peers. Chaplin exemplified the Horatio Alger legend come alive on the screen. Literally, he rose from rags to riches through his extraordinary depiction of the inner tragedy of the little man—comic, anguished, mute, ingloriously frustrated, pathetically buffeted by fate—but winning the hearts of millions. In such classics as "The Tramp," "The Gold Rush," and even in his later films such as "The Great Dictator," a serio-comic representation of the Hitler mythology, Chaplin epitomized the poor soul of his day, the brow-beaten tramp who aroused a unique combination of sympathy and laughter. In 1972, at the annual Academy Awards ceremonies, 82-year-old Charles Spencer (Charlie) Chaplin, an exile from America for more than 20 years, received a special award from the Academy of Motion Picture Arts and Sciences for his unique contribution to motion pictures.

There were contemporaries of Chaplin whose success as stars was legendary, but whose charisma could not come across on the screen as it is constituted today. Mary Pickford, "America's Sweetheart," was the first feminine star, the first to become rich in an acting career in Hollywood. An incredible mixture of Pollyanna and sentimental romanticism, Mary Pickford was probably the best-known name in America during her reign as the industry's premiere leading lady. And America's leading cinema idol was Douglas Fairbanks, famous for the Fairbanks smile, calisthenics and penchant for swashbuckling romance. His films were highly romanticized, intricate in plot and laced with dynamic action and glamour. At the same time, William S. Hart, who acted in, wrote and directed his own westerns, epitomized the grim-visaged star whose pictures set the pattern for the good-guys-versus-bad-guys kind of western.

Motion Picture Palaces

The growth and expansion of the film industry lead to the construction of thousands of movie theatres. Between 1914 and 1922 an estimated 4,000 new theatres opened. In April 1914, the Strand, which had a seating capacity of 3,300, opened in New York City.

The manager of the Strand, Samuel Rothafel, nicknamed Roxy, soon went on to develop extraordinary movie palaces. He was responsible for creating the palatial atmosphere of such theatres as the Rialto, Rivoli, Capital, Roxy, and, that last survivor of the movie palace, Radio City Music Hall. Roxy's theatres supplemented the film with symphony orchestras, a melange of song and ballet, and live variety acts. Gargoyles, copies of Greek statues, elaborate fountains, and thick carpets adorned his theatres. The ushers wore silken uniforms which matched the color pattern of the theatre.

On the west coast, Roxy was rivaled by Sidney Patrick Grauman who, in 1922, constructed Grauman's Egyptian Theatre on Hollywood Boulevard at a cost of $800,000. One critic characterized its architecture as "early Frankenstein." The theatre seated 1,760 people who were attended by 28 usherettes attired in Egyptian-style costumes. Gilt sphinxes framed the proscenium. Five years later, Grauman opened his Chinese Theatre with the premiere showing of Cecil B. De Mille's "King of Kings." The Chinese motif of his new theatre included *objets d'art,* draperies and statues imported from the Orient. Celebrity footprints decorate the long forecourt of the theatre.

Before the Roxy theatre opened in New York City, it was purchased by William Fox. The trend toward monopolization over production, distribution and exhibition was spreading rapidly. The control of first-run and the bigger neighborhood theatres was thought essential to the success of the production companies.

Hollywood After the War

The motion picture industry suffered during World War I, but the post-war years, the frenzied and plush years of the 1920s, saw Hollywood established as the unquestioned film center of the world. Foreign competition, particularly from the French, had virtually disappeared as a result of the war. By 1920 most of the films shown throughout the world were made in Hollywood. As theatres proliferated throughout the United States, distributing companies engaged in the practice of "block booking" which forced the exhibitor to take many of the films distributed by a given company in order to secure the few major box office attractions. Certainly block booking produced substantial revenue, but it was less efficient than actually owning the theatres. The best guarantee of profit for a producer of films was to own theatres in which to show his products.

European Influences

While American film companies were building empires, the impetus toward film-making as an art form came from abroad, not from Hollywood. In Germany, France and Russia economic considerations did not thwart the desire for genuine experimentation. The flowering of a post-war art in Germany, misanthropic and disillusioned but nevertheless striking and effective, was also evident in films where there was an effort to probe the emotions and tensions of the post-war generation. In a period which saw the production of a number of sordid, pathological and realistic films, Robert Wiene's "The Cabinet of Dr. Caligari," a brilliant and highly expressionistic treatment of madness and evil, is still exhibited today as one of the great achievements in foreign film-making. From post-war Germany came other memorable motion pictures such as Joseph Von Sternberg's "The Blue Angel," with Emil Jannings and Marlene Dietrich. Symbolism and expressionism were exemplified by G. W. Pabst's "The Joyless Street," a film typical of the dour temper of the period as revealed in the behavior of ordinary citizens brooding dispiritedly about their frustrations on the streets of German cities.

In France and Russia there were manifestations of authentic talent, particularly in France where film was influenced by the fashion of surrealism, impressionism and Dadaism in the *ateliers* of contemporary artists. René Clair, in France, used film to achieve a truly comic effect with a sophisticated and light gloss. Jean Renoir, son of the impressionist painter, produced motion pictures with the touch of a poet. Jean Cocteau experimented with surrealist and symbolist themes and Luis Bunuel, perhaps the most brilliant director of the period, turned toward a naturalistic approach that did not eschew the most sordid aspects of the human condition. All of these directors were, to an extent, experimentalists. And all set a pattern of growth and sophistication in the development of the motion picture as a communicative art, while in the United States the Hollywood factories turned out products designed to further the development of the movies as a medium for mass entertainment.

One of the most controversial philosophers of the film art was the Russian director, Sergei Eisenstein, whose "Ten Days That Shook The World" and "Potemkin" are representative of the use of film to reveal the struggle of the Russian people in a period of revolutionary change. In Eisenstein's films the Russian people, the disenfranchised masses, are the true heroes, symbolically represented so that one significant event epitomizes an entire social movement through the crucible of the motion picture. Eisenstein theorized widely in books and articles, but it is his works which most brilliantly exemplify the use of the camera to reveal the symbolic impact of time and space. Eisenstein's films combine expressionism, realism and symbolism, but his refusal to accept the restrictive tenets of the Soviet propagandists brought him into repeated conflicts with the political authorities. His work is primarily aesthetic, and only secondary political. His juxtaposition of time and space, his handling of large crowd scenes, his ability to extract every symbolic significance of social contrast, and his use of montage gave a new luster to movie-making and greatly influenced serious students of cinema in this country.

The Dream Factory

Meanwhile, the Hollywood studios distilled dream packages for the delectation of millions of weekly fans at the local palaces. The movie fan magazines became imperative reading for the teenager, and the stars bathed in an *ambience* of money, power, glamour and glory. The movie moguls, intent on achieving what the trade journal, *Variety,* called "boffo" at the box-office, thwarted any remote tendency that directors might have manifested toward sensitivity or artistry. Westerns, comedies, and sophisticated romance predominated. The stars of the era were typified by Rudolph Valentino, an enormously popular Latin romantic figure, and Gloria Swanson who acted in what were then considered daring sex comedies. Ironically, it was Miss Swanson who years later distilled the curious mixture of tragi-comedy that characterized the period in the film "Sunset Boulevard." Erich Von Stroheim, who also appeared in "Sunset Boulevard" with Miss Swanson, was one of the leading directors of the period, along with Cecil B. De Mille. Von Stroheim's films, concerned with dramatic studies of moral values, were a cut above the bland comedies and the action westerns that predominated.

Cecil B. De Mille's success, in part, may be attributed to his ability to adapt to the changing tastes of the audience. In the pre-World War I period he capitalized on the public's interest in westerns and then moved on to screen adaptations of stage plays. After the war, he catered to the looser moral standards prevalent during the early 1920s. With the advent of the Hays office, he switched to biblical themes. His extravaganza "The Ten Commandments" (1924) moralized against breaking the commandments, while at the same time displaying enough sex and sin to rivet audience attention.

The Arrival of Sound

In 1927, the motion picture industry underwent a dramatic metamorphosis when the Warner Bros. studio presented "The Jazz Singer" in which Al Jolson uttered the prophetic words, "You ain't heard nothin' yet. . . ." This film ushered in the era of sound movies and unalterably changed the power structure of Hollywood. The hierarchy of the movie industry was understandably disquieted by the coming of sound motion pictures.

The Warners' film, which used large gramophone discs run in mechanical synchronization with the cinema projector, was not the first sound movie. Lee DeForest, whose significant contributions to radio communication are chronicled in a following chapter, demonstrated sound-on-film motion pictures at the Rivoli Theatre in New York City as early as 1923. But it was ''The Jazz Singer'' that revolutionized the motion picture industry. The public's enthusiasm could not be ignored. The introduction of ''talking'' pictures affected all aspects of the motion picture industry from initial studio production to the final presentation in the theatre.

5

The Hierarchy of Hollywood

THE COLLAPSE OF THE stock market in 1929 had a dramatic impact on the movie business. The stock valuations of all the major film companies dropped at an alarming rate. The entire industry underwent major financial readjustment and reorganization. The sharp decline in stock values, combined with the enormous expense of installing sound equipment, resulted in concentration of control over the movie industry by eastern banking firms, particularly the Morgan group (telephone interests) and the Rockefeller group (radio interests). By 1929 sound production pervaded the film industry. Both the studios and the theatres became dependent on the banks in order to convert to sound.

Eight major companies survived the depression years intact: Loew's-MGM, 20th Century-Fox, Radio Keith Orpheum, Warner Brothers, Paramount Pictures, Universal Pictures, Columbia Pictures, and United Artists. These eight turned out practically all the high rental films. The first five companies owned the controlling interest in 70 per cent of the first-run theatres in cities with populations exceeding 100,000. Control of exhibition became the major means of curtailing competition by keeping rival productions off the screen. By the late 1930s only a fringe of theatres existed outside the control of the eight major motion picture companies which, as distributors, released 95 per cent of all feature films and got 95 per cent of all domestic film rentals.

The Major Studios

Loew's-MGM emerged the undoubted leader of the movie industry. The company stemmed from Loew's Inc., an exhibiting concern which purchased Metro Pictures in 1920 to provide productions for its theatres. In 1924, Metro was merged with the Goldwyn production company (Samuel Goldwyn was no longer directly associated with the organization). In the same year, Louis B. Mayer Pictures joined to form Metro-Goldwyn-Mayer, with Loew's Inc. as the parent corporation. Louis B. Mayer was designated first vice-president and head of the studio. Twenty-four year old Irving Thalberg became second vice-president in charge of production. For six successive years during the '30s, Louis B. Mayer was the highest salaried individual in the United States. In 1937, his salary and bonus totaled $1,296,503, ten times greater than the pay of the President of the United States. MGM's motto was "more stars than there are in Heaven." Such stars as Clark Gable, Wallace Beery, Spencer Tracy, Lionel Barrymore, William Powell, and Judy Garland were under contract to MGM.

After the death of Marcus Loew in 1927, Nicholas Schenck, the Loew's family representative, ascended to the presidency of Loew's Inc. William Fox, with the financial backing of several organizations including one of AT&T's affiliates, Electrical Research Products Inc. (ERPI), purchased controlling interest in Loew's Inc. Fox agreed to use the sound equipment of AT&T's manufacturing subsidiary, Western Electric. In the aftermath of the 1929 stock crash, Fox was forced to sell his stock interests at a substantial loss.

During the era of realignment which occurred in the early 1930s, Joseph Schenck (Nicholas' brother) and Darryl Zanuck formed a corporation which they named Twentieth Century Pictures. In 1935, Twentieth Century merged with the Fox Film Corporation to form 20th Century-Fox. The new company acquired Fox Metropolitan Theatres. Spyros Skouras was placed in charge of the theatre operation. Joseph Schenck became chairman of the board of 20th Century-Fox. Sidney Kent was appointed president, and Darryl Zanuck became vice-president and chief of production. Spyros Skouras was elected to the presidency of 20th Century-Fox after the death of Sidney Kent in 1942. Skouras reigned over the Fox empire for 20 years. Wendell Willkie, the 1940 Republican presidential candidate, was elected chairman of the board in 1942 to replace Joseph Schenck who had been imprisoned for committing perjury. Schenck served four months of a one-year prison sentence and upon release he was restored to a position of power at 20th Century-Fox. In 1947, he received a full pardon from President Truman.

In October 1928 the Radio Corporation of America (RCA), to secure a market for its sound-on-film system, consolidated the Film Booking Office (FBO), a film producing company controlled by Joseph P. Kennedy, father of the late President John F. Kennedy, and the Keith-Albee-Orpheum theatre chain to form Radio Keith Orpheum (RKO). David Sarnoff became chairman of the board of RKO, and Joseph Kennedy was appointed president and general manager. The Rockefellers became indirectly associated with RKO in 1930 through their financial control of RCA via the Chase National Bank.

Joseph P. Kennedy helped movie star Gloria Swanson set up a film company under the label of Gloria Productions, Inc. and he became the managing director of this enterprise. Kennedy engaged Erich Von Stroheim in 1928 to write, direct, and act in the movie "Queen Kelly" starring Ms. Swanson. The film contained several controversial scenes including one of a convent girl being seduced. Kennedy dismissed Von Stroheim and tried to salvage the film by engaging another director, Edmund Goulding. After spending over $800,000, the whole venture was scrapped. "Queen Kelly" was never released. Kennedy and Swanson made another picture together called "What a Widow," which was modestly successful.

Kennedy, although maintaining some holdings in the movie industry, returned to Wall Street and was succeeded as president of RKO by Hiram Brown. Early in 1932, Merlin Aylesworth replaced Brown as president of RKO. At the time Aylesworth accepted the presidency of RKO, he was president of the National Broadcasting Company, a post he continued to hold. Although RKO enjoyed occasional periods of success, the company struggled for survival throughout most of its existence and RCA eventually sold off its stock. RKO at one time boasted such stars as Fred Astaire, Cary Grant and Katharine Hepburn. Samuel Goldwyn, Walt Disney and David O. Selznick all released their pictures through RKO at its peak. In 1948, Howard Hughes acquired controlling interest in the company. Under Hughes' whimsical direction, RKO was reduced to a corporate shell.

By late 1954, Howard Hughes owned RKO outright, making him the only person in history who was the sole owner of a major producing-distributing company. A year later Hughes sold RKO at a small profit to the General Tire and Rubber Company for $25 million.

Warner Bros. Pictures was a family enterprise started by Samuel, Harry, Albert and Jack L. Warner in 1923. All four brothers had experience in various phases of the motion picture industry. Warner Bros. teetered on the brink of financial instability during its first few years of operation. The company began experimenting with sound in 1925 in association with Western Electric. Their initial efforts involved the use of a synchronized disc system. The daring venture into sound films catapulted Warner Bros. to enormous success and it became prosperous enough to acquire the Stanley chain of theatres with its subsidiary, First National, a producing company which had been established by exhibitors. The Warner empire expanded into a giant complex. Samuel Warner died 24 hours before the October 6, 1927 premiere of "The Jazz Singer." Harry and Albert were president and treasurer of Warner's, respectively. Jack was vice-president in charge of production. The Skouras Brothers (Charles, George and Spryros) were placed in charge of Warner's theatre operation. Impoverished immigrants from Greece, they had risen to control their own theatre chain before being absorbed by the Warners. The Warner studio's impressive list of stars included Edward G. Robinson, James Cagney, Humphery Bogart, Errol Flynn, Bette Davis, Olivia de Haviland, and Ann Sheridan. (Bette Davis once tried to break her Warner contract by fleeing to England but, in a celebrated court case, she was told she must honor her contractual obligation.) In 1969, Jack L. Warner, the surviving brother, retired.

Paramount Pictures was created primarily by merging several companies which were founded by Benjamin Schulberg, Cecil B. De Mille, Jesse Lasky, and Adolph Zukor. Schulberg, who was Paramount's production head from 1925 to 1932, succumbed to alcohol and to an ill-fated romance with a popular movie actress of the period. Cecil B. De Mille severed ties with Paramount in 1925 to set up his own production company. Jesse Lasky was fired in the managerial upheavals of the early 1930s but went on to achieve success as an independent producer with the award-winning "Sergeant York" starring Gary Cooper. Through the series of complex mergers, Adolph Zukor, a Hungarian immigrant who had worked as an upholsterer for $2 a week, emerged as the dominant force within Paramount. Under Zukor's direction, Paramount acquired enormous theatre holdings. During the silent era, Paramount's contract players included Rudolph Valentino, Gilbert Roland, Maurice Chevalier, Mary Pickford, Gloria Swanson, Pola Negri, and Clara Bow. Stars such as Mae West, the Marx Brothers, Bing Crosby, Bob Hope, and a host of others helped Paramount through the turbulent '30s. The company had several names: in 1927, it was called Paramount-Famous Lasky; three years later its name was changed to Paramount Publix.

In 1928, Paramount purchased 49 per cent of the Columbia Broadcasting System. Paramount underwent a dramatic financial upheaval in 1932 and William Paley, then CBS president, and his associates purchased back its holdings of CBS stock. That same year, Paramount Publix, was reorganized and renamed Paramount Pictures, Inc. Adolph Zukor was asked to serve as chairman of the board although his power was substantially diminished. He remained active in the company for many years.

The founder of Universal Pictures, Carl Laemmle, was the prototype of the early movie magnate, an impoverished Jewish immigrant with negligible education and overriding ambition. Born in the South German kingdom of Würtemberg in 1867, he arrived in America on February 27, 1884. After working at various menial jobs, he achieved modest success in the haberdashery business. In 1906, at the age of 39, he embarked on a career in the film industry as a nickelodeon operator. Within three years, he developed one of the largest film distribution companies in the United States. In 1909, Laemmle collided with the Motion Picture Patents Company (MPPC) which attempted to force him out of business. He decided to fight the MPPC by going into independent production to supply his exhibitors. His production company was called the Independent Moving Pictures Company (IMP). Since the MPPC maintained an exclusive contract with George Eastman for raw film, Laemmle purchased his celluloid from the French firm, Lumière. By the close of 1910, IMP had produced over one hundred films.

Laemmle is credited with inaugurating the star system. The MPPC intentionally kept its performers anonymous in an effort to hold salaries to a minimum. IMP made an unknown Biograph studio player, Florence Lawrence, into a public sensation by affording her vast publicity.

In 1912, the IMP name was changed to the Universal Film Manufacturing Company. The "Universal" title symbolized Laemmle's intent to supply entertainment for all. In 1915, Carl Laemmle and his associates established Universal City on a 230-acre tract in the San Fernando Valley, 10 miles northwest of Hollywood. The new municipality, which had its own police force, railroad, post office, hospital and private reservoir, was founded for the sole purpose of producing motion pictures. During the 1920s, Universal produced mostly low-budget westerns and comedies, since it was unable to obtain theatre affiliates in the major markets. Its contract players included William Powell, Boris Karloff, and Zasu Pitts. In 1930, Carl Laemmle Jr., who was placed in charge of the studio operation by his father as a 21st birthday present, produced the Academy Award-winning, anti-war classic "All Quiet on the Western Front," directed by Lewis Milestone. Other Universal classics included "Dracula" and "Frankenstein," the precursors of an endless procession of horror pictures.

By 1935, the eastern banking interests were securely rooted in the motion picture field. Carl Laemmle, the last of the pioneer filmmoguls to maintain control of his company, sold his Universal stock in 1936. Three years later, at the age of 72, he died. Among the majors, Universal became one of the "little three" (the other two being Columbia Pictures and United Artists). In the 1940s the company merged with International Pictures, a small company run by William Goetz and Leo Spitz, to become Universal-International. Decca Records bought control of Universal and sold the studio in 1959 to Revue Productions, the television subsidiary of MCA, a corporation that had begun as a talent agency. Within a few years, MCA took control of Decca and Universal's production and distribution operations. Universal City became the home of "McHale's Navy," "The Virginian," and scores of other television programs.

Columbia Pictures was founded by Harry Cohn and his associates in 1924, as the outgrowth of an earlier endeavor, the C.B.C. Film Sales Company. Harry Cohn, one of film capital's most colorful and controversial figures, became chief of production and a principal stockholder in the new company. Hollywood gossip columnist, Hedda Hopper, once characterized Harry Cohn as "a man you had to stand in line to hate." In 1932, Harry Cohn became president of Columbia, as well as remaining in charge of production; his brother, Jack, became vice-president and treasurer. Columbia specialized in competent co-features, occasionally making a film of merit. The company had a scant list of contract players. Columbia received the critics' accolades and ascended to major studio status with its 1934 production of "It Happened One Night" starring Clark Gable (on loan from MGM), and Claudette Colbert (exercising a Paramount contractual option that permitted her to make one outside picture a year). The film was directed by Frank Capra, who was under contract to Columbia.

Columbia's greatest asset during the 1940s was a former Spanish dancer, Margarita Cansino, whom Harry Cohn renamed Rita Hayworth. Beginning in the late '40s, Columbia produced a series of distinguished films including "All the King's Men," "From Here to Eternity," and "On the Waterfront." One of Jack Cohn's three sons, Ralph, founded Screen Gems, Columbia's television subsidiary, in 1951. Screen Gems grew rapidly and became an enormous asset to its parent company. It was recently renamed Columbia Television Inc. By the time of Harry Cohn's death in 1958, Columbia Pictures was a leader in international co-production.

United Artists was founded in 1919 by Mary Pickford, Douglas Fairbanks, Charlie Chaplin and D. W. Griffith as a film distribution company with each of the four artists retaining control of his or her respective producing activities. The company had no studio of its own nor did it have a large roster of stars under contract. Joseph Schenck became its president during the 1920s. In 1930, United Artists released Howard Hughes' aerial spectacular of World War I, "Hell's Angels" starring Jean Harlow. United Artists financed many independent producers, foreshadowing the commercial practices of today. Samuel Goldwyn, David O. Selznick and Stanley Kramer released through United Artists. By the late '40s, the company did not produce enough films to sustain its expensive distribution apparatus but after undergoing reorganization in 1951, United Artists achieved enormous success and its pattern of operation had a profound effect upon the movie industry. The company was acquired in 1967 by the Transamerica Corporation, a conglomerate with interests in insurance and other financial services.

Film Content

The first "talkies" were primitive. Directors, writers, producers and players were groping for a way to use the new technology. Unfortunately, many of the great stars of the silent film could not make the transition, even with the help of voice specialists. Even John Gilbert, who had made feminine hearts flutter in dozens of silent films, was unable to make his high-pitched voice sound romantic. A new crop of players emerged to star in sound dramas and musicals. Jeanette MacDonald and Maurice Chevalier played in musicals directed by Ernst Lubitsch. Warner Brothers offered a plethora of singing and dancing musical comedies under the direction of Busby Berkeley, whose characteristic penchant for dance routines of lavishly gowned women in long shots against sylvan fountains became a standard presentation and, ultimately, an object of satire. James Cagney and Edward G. Robinson starred in a series of gangster films of the "Little Caesar" variety, films which were really caricatures of gangland, with none of the sordid naturalism of such pictures today—a far cry from the realism, for example, of Al Pacino in "Godfather II." The Marx Brothers and the magnificent W. C. Fields elicited unrestrained laughter—genuine and not "canned"—from audiences, with the Marx Brothers satiric and absurd, and Fields uproariously and sardonically pathetic. Westerns and comedies, of course, continued their inevitable course.

The technical proficiency which Hollywood had achieved by the early '30s is evidenced in the special effects employed by Willis O'Brien in the RKO movie "King Kong" (1933). The film took a year to complete at a cost of $650,000. The animation of Kong, and the 16-inch doll replicas of human performers were achieved through stop-motion photography—after each slight movement, the model was photographed, the camera stopped, and the model reset. A dozen separate exposures were required for each of Kong's steps. Live actors were combined with the animated models by miniature rear projection, multiple printing, and traveling mattes. A full-scale bust and hand of Kong were built for closeup shots. Some of the special effects achieved are unsurpassed to this day.

Gone with the Wind

In 1939, David O. Selznick produced one of the most successful films of all time, "Gone with the Wind." Based on Margaret Mitchell's best-selling novel of the same title, the film starred Clark Gable as Rhett Butler and Vivian Leigh as Scarlett O'Hara. Dozens of actresses coveted the role of Scarlett, including Katherine Hepburn and Bette Davis. Even Lucille Ball auditioned for the part. Gary Cooper and Errol Flynn were considered for the role of Rhett, but Selznick reluctantly decided to negotiate with his father-in-law, Louis B. Mayer, MGM production head, to secure Clark Gable for the part. MGM supplied Gable and half the estimated production cost of $2,500,000 in return for the releasing rights to the film plus half the profits. Gable, who was under contract to MGM, was given a $100,000 bonus. "Gone with the Wind" cost close to $4 million to produce but MGM provided no additional funds.

George Cukor began directing "Gone with the Wind" but he was fired after several weeks. Victor Fleming was hired to complete the film, but he suffered a nervous breakdown and was temporarily replaced by Sam Wood. Sidney Franklin and William Wellman also directed some of the dramatic sequences. The final scene of the movie had been filmed and previewed with the line, "Frankly, my dear, I don't care." Selznick decided the "damn" line from the book was essential. The Production Code Administration refused to approve the word, but Will Hays, after receiving a lengthy "memo" from Selznick, permitted Rhett Butler to say, "Frankly, my dear, I don't give a damn."

"Gone with the Wind" has sold more movie tickets than any other film in history. It was technically renovated in 1967 for large-screen, 70mm projection, with enhanced color and stereophonic sound. NBC paid an estimated $5 million for its television showing of "Gone with the Wind" in April 1976.

A film which many consider one of the greatest in Hollywood history is Orson Welles' "Citizen Kane," a brilliant psychological and biographical study loosely based on the career of one of America's most powerful and enigmatic publishing figures, William Randolph Hearst. A large part of the film's acclaim stems from its technical innovation. Welles employed extreme up-angle shots, dramatic contrasts of dark and light, and vast in-depth perspectives. He demonstrated unique cinematic imagination in editing several of the sequences. Some critics contend that the film techniques employed by Welles detract from the human drama. The public apparently agreed, since the film was a dismal failure at the box office.

Newsreels

A standard staple of virtually every movie theatre's program during the 1930s and '40s was the *newsreel*. Generally about 10-minutes long, newsreels were released through the major studios twice weekly to motion picture theatres throughout the country. The largest and best financed of the newsreel organizations was "Fox Movietone," which featured Lowell Thomas as its chief commentator. A Fox reel consisted of a potpourri of news footage which was compartmentalized into a series of categories, such as sports and women's fashions. "Pathé News," the RKO newsreel, featured radio announcer Harry Von Zell. William Randolph Hearst's "News of the Day," released by MGM, arranged its material on the basis of newsworthiness. Hearst was criticized by various liberal groups for using the newsreel to propagandize the American public, and theatres featuring "News of the Day" were sometimes boycotted and picketed. Jean Paul King of NBC was the principal narrator. Paramount News emphasized international coverage. Graham McNamee narrated Universal's low-budgeted newsreel. Although the newsreels occasionally presented events of great magnitude, such as the on-the-spot newsreel footage by "Fox Movietone" of the assassination of King Alexander I of Yugoslavia in 1934, they were more a product of show business than journalism.

In the spring of 1935, Time Inc., introduced a new concept in newsreels called "The March of Time." Really more of a film documentary than a newsreel, it was released once a month. For the first years "March of Time" dealt with several subjects, but after May 1938 it concentrated on one topic in each 20-minute issue. Unlike its competitors which eschewed controversy, "March of Time" sought to provoke discussion of politically sensitive topics and often openly editorialized. "March of Time" survived for 16 years. Competition from television-news services eventually eliminated newsreels from the movie screen.

Over 4,000 films were produced in Hollywood between 1940 and

1949. By the middle '40s, attendance at the motion picture theatres was at an all-time high. In 1946, the peak box-office year in motion picture history, an average of 90 million people were attending the movies each week.

The Decline of the Old Order

Beginning late in 1947, Hollywood was beset with a series of ills from which it has never fully recovered. A Sub Committee of the House Committee on Un-American Activities, chaired by Rep. J. Parnell Thomas of New Jersey, descended on the film community in October, 1947 to investigate alleged Communist infiltration into the film industry. In a caucus room of the House Office Building in Washington, D.C. the hierarchy of Hollywood testified before Parnell and his four-member committee, which included an ambitious young Congressman, Richard M. Nixon.

Scores of news gathering agencies, some equipped with newsreel and television cameras, covered the spectacle. The first to testify were the "friendly" witnesses. They produced very little evidence of Communist activity, but provided some amusement. Mrs. Lela Rogers, mother of screen actress Ginger Rogers, told of a communistic line that her daughter refused to speak in a Dalton Trumbo picture, "Tender Comrades." The line was "Share and share alike, that's democracy." Walt Disney explained that attempts had been made to have Mickey Mouse follow the party line. Adolphe Menjou, the well-dressed screen actor, identified himself as a close friend of J. Edgar Hoover and an expert on Communism, but he was unable to identify specific examples of subversive propaganda in Hollywood films.

A week later the "unfriendly" witnesses appeared. Ten prominent producers, directors and screen writers refused to cooperate and expressed opposition to the invasion of their civil rights. Known as the "Hollywood Ten," they were held in contempt of the Committee and subsequently went to jail for sentences of up to a year. The U.S. Supreme Court, in a 5-to-4 decision, refused to review the convictions. Ironically, J. Parnell Thomas, who was convicted of conspiracy to defraud the government for adding mythical names to his payroll, ended up at the Federal Correctional Institution in Danbury, Connecticut with two of the convicted ten, Ring Lardner Jr. and Lester Cole. The hearings, which were suspended during the ten's various court appeals, were resumed again in 1951 under the direction of Representative John S. Wood. Hollywood entered a period of fear. Political discussion became minimal, and those who were not "cleared" by the Committee had to find another line of work. Blacklists were compiled and distinguished careers were destroyed. It was not a period that Hollywood could look back on with pride.

The Paramount Case

The crushing blow to Hollywood's economic structure came with the U.S. Supreme Court's decision in *U.S.* vs. *Paramount et al.* [334 U.S. 131 (1948)]. The proceedings in this case were initiated in 1938 with a suit filed by the Justice Department against the major motion picture companies, alleging that they violated Section 4 of the Sherman Act. The complaint specifically charged that the major studios had conspired to restrain and monopolize interstate trade in the exhibition of films and that the vertical combination of producing, distributing, and exhibiting films was contrary to the provisions of the Sherman Act. The Federal District Court, after lengthy proceedings, found the motion picture companies guilty of most of the allegations made by the Justice Department. On May 3, 1948, the U.S. Supreme Court affirmed the lower court's decision with respect to the charges of unreasonable restraint of trade, finding that the major studios discriminated against independent exhibitors through various kinds of contract provisions. The studios were enjoined from engaging in "block booking" whereby the licensing of one film is conditioned upon the exhibitor's taking one or more other features. The District Court concluded that five major firms (Loew's-MGM, 20th Century-Fox, RKO, Warner Brothers, and Paramount) had a particular monopoly in the ownership of theatres and enjoined them from expanding their theatre holdings. The U.S. Supreme Court remanded the question of theatre ownership to the lower court.

In the next several years, through a series of consent decrees, the "Big Five" divested themselves of their theatre holdings. Paramount Pictures, Inc. separated into Paramount Pictures Corporation and United Paramount Theatres. The former became a part of Gulf and Western Industries in 1966 and the latter merged with the American Broadcasting Company. RKO became RKO Pictures and RKO Theatres. The theatre operation was acquired by List Industries, Inc. which later merged with Glen Alden Corporation, an organization that began as a coal company. List had holdings in textiles, restaurant services, real estate and electronics. In 1955, General Teleradio, a subsidiary of the General Tire and Rubber Company, bought RKO Pictures, stopped production and sold the RKO film library for television use. Desilu, the TV empire created by Desi Arnaz and Lucille Ball, acquired the RKO studios for television production. 20th Century-Fox transferred its theatre holdings in 1951 to a new company, National Theatres. George Skouras (Spyros' brother) became president of the theatre operation. Of the former "Big Five," only 20th Century-Fox is still primarily in the motion picture production and distribution business.

In 1953, Warner Bros. became Warner Bros. Pictures and the Stanley-Warner movie chain. Warner Pictures was taken over in 1967 by Seven Arts Productions Ltd., a company that sold motion pictures to television stations, and was renamed Warner-7 Arts. Two years later, the new company merged with Kinney National Service Inc. ultimately to become a subsidiary of a huge conglomerate, Warner Communications. Kinney's varied interests included parking lots, funeral homes, hearse and limousine rental, and a host of other non-media related areas. In addition the company also owned Ashley-Famous, a talent agency; National Periodical Publications, publishers of *Mad, Superman* and *Batman* magazines and distributors of numerous magazines ranging from *Playboy* to *Yachting;* and Panavision Inc., a motion picture production equipment-leasing organization. Loew's-MGM, the last of the majors to undergo divorcement transferred its U.S. and Canadian theatre holdings to a new holding company, Loew's Theatres, Inc. starting in 1954.

The New Order

No longer having a guaranteed outlet for their product, and spurred on by the threat of television which was beginning to capture the American public's fancy in 1948, the major studios substantially cut back production and attempted to reduce costs by dropping their leading contract players and directors. United Artists began to finance the independent productions of stars as well as directors in the early 1950s. Other companies followed United's lead. Several stars, for example Gary Cooper in "High Noon," took a salary cut in exchange for a share of the profits. For his work in "Bridge on the River Kwai,"

William Holden received 10 per cent of the film's gross income with the understanding that his percentage would be paid to him at the rate of $50,000 a year. To date, the film has grossed over $17 million in domestic film rentals alone. Stars of the magnitude of Cary Grant were given all rights to the negatives of their films after a designated number of years. By the early 1960s the major studios would, more often than not, merely distribute a picture that had been filmed by an independent producer.

Technological gimmickry enjoyed a brief vogue in the early 1950s. In November 1952 "Bwana Devil," starring Robert Stack and Nigel Bruce, was presented in 3-D. The process achieved the illusion of three dimensions by projecting two slightly overlapping images on the screen. The movie was shot through two camera lenses simultaneously at a specified distance apart. The viewer wore plastic polaroid glasses which merged the two images giving the impression of three-dimensionality. Objects, such a spears, arrows and knives, appeared to jump out of the screen. "Bwana Devil," which caused audiences to drop to the floor for cover, was followed by several 3-D pictures including "House of Wax," "The French Line," and "Murders in the Rue Morgue." Alfred Hitchcock shot "Dial M for Murder" in 3-D, but decided to release it in conventional form. The novelty of 3-D soon diminished and despite recent attempts to revive the technique in such films as "The Stewardesses" and Andy Warhol's "Frankenstein," it is rarely employed in current films.

Another process, called Cinerama, used peripheral vision to create a sense of depth. Invented by Fred Waller in 1938, the system employs three projectors, electronically synchronized, to put the pictures on a deeply curved screen in three sections. Although its effects were spectacular, the system proved economically unfeasible. Cinerama requires a large theatre to accommodate a small audience. Eventually compromise systems such as Cinemascope and Panavision were utilized by most film companies, since they were adaptable to conventional theatres.

Ultimately, it was film content, not technical gimmicks, which attracted audiences away from television. Several films of distinction emerged from the 1950s, including Elia Kazan's "On the Waterfront," Delbert Mann's "Marty" and Sidney Lumet's "Twelve Angry Men." Interestingly, all three of these films were produced in

New York—not Hollywood. Several other important films were shot at domestic locales outside the film capital. Throughout the '50s, the number of "runaway" films—pictures produced abroad—also increased. Films produced outside the United States had several economic advantages. Lower production costs, particularly cheaper labor for pictures requiring large casts, provided a financial incentive for film production in certain countries. Creative artists in the high income tax brackets found the tax advantages of foreign production particularly inviting. In addition, the use of international stars and locales generally made the film attractive to a greater number of countries. By the early 1960s Hollywood was becoming more of a metaphor for the film industry than a center for motion picture production. The popular mythology of Hollywood as a place of glamour and luminosity, of romance laced with decadence, of stars in white limousines and directors in characteristically movie-set accoutrements, of vulgarian moguls in front offices, gradually receded before a more pragmatic and mundane image.

Many films of the blockbuster variety were made at enormous costs and at great financial risk. In order to realize a profit, a film must exceed 2½ times its negative cost—total cost of producing a film—in gross film rentals. "Ben Hur," the 1959 extravaganza starring Charlton Heston, is said to have cost $15 million. By 1963, the cost of "Cleopatra," beset by production delays, escalated to an estimated $31 million, although the film had been originally budgeted for only $2 million. Advertising, promotion and distribution costs brought the total to a whopping $40 million.

There were, of course, highly successful low-budget films. Joseph E. Levine, a modest theatre owner and regional distributor in Boston, purchased the U.S. and Canadian distribution rights to an Italian produced film titled "Hercules," starring muscular Steve Reeves, for less than $150,000. Levine made 600 prints of the film for "saturation booking" throughout the United States and spent an estimated $1.5 million on advertising and publicity. The film's gross box office receipts exceeded $20 million, catapulting his investment into enormous profits.

But, despite the cinematic gimmicks, the emphasis on spectacle and extravaganza, and the occasional big money maker, overall movie income and movie admissions declined throughout the 1950s. Television had proved itself to be a formidable opponent.

Changing Patterns of Exhibition

By the mid-1960s the number of motion picture houses decreased by over 50 per cent from the 20,355 estimated to exist in 1945. During the same period, "drive-in" theatres multiplied at a near geometric rate—from about 100 in 1945 to over 4,000 in 1965. Overall, motion picture theatres declined by about one-third between the 1950s and '60s. Many of the "movie palaces" were closed down because they were uneconomical to operate. Some were converted to a complex of two or more smaller theatres, each with reduced seating capacity. Recently constructed theatres, whether single units or "quad-complexes," are generally designed for operating efficiency and audience convenience. Many of the new motion picture houses are located adjacent to or within major shopping centers. Today there are about 10,000 motion picture houses and 3,500 "drive-in" theatres throughout the United States.

Corporate Commotion

During the 1960s the motion picture industry was characterized by corporate commotion and turbulence. Three companies in particular underwent dramatic upheaval: Paramount Pictures, Columbia Pictures and MGM. Despite the fact that these companies were not consistently profitable ventures, those seeking to gain control were attracted by the liquidation value of the corporate assets—such as: potential television license fees from feature films; the sale and development of real estate; and the sale of music and literary copyrights. Because of their financially precarious position, the film companies were thought to have greater value dead than alive.

When the battle for control over Paramount began in the spring of 1965, the chairman of the board, Adolph Zukor, was in his 90s, the president of the company, Barney Balaban, was in his late 70s, and Paramount itself was sinking financially. The company was suffering heavy losses on its feature-film productions, and was reluctant to enter into the production of television programs. Its old movies were being unsystematically leased to television on comparatively disadvantageous terms. Paramount's elderly executives attempted to prop up earnings by selling off assets, including some TV stations and the Paramount Building in Times Square. In the ensuing struggle for control of Paramount, Gulf and Western Industries emerged victorious. Charles Bludhorn, chairman of G&W, negotiated a deal in which he was able to acquire Paramount's $300 million assets for only $125 million. Gulf and Western Industries is an enormous conglomerate with holdings in auto parts, zinc mining, cigars, and meatpacking. Between 1958, when Bludhorn established G&W, and 1966 when he concluded his purchase of Paramount Pictures, he acquired almost 70 other companies at a rate of nearly one every six weeks.

At about the same time as the Paramount acquisition, Columbia Pictures also found itself in an extremely vulnerable position for a corporate takeover. While Columbia's earnings were disappointing, its film assets were rising in value. Maurice Clairmont of Lee National Corp. acquired a considerable amount of Columbia Pictures stock in mid-1966 in his bid for control. In a seemingly coordinated move, the Banque de Paris acquired 34.4 per cent of Columbia's outstanding stock. Attorneys for the Banque de Paris failed to consider Section 310(a) of the Communications Act of 1934 which prohibits aliens from owning more than 25 per cent of a company with broadcasting interests. This was a critical oversight since Columbia Pictures' subsidiary, Screen Gems, Inc., held an interest in several broadcasting stations. After months of negotiations and several warnings by the Federal Communications Commission, the Banque de Paris pledged to support the incumbent Columbia management. A few months later, the bank sold its stock to interests supportive of the then-current Columbia regime. The existing management remained intact.

The fierce power struggles which have occurred in the movie industry since its inception are exemplified by the changes in management at MGM. The company had declined rapidly in the post-war years under Nicholas Schenck. Shareholders became increasingly more concerned about the studio's losses. Dore Schary, who had been production chief at RKO, was appointed as head of production at MGM in 1948. Louis B. Mayer continued as studio head. Schary's first picture, "Battleground," starring Van Johnson, became a great success. However, his success was short-lived and a series of flops followed. "Jupiter's Darling," an Esther Williams vehicle, lost over

$2 million and the story of the Seventeenth Century settlers who came to Massachusetts, "Plymouth Adventure," lost a reported $1.8 million. Schary was fired in 1956, while the power at MGM shifted from Nicholas Schenck—forced out as chairman of the board—to Arthur Loew, son of the company's founder, Marcus Loew. Wall Street bankers, Lazard Frères and Lehman Brothers, were brought in to help bolster its shaky finances. After little more than a year in office Arthur Loew left the MGM presidency, to be succeeded by Joseph Vogel, former head of Loew's theatre operation. Vogel quickly came into conflict with Louis B. Mayer, who plotted his downfall. Mayer's attempts were unsuccessful and Vogel emerged temporarily victorious. However, MGM's earnings continued to plummet. Between 1961 and 1963 MGM's earnings had plunged from more than $12 million to less than $3 million. Vogel was moved up as chairman in 1963 and replaced as president by Robert H. O'Brien, a former Commissioner with the Securities Exchange Commission, who had joined MGM in 1957 as treasurer and vice president. Within a few months, Vogel was removed as chairman. His greatest financial fiasco had been the 1962 remake, "Mutiny on the Bounty," starring the temperamental actor, Marlon Brando. The movie lost an estimated $10 million.

In 1967, just 10 years after MGM's fierce struggle over corporate control, Philip J. Levin, a wealthy real estate builder-developer and a member of the MGM board of directors, led a proxy fight to take control of MGM from the company's management team headed by Robert H. O'Brien. By 1965 Levin became MGM's largest stockholder, holding more than 14 percent of the outstanding stock. He attempted to pressure management into a program of diversification and acquisition, a reduction in operating costs, and an accelerated schedule of low-budget film production. He also advocated the conversion of MGM's Culver City, California studio lot—more than 180 acres in size—into a profitable real estate development. Levin received virtually no support from the other members of the board. On the contrary, they openly praised O'Brien's three-year record of rising corporate profits, beginning in 1964 and aggregating more than $25 million. By comparison, in 1963, the year that O'Brien assumed the presidency, MGM reported a loss of more than $30 million.

Levin hired Price, Waterhouse & Co., an accounting firm, to prepare a financial report for the benefit of the MGM stockholders, charging O'Brien and his team with poor fiscal management. The report lost much of its credibility when Price, Waterhouse admitted that in its financial analysis, it had failed to include revenues from 16 of MGM's most recent film releases, including "Doctor Zhivago," which went on to gross over $40 million in film rentals and now ranks among the 10 top-grossing feature films of all time.

Although the O'Brien group owned more MGM stock than Levin and his supporters—40 per cent versus 34 per cent—the balance of power rested with several large mutual funds that controlled more than 20 per cent of the stock. When the votes were finally tallied in March 1967, O'Brien managed to stave off the challenge to his control of the corporation.

However, by late 1968, MGM had virtually disintegrated into a deficit-ridden operation deriving its primary fiscal gain from leasing films to television. O'Brien followed the path of his vanquished predecessor, Joseph Vogel, from president to chairman and then out altogether. Louis Polk, a former General Mills executive, succeeded O'Brien as president in 1968 and MGM's biggest shareholder, Edgar Bronfman,* ascended to the chairmanship. Under Polk, the company in 1968 reported more than $35 million deficit.

In October 1969, Tracy Investment, Inc., a company controlled by Las Vegas businessman Kirk Kerkorian, acquired controlling interest in MGM. The following month Kerkorian ousted Polk, whose reign had lasted only 10 months, and appointed James T. Aubrey, a former CBS executive, as president of MGM. Aubrey set the company on a disastrous course by producing low-budgeted films, most of which failed at the box office. During his presidency at CBS-TV, Aubrey made the television network's ratings soar with such programs as "The Andy Griffith Show," "The Beverly Hillbillies," and "Petticoat Junction." He badly misjudged the tastes of motion picture audiences, however, and resigned as MGM president in the fall of 1973.

In September 1973, the company announced it would make only six to eight "special" movies a year. MGM also has withdrawn from film distribution, assigning its domestic distribution rights to United Artists for 10 years and its foreign distribution rights to Cinema International, a joint venture of Paramount and MCA. MGM at present

* Father of Samuel Bronfman II, whose kidnapping for ransom in 1975 was a featured news story.

concentrates on television programming, and Las Vegas hotel and gambling operations.

Ironically, motion picture companies had achieved their new-found desirability through their relationship to television. By the second half of the 1960s, the TV networks turned to motion pictures as a basic staple of their prime-time program fare. Box office hits became a very saleable commodity. ABC was the first to demonstrate their enormous appeal to television audiences when it presented in October 1966 a nine-year-old, three-hour feature film, "The Bridge on the River Kwai." ABC had purchased the film from Screen Gems, Inc. for two showings at a reported price of $2 million. The Ford Motor Company paid $1.8 million for the first telecast of the film—the largest price then paid for a television special by a single sponsor. It attracted the largest audience of any movie ever presented on television up to that time—an estimated 60 million people viewed this film. Motion picture executives began to view television as an extension of the movie theatre box office. In a one-week period in October 1966 over $93 million worth of movies were licensed to network television. MGM received $63 million for 51 films already released, plus an additional 18 still to be produced. Paramount received $20 million from ABC for a package of 32 films. And 20th Century-Fox sold 17 of its most recent attractions, including "Cleopatra," to ABC for $19.5 million.

The record prices the studios received for the sale of feature-film rights to television were short-lived as the television networks soon acquired a large feature-film inventory sufficient to last several years. The end of the 1960s saw MGM take a pre-tax loss of $22 million and 20th Century-Fox register a pre-tax loss of $29.8 million. Universal's drain upon MCA's other profitable operations ran into millions of dollars and executives at Paramount acknowledged that the company was operating at a loss. In all, five of the major companies reported an aggregate loss of $110 million. By the end of 1971, the major producer-distributors had losses totaling more than $500 million. Huge budgeted films like "Tora! Tora! Tora!" ($20 million) and "Hello, Dolly!" ($21 million), both released in 1970, were boxoffice disasters. Hollywood then embarked on a policy of producing $2-million-and-under films. With few exceptions, this concept proved unsuccessful.

The record-breaking success of "The Godfather" in late 1971, closely followed by the "Poseidon Adventure" in 1972, restored the reputation of the big-budget motion picture. The public's taste for "blockbuster" films was further reflected by phenomenal successes of "The Sting," "Chinatown," and "The Exorcist." The latter film, which cost about $10 million to produce, has grossed over $110 million worldwide.

An occasional low-budgeted film has proven to be successful. "American Graffiti," which cost $830,000 to produce, is expected eventually to gross some 40 to 50 times that amount. However, its success has not been duplicated by most low-budget films. Most of the majors have scrapped their low-budget film projects and have moved back to an emphasis on stars and spectacular settings.

The major companies are producing fewer films than in the past, but spending more money on them. The decline in feature film production is responsible, in part, for the high rate of unemployment in the film industry. Some 85 per cent of the Screen Actors Guild's 30,000 active members cannot find work in the entertainment field. With the trend toward expensive movies has come a resurgence of concentration and centralization of control in the film industry. Theatre owners are becoming progressively more dependent on a small group of producers. Five producers and distributors (Warner Bros., Universal, 20th Century-Fox, Paramount, and United Artists) accounted for 71 per cent of the domestic film market in 1974. The significant boxoffice successes of 1975 reflected a continuation of this trend. "Towering Inferno," "Murder on the Orient Express," "Godfather II," "Earthquake," and "Jaws" were all produced by these dominant companies. "Jaws," the 1975 Universal release based on Peter Benchley's best-selling novel about a marauding shark, cost $8 million to produce and had reported boxoffice receipts of $25.7 million for the first 13 days of showings around the world.

Most of the major film companies have proven to be more resilient than the prophets of doom had anticipated. Although the despotic moguls of moviedom have been deposed by conglomerates, financiers, lawyers and computers, the oligarchical character of the movie industry remains intact.

6

Motion Picture
Self-Regulation

THE PERIOD FOLLOWING World War I was characterized by a general relaxation of moral standards which was mildly reflected on the screen. Since profits depended on maintaining the screen as a family institution, sex, for the most part, was approached cautiously. Nevertheless, divorce, seduction, consumption of alcohol and even the use of drugs were hinted at in the early postwar films. Although there were some strictures offered against the alleged immorality of these films, the moral concern about Hollywood in the 1920s centered more around the newspapers' and magazines' exposés of the private lives of the stars than what happened on the screen. In the early '20s the foundation of the movie capital was shaken by events which shocked and outraged various sectors of the American public.

Hollywood Scandals

In 1920 Mary Pickford, "America's Sweetheart," established residence in Nevada and secured a divorce from her husband, Owen Moore. Three weeks later, she and Douglas Fairbanks were married in California. Accusations concerning the legality of her divorce created a brief, but disturbing, turmoil. Nevada officials never took formal action against her, but the incident provided fuel for the anti-Hollywood flames, particularly since Mary's screen image was always the personification of goodness, innocence, and purity. She was the woman every man wanted to have—as a sister.

In September, 1921 the Roscoe ("Fatty") Arbuckle scandal rocked Hollywood. Arbuckle, who had weighed 16 lbs. at birth, achieved fame as the lovable fat clown in the silent screen era. In the early '20s he was as famous as Chaplin and Keaton, and in 1921 he was the first screen actor to be offered a $3 million contract.

Arbuckle spent his money lavishly and was known to give wild parties. On Labor Day, in 1921, he gave a party at the St. Francis Hotel in San Francisco. One of the guests, a minor screen actress named Virginia Rappe, was later found in the bedroom holding her abdomen and moaning, apparently in a great deal of pain. Several guests at the party testified that Ms. Rappe had spent the latter part of the evening with Arbuckle in the locked bedroom. Four days later she died and Arbuckle was indicted for involuntary manslaughter. Newspapers gave the case front-page coverage. William Randolph Hearst ordered six extra editions to be printed every day and the Arbuckle case was the main item of news. After three highly publicized trials (the first two were inconclusive) Arbuckle was found "not guilty," but his acting career was destroyed. He later did some directing for Buster Keaton under the assumed name of Will B. Good.

In 1922, an English director, William Desmond Taylor, was murdered in his home in Los Angeles. Newspapers increased their circulation by intimating that the case involved sex and drugs. Two Hollywood actresses, Mary Miles Minter and Mabel Normand were featured prominently in the case. Although the facts of the case were never made clear, and the murder is still unsolved, Minter's and Normand's careers were permanently damaged.

Later in the same year that Taylor mysteriously died, the death of actor Wallace Reid generated posthumous scandal when it was revealed that he was addicted to drugs. The notoriety and scandal that seemed to engulf Hollywood encouraged many states and municipalities to enact laws requiring the licensing of films. Within a few years there were more than 20 states where municipal or statewide censorship was enforced.

While the Arbuckle case was being tried on the front pages of newspapers throughout the country, the major motion picture companies recognized the necessity for immediate and decisive action to thwart a swelling movement that was hostile to the movie industry and demanding restrictive national legislation. The Southern Baptist Conference, the Christian Endeavor, the General Federation of Women's

Clubs and various other groups all passed resolutions condemning the evil depicted in films, the open and wanton display of deviant moral behavior by movie talent, and the sensationalism of movie advertising. Often, the advertising for a motion picture was more lurid than the film itself.

Will H. Hays

The major movie companies decided that a new organization was needed to represent their common interest. They realized that the individual selected to head this association could ultimately determine the fate of the movies as a medium of mass entertainment. The person they sought had to have no previous involvement with the movie industry. In addition, their prospective leader would have to be an effective administrator, someone with good political contacts to stave off any enactment of federal censorship legislation, an individual who could lend his personal prestige, dignity and respectability to the business of movie-making. All of these attributes seemed to be embodied in one man: Will H. Hays, President Warren G. Harding's Postmaster General. An offer was made to him early in 1922 in a letter signed by a number of movie executives, including Adolph Zukor, William Fox, Samuel Goldwyn, Lewis J. Selznick and Carl Laemmle. Hays accepted their offer—a three-year contract at an annual salary of $100,000—and on March 4, 1922 he resigned his government post, the first Harding cabinet member to do so. Eight days later, the Motion Picture Producers and Distributors of America (MPPDA) was incorporated and Hays was formally appointed its president, chairman of the board of directors and chairman of the executive committee. The organization, which was financed by a small percentage of the gross receipts of each of its members, set up a policy of self-regulation in which each of the studios submitted synopses of questionable books, plays and original properties they planned to film. The MPPDA advised the studios as to the feasibility of using the material. In addition, Hays prepared a list of prohibited books and plays. In 1927, Hays provided movie producers with a list of rejected and deleted scenes from pictures screened before governmental censor boards which he labeled the "Don'ts and Be Carefuls." In an effort to fight off national censorship, Hays launched a national campaign to rehabilitate the movie industry and untarnish its image.

On March 30, 1930, the movie industry adopted the Motion Picture Production Code which was written by Martin Quigley, a trade publication editor and an influential Catholic layman, and Father Daniel Lord, a Jesuit. The Code was extremely proscriptive, and interpretations of its specific provisions sometimes bordered on the absurd. A couple could kiss while sitting on the edge of the bed, for example, but the woman had to have one foot touching the floor. Double beds were discouraged. The Code authority, operating under a self-imposed set of taboos, became more restrictive than the state censors. Here, in its entirety, is the 1930 Motion Picture Production Code, as amended.

THE MOTION PICTURE PRODUCTION CODE

PREAMBLE

Motion picture producers recognize the high trust and confidence which have been placed in them by the people of the world and which have made motion pictures a universal form of entertainment.

They recognize their responsibility to the public because of this trust and because entertainment and art are important influences in the life of a nation.

Hence, though regarding motion pictures primarily as entertainment without any explicit purpose of teaching or propaganda, they know that the motion picture within its own field of entertainment may be directly responsible for spiritual or moral progress, for higher types of social life, and for much correct thinking.

During the rapid transition from silent to talking pictures they realized the necessity and the opportunity of subscribing to a Code to govern the production of talking pictures and of reacknowledging this responsibility.

On their part, they ask from the public and from public leaders a sympathetic understanding of their purposes and problems and a spirit of cooperation that will allow them the freedom and opportunity necessary to bring the motion picture to a still higher level of wholesome entertainment for all the people.

GENERAL PRINCIPLES

1. No picture shall be produced which will lower the moral standards of those who see it. Hence the sympathy of the audience shall never be thrown to the side of crime, wrong-doing, evil or sin.

2. Correct standards of life, subject only to the requirements of drama and entertainment, shall be presented.

3. Law, natural or human, shall not be ridiculed, nor shall sympathy be created for its violation.

PARTICULAR APPLICATIONS

I. Crimes against the law *

These shall never be presented in such a way as to throw sympathy with the crime as against law and justice or to inspire others with a desire for imitation.

1. *Murder*
   a) The technique of murder must be presented in a way that will not inspire imitation.
   b) Brutal killings are not to be presented in detail.
   c) Revenge in modern times shall not be justified.
2. *Methods of crime* should not be explicitly presented.
   a) Theft, robbery, safe-cracking, and dynamiting of trains, mines, buildings, etc., should not be detailed in method.
   b) Arson must be subject to the same safeguards.
   c) The use of firearms should be restricted to essentials.
   d) Methods of smuggling should not be presented.
3. *The illegal drug traffic* must not be portrayed in such a way as to stimulate curiosity concerning the use of, or traffic in, such drugs; nor shall scenes be approved which show the use of illegal drugs, or their effects, in detail (as amended September 11, 1946).
4. *The use of liquor* in American life, when not required by the plot or for proper characterization, will not be shown.

II. Sex

The sanctity of the institution of marriage and the home shall be upheld. Pictures shall not infer that low forms of sex relationship are the accepted or common thing.

1. *Adultery and illicit sex,* sometimes necessary plot material, must not be explicitly treated or justified, or presented attractively.
2. *Scenes of passion*
   a) These should not be introduced except where they are definitely essential to the plot.
   b) Excessive and lustful kissing, lustful embraces, suggestive postures and gestures are not to be shown.
   c) In general, passion should be treated in such manner as not to stimulate the lower and baser emotions.

* See "Special Regulations on Crime in Motion Pictures," pp. 84–85.

3. *Seduction or rape*

    a) These should never be more than suggested, and then only when essential for the plot. They must never be shown by explicit method.

    b) They are never the proper subject for comedy.

4. *Sex perversion* or any inference to it is forbidden.

5. *White slavery* shall not be treated.

6. *Miscegenation* (sex relationship between the white and black races) is forbidden.

7. *Sex hygiene* and venereal diseases are not proper subjects for theatrical motion pictures.

8. Scenes of *actual childbirth,* in fact or in silhouette, are never to be presented.

9. *Children's sex organs* are never to be exposed.

III. Vulgarity

The treatment of low, disgusting, unpleasant, though not necessarily evil, subjects should be guided always by the dictates of good taste and a proper regard for the sensibilities of the audience.

IV. Obscenity

Obscenity in word, gesture, reference, song, joke, or by suggestion (even when likely to be understood only by part of the audience) is forbidden.

V. Profanity *

Pointed profanity and every other profane or vulgar expression, however used, is forbidden.

No approval by the Production Code Administration shall be given to the use of words and phrases in motion pictures including, but not limited to, the following:

Alley cat (applied to a woman); bat (applied to a woman); broad (applied to a woman); Bronx cheer (the sound); chippie; cocotte; God, Lord, Jesus, Christ (unless used reverently); cripes; fanny; fairy (in a vulgar sense); finger (the); fire, cries of; Gawd; goose (in a vulgar sense); "hold your hat" or "hats"; hot (applied to a woman); "in your hat"; louse; lousy; Madam (relating to prostitution); nance; nerts; nuts (except when meaning crazy); pansy; razzberry (the sound); slut (applied to a woman); S.O.B.; son-of-a; tart; toilet gags; tom cat (applied to a man); traveling salesman and farmer's daughter jokes; whore; damn, hell (excepting when the use of said last two words shall be essential and required for portrayal, in proper historical context, of any scene or dialogue based

* As amended by resolution of the Board of Directors, November 1, 1939.

upon historical fact or folklore, or for the presentation in proper literary context of a Biblical, or other religious quotation, or a quotation from a literary work provided that no such use shall be permitted which is intrinsically objectionable or offends good taste.

In the administration of Section V of the Production Code, the Production Code Administration may take cognizance of the fact that the following words and phrases are obviously offensive to the patrons of motion pictures in the United States and more particularly to the patrons of motion pictures in foreign countries:

Chink, Dago, Frog, Greaser, Hunkie, Kike, Nigger, Spig, Wop, Yid

VI. Costume *

1. *Complete nudity* is never permitted. This includes nudity in fact or in silhouette, or any licentious notice thereof by other characters in the pictures.
2. *Undressing scenes* should be avoided, and never used save where essential to the plot.
3. *Indecent or undue exposure* is forbidden.
4. *Dancing costumes* intended to permit undue exposure or indecent movements in the dance are forbidden.

VII. Dances

1. Dances suggesting or representing sexual actions or indecent passion are forbidden.
2. Dances which emphasize indecent movements are to be regarded as obscene.

VIII. Religion

1. No film or episode may throw *ridicule* on any religious faith.
2. *Ministers of religion* in their character as ministers of religion should not be used as comic characters or as villains.
3. *Ceremonies* of any definite religion should be carefully and respectfully handled.

IX. Locations

The treatment of bedrooms must be governed by good taste and delicacy.

X. National feelings

1. *The use of the flag* shall be consistently respectful.
2. *The history,* institutions, prominent people and citizenry of all nations shall be represented fairly.

* See "Special Resolution on Costumes, p. 85.

XI. Titles

Salacious, indecent, or obscene titles shall not be used.

XII. Repellent subjects

The following subjects must be treated within the careful limits of good taste:

1. *Actual hangings or electrocutions* as legal punishments for crime.
2. *Third-degree* methods.
3. *Brutality* and possible gruesomeness.
4. *Branding* of people or animals.
5. *Apparent cruelty* to children or animals.
6. *The sale of women,* or a woman selling her virtue.
7. *Surgical operations.*

SPECIAL REGULATIONS ON CRIME IN MOTION PICTURES

Resolved, That the Board of Directors of the Motion Picture Producers and Distributors of America, Incorporated, hereby ratifies, approves, and confirms the interpretations of the Production Code, the practices thereunder, and the resolutions indicating and confirming such interpretations heretofore adopted by the Association of Motion Picture Producers, Incorporated, all effectuating regulations relative to the treatment of crime in motion pictures, as follows:

1. Details of crime must never be shown and care should be exercised at all times in discussing such details.
2. Action suggestive of wholesale slaughter of human beings, either by criminals, in conflict with police, or as between warring factions of criminals, or in public disorder of any kind, will not be allowed.
3. There must be no suggestion, at any time, of excessive brutality.
4. Because of the increase in the number of films in which murder is frequently committed, action showing the taking of human life, even in the mystery stories, is to be cut to the minimum. These frequent presentations of murder tend to lessen regard for the sacredness of life.
5. Suicide, as a solution of problems occurring in the development of screen drama, is to be discouraged as morally questionable and as bad theatre—unless absolutely necessary for the development of the plot.
6. There must be no display, at any time, of machine guns, sub-machine guns or other weapons generally classified as illegal weapons in the hands of gangsters, or other criminals, and there are to be no off-stage sounds of the repercussions of these guns.
7. There must be no new, unique or trick methods shown for concealing guns.

8. The flaunting of weapons by gangsters, or other criminals, will not be allowed.

9. All discussions and dialogue on the part of gangsters regarding guns should be cut to the minimum.

10. There must be no scenes, at any time, showing law-enforcing officers dying at the hands of criminals. This includes private detectives and guards for banks, motor trucks, etc.

11. With special reference to the crime of kidnapping—or illegal abduction—such stories are acceptable under the Code only when the kidnapping or abduction is (a) not the main theme of the story; (b) the person kidnapped is not a child; (c) there are no details of the crime of kidnapping; (d) no profit accrues to the abductors or kidnappers; and (e) where the kidnappers are punished.

It is understood, and agreed, that the word kidnapping, as used in paragraph 11 of these Regulations, is intended to mean abduction, or illegal detention, in modren times, by criminals for ransom.

12. Pictures dealing with criminal activities, in which minors participate, or to which minors are related, shall not be approved if they incite demoralizing imitation on the part of youth.

SPECIAL RESOLUTION ON COSTUMES

On October 25, 1939, the Board of Directors of the Motion Picture Producers and Distributors of America, Inc., adopted the following resolution:

Resolved, That the provisions of Paragraphs 1, 3 and 4 of subdivision VI of the Production Code, in their application to costumes, nudity, indecent or undue exposure and dancing costumes, shall not be interpreted to exclude authentically photographed scenes photographed in a foreign land, of natives of such foreign land, showing native life, if such scenes are a necessary and integral part of a motion picture depicting exclusively such land and native life, provided that no such scenes shall be intrinsically objectionable nor made a part of any motion picture produced in any studio; and provided further that no emphasis shall be made in any scenes of the customs or garb of such natives or in the exploitation thereof.

SPECIAL REGULATIONS ON CRUELTY TO ANIMALS

On December 27, 1940, the Board of Directors of the Motion Picture Producers and Distributors of America, Inc., approved a resolution adopted by the Association of Motion Picture Producers, Inc., reaffirming previous resolutions of the California Association concerning brutality and possible gruesomeness, branding of people and animals, and apparent cruelty to children and animals:

Resolved, by the Board of Directors of the Association of Motion Picture Producers, Inc., That

(1) Hereafter, in the production of motion pictures there shall be no use by the members of the Association of the contrivance or apparatus in connection with animals which is known as the "running W," nor shall any picture submitted to the Production Code Administration be approved if reasonable grounds exist for believing that use of any similar device by the producer of such picture resulted in apparent cruelty to animals; and

(2) Hereafter, in the production of motion pictures by the members of the Association, such members shall, as to any picture involving the use of animals, invite on the lot during such shooting and consult with the authorized representative of the American Humane Association; and

(3) Steps shall be taken immediately by the members of the Association and by the Production Code Administration to require compliance with these resolutions, which shall bear the same relationship to the sections of the Production Code quoted herein as the Association's special regulations re: Crime in Motion Pictures bear to the sections of the Production Code dealing therewith; and it is

Further resolved, That the resolutions of February 19, 1925 and all other resolutions of this Board establishing its policy to prevent all cruelty to animals in the production of motion pictures and reflecting its determination to prevent any such cruelty, be and the same hereby are in all respects reaffirmed.

REASONS SUPPORTING PREAMBLE OF CODE

1. Theatrical motion pictures, that is, pictures intended for the theatre as distinct from pictures intended for churches, schools, lecture halls, educational movements, social reform movements, etc., are primarily to be regarded as ENTERTAINMENT.

   Mankind has always recognized the importance of entertainment and its value in rebuilding the bodies and souls of human beings.

   But it has always recognized that entertainment can be of a character either HELPFUL or HARMFUL to the human race, and in consequence has clearly distinguished between:

   a) *Entertainment which tends to improve* the race, or at least to re-create and rebuild human beings exhausted with the realities of life; and

b) Entertainment which tends to degrade human beings, or to lower their standards of life and living.

Hence the MORAL IMPORTANCE of entertainment is something which has been universally recognized. It enters intimately into the lives of men and women and affects them closely; it occupies their minds and affections during leisure hours; and ultimately touches the whole of their lives. A man may be judged by his standard of entertainment as easily as by the standard of his work.

So *correct entertainment raises* the whole standard of a nation.

Wrong entertainment lowers the whole living conditions and moral ideals of a race.

> *Note,* for example, the healthy reactions to healthful sports, like baseball, golf; the unhealthy reactions to sports like cockfighting, bullfighting, bear baiting, etc.

> Note, too, the effect on ancient nations of gladiatorial combats, the obscene plays of Roman times, etc.

2. Motion pictures are very important as ART.

Though a new art, possibly a combination art, it has the same object as the other arts, the presentation of human thought, emotion, and experience, in terms of an appeal to the soul through the senses.

Here, as in entertainment,

Art *enters intimately* into the lives of human beings.

Art can be *morally good,* lifting men to higher levels. This has been done through good music, great painting, authentic fiction, poetry, drama.

Art can be *morally evil* in its effects. This is the case clearly enough with unclean art, indecent books, suggestive drama. The effect on the lives of men and women is obvious.

Note: It has often been argued that art in itself is unmoral, neither good nor bad. This is perhaps true of the THING which is music, painting, poetry, etc. But the thing is the PRODUCT of some person's mind, and the intention of that mind was either good or bad morally when it produced the thing. Besides, the thing has its EFFECT upon those who come into contact with it. In both these ways, that is, as a product of a mind and as the cause of definite effects, it has a deep moral significance and an unmistakable moral quality. Hence: The motion pictures, which are the most popular of modern arts for the masses, have their moral quality from the intention of the minds which produce them and from their effects on the moral lives and reactions of their audiences. This gives them a most important morality.

1. They *reproduce* the morality of the men who use the pictures as a medium for the expression of their ideas and ideals.

2. They *affect* the moral standards of those who, through the screen, take in these ideas and ideals.

In the case of the motion pictures, this effect may be particularly emphasized because no art has so quick and so widespread an appeal to the masses. It has become in an incredibly short period *the art of the multitudes*.

3. The motion picture, because of its importance as entertainment and because of the trust placed in it by the peoples of the world, has special MORAL OBLIGATIONS:

A. Most arts appeal to the mature. This art appeals at once *to every class,* mature, immature, developed, undeveloped, law abiding, criminal. Music has its grades for different classes; so has literature and drama. This art of the motion picture, combining as it does the two fundamental appeals of looking at a *picture* and *listening to a story,* at once reaches every class of society.

B. By reason of the mobility of a film and the ease of picture distribution, and because of the possibility of duplicating positives in large quantities, this art *reaches places* unpenetrated by other forms of art.

C. Because of these two facts, it is difficult to produce films intended for only certain classes of people. The exhibitor's theatres are built for the masses, for the cultivated and the rude, the mature and the immature, the self-respecting and the criminal. Films, unlike books and music, can with difficulty be confined to certain selected groups.

D. The latitude given to film material cannot, in consequence, be as wide as the latitude given to *book material*. In addition:

a) A book describes; a film vividly presents. One presents on a cold page; the other by apparently living people.

b) A book reaches the mind through words merely; a film reaches the eyes and ears through the reproduction of actual events.

c) The reaction of a reader to a book depends largely on the keenness of the reader's imagination; the reaction to a film depends on the vividness of presentation.

Hence many things which might be described or suggested in a book could not possibly be presented in a film.

E. This is also true when comparing the film with the newspaper.

a) Newspapers present by description, films by actual presentation.

b) Newspapers are after the fact and present things as having taken place; the film gives the events in the process of enactment and with apparent reality of life.

F. Everything possible in a *play* is not possible in a film:

a) Because of the *larger audience of the film,* and its consequential mixed character. Psychologically, the larger the audience, the lower the moral mass resistance to suggestion.

b) Because through light, enlargement of character, presentation, scenic emphasis, etc., the screen story is *brought closer* to the audience than the play.

c) The enthusiasm for and interest in the film *actors* and *actresses,* developed beyond anything of the sort in history, makes the audience largely sympathetic toward the characters they portray and the stories in which they figure. Hence the audience is more ready to confuse actor and actress and the characters they portray, and it is most receptive of the emotions and ideals presented by their favorite stars.

G. *Small communities,* remote from sophistication and from the hardening process which often takes place in the ethical and moral standards of groups in larger cities, are easily and readily reached by any sort of film.

H. The grandeur of mass settings, large action, spectacular features, etc., affects and arouses more intensely the emotional side of the audience.

In general, the mobility, popularity, accessibility, emotional appeal, vividness, straightforward presentation of fact in the film make for more intimate contact with a larger audience and for greater emotional appeal.

Hence the larger moral responsibilities of the motion pictures.

REASONS UNDERLYING THE GENERAL PRINCIPLES

1. No picture shall be produced which will lower the moral standards of those who see it. Hence the sympathy of the audience should never be thrown to the side of crime, wrong-doing, evil or sin.

   This is done:

   1. When *evil* is made to appear *attractive* or *alluring,* and good is made to appear *unattractive.*
   2. When the *sympathy* of the audience is thrown on the side of crime, wrong-doing, evil, sin. The same thing is true of a film that would throw sympathy against goodness, honor, innocence, purity or honesty.

   Note: Sympathy with a person who sins is not the same as sympathy with the sin or crime of which he is guilty. We may feel sorry for the plight of the murderer or even understand the circumstances which led him to his crime. We may not feel sympathy with the wrong which he has done.

   The *presentation of evil* is often essential for art or fiction or drama. This in itself is not wrong provided:

a) That evil is *not presented alluringly*. Even if later in the film the evil is condemned or punished, it must not be allowed to appear so attractive that the audience's emotions are drawn to desire or approve so strongly that later the condemnation is forgotten and only the apparent joy of the sin remembered.

b) That throughout, the audience feels sure that *evil is wrong* and *good is right*.

2. Correct standards of life shall, as far as possible, be presented. A *wide knowledge of life and of living* is made possible through the film. When right standards are consistently presented, the motion picture exercises the most powerful influences. It builds character, develops right ideals, inculcates correct principles, and all this in attractive story form.

If motion pictures consistently *hold up for admiration high types of characters* and present stories that will affect lives for the better, they can become the most powerful natural force for the improvement of mankind.

3. Law, natural or human, shall not be ridiculed, nor shall sympathy be created for its violation.

By *natural law* is understood the law which is written in the hearts of all mankind, the great underlying principles of right and justice dictated by conscience.

By *human law* is understood the law written by civilized nations.

1. *The presentation of crimes* against the law is *often necessary* for the carrying out of the plot. But the presentation must not throw sympathy with the crime as against the law nor with the criminal as against those who punish him.

2. *The courts of the land* should not be presented as unjust. This does not mean that a single court may not be represented as unjust, much less that a single court official must not be presented this way. But the court system of the country must not suffer as a result of this presentation.

REASONS UNDERLYING PARTICULAR APPLICATIONS

1. *Sin and evil* enter into the story of human beings and hence in themselves *are valid dramatic material*.

2. In the use of this material, it must be distinguished between *sin which repels* by its very nature, and *sins which often attract*.

a) In the first class come murder, most theft, many legal crimes, lying, hypocrisy, cruelty, etc.

b) In the second class come sex sins, sins and crimes of apparent heroism, such as banditry, daring thefts, leadership in evil, organized crime, revenge, etc.

The first class needs less care in treatment, as sins and crimes of this class are naturally unattractive. The audience instinctively condemns all such and is repelled.

Hence the important objective must be to avoid the hardening of the audience, especially of those who are young and impressionable, to the thought and fact of crime. People can become accustomed even to murder, cruelty, brutality, and repellent crimes, if these are too frequently repeated.

The second class needs great care in handling, as the response of human nature to their appeal is obvious. This is treated more fully below.

3. A careful distinction can be made between films intended for *general distribution,* and films intended for use in theatres restricted to a *limited audience.* Themes and plots quite appropriate for the latter would be altogether out of place and dangerous in the former.

Note: The practice of using a general theatre and limiting its patronage during the showing of a certain film to "Adults Only" is not completely satisfactory and is only partially effective.

However, maturer minds may easily understand and accept without harm subject matter in plots which do younger people positive harm.

Hence: If there should be created a special type of theatre, catering exclusively to an adult audience, for plays of this character (plays with problem themes, difficult discussions and maturer treatment) it would seem to afford an outlet, which does not now exist, for pictures unsuitable for general distribution but permissible for exhibitions to a restricted audience.

I. Crimes against the law

The *treatment of crimes* against the law must not:

1. *Teach methods* of crime.
2. *Inspire potential criminals* with a desire for imitation.
3. *Make criminals seem heroic* and justified.

Revenge in modern times shall not be justified. In lands and ages of less developed civilization and moral principles, revenge may sometimes be presented. This would be the case especially in places where no law exists to cover the crime because of which revenge is committed.

Because of its evil consequences, *the drug traffic* should not be presented in any form. The existence of the trade should not be brought to the attention of audiences.

The use of liquor should never be excessively presented. In scenes from American life, the necessities of plot and proper characterization alone justify its use. And in this case, it should be shown with moderation.

II. Sex

Out of regard for the sanctity of marriage and the home, the *triangle,* that is, the love of a third party for one already married, needs careful handling. The treatment should not throw sympathy against marriage as an institution.

Scenes of passion must be treated with an honest acknowledgment of human nature and its normal reactions. Many scenes cannot be presented without arousing dangerous emotions on the part of the immature, the young or the *criminal classes*.

Even within the limits of *pure love,* certain facts have been universally regarded by lawmakers as outside the limits of safe presentation.

In the case of *impure love,* the love which society has always regarded as wrong and which has been banned by divine law, the following are important:

1. Impure love must *not* be presented as *attractive and beautiful*.
2. It must *not* be the subject of *comedy or farce,* or treated as material *for laughter*.
3. It must *not* be presented in such a way as *to arouse passion* or morbid curiosity on the part of the audience.
4. It must *not* be made to seem *right and permissible*.
5. In general, it must *not* be *detailed* in method and manner.

III. Vulgarity; IV. Obscenity; V. Profanity, hardly need further explanation than is contained in the Code.

VI. Costume

General principles:

1. *The effect of nudity or semi-nudity* upon the normal man or woman, and much more upon the young and upon immature persons, has been honestly recognized by all lawmakers and moralists.
2. Hence the fact that the nude or semi-nude body may be *beautiful* does not make its use in the films moral. For, in addition to its beauty, the effect of the nude or semi-nude body on the normal individual must be taken into consideration.
3. Nudity or semi-nudity used simply to put a *''punch''* into a picture comes under the head of immoral actions. It is immoral in its effect on the average audience.
4. Nudity can never be permitted as being *necessary for the plot*. Semi-nudity must not result in undue or indecent exposures.
5. *Transparent* or *translucent materials* and silhoutte are frequently more suggestive than actual exposure.

VII. Dances

Dancing in general is recognized as an *art* and as a *beautiful* form of expressing human emotions.

But dances which suggest or represent sexual actions, whether performed solo or with two or more; dances intended to excite the emotional reaction of an audience; dances with movement of the breasts, excessive body movements while the feet are stationary, violate decency and are wrong.

VIII. Religion

The reason why ministers of religion may not be comic characters or villains is simply because the attitude taken toward them may easily become the attitude taken toward religion in general. Religion is lowered in the minds of the audience because of the lowering of the audience's respect for a minister.

IX. Locations

Certain places are so closely and thoroughly associated with sexual life or with sexual sin that their use must be carefully limited.

X. National feelings

The just rights, history, and feelings of any nation are entitled to most careful consideration and respectful treatment.

XI. Titles

As the title of a picture is the brand on that particular type of goods, it must conform to the ethical practices of all such honest business.

XII. Repellent subjects

Such subjects are occasionally necessary for the plot. Their treatment must never offend good taste nor injure the sensibilities of an audience.

Colonel Jason Joy was put in charge of administering the Code. He was succeeded by James Wingate in 1932. Studios were not compelled to adhere to the Code. By the end of 1933, many Catholic leaders and members of the clergy saw no evidence of reform in motion picture content. They looked upon the Motion Picture Production Code as a complete failure and decided that, since the motion picture industry was incapable of cleaning its own house, perhaps the threat of economic boycott might prove more effective than industry self-regulation or even governmental regulation. This resulted in the formation of the National Legion of Decency (NLOD) which, in 1965, was renamed the National Catholic Office for Motion Pictures. The NLOD established its own rating system designed to determine the suitability of various films for Catholic viewers. Until the late 1950s, a movie "condemned" by the Legion had little chance of realizing a profit. Consequently, the Catholic Church wielded great power over the movie industry for almost 30 years.

Pressure from the newly formed Legion forced the studios to establish enforcement procedures. The MPPDA created the Production Code Administration (PCA) in 1934 to administer the Code and provided for the issuance of a certificate. of approval and a seal to be placed on each film meeting the requirements of the Production Code. To receive a certificate of approval a producer or distributor had to agree to submit all advertising in connection with his picture to the MPPDA's Advertising Code Administration (ACA) for approval. The Production Code Administration was empowered to impose a $25,000 fine against any MPPDA member who sold, distributed, or exhibited a film not bearing its seal of approval. There is no public record which indicates that the fine was ever invoked. Joseph Breen, a former journalist, became chief administrator of the Code's provisions, a position he held for almost 20 years. (Breen took a one year leave of absence in 1941 to serve as head of production at RKO Pictures.) The PCA was financed separately from the other activities of the MPPDA. A fee was charged, based upon total production cost of each picture submitted for approval.

In 1942, the MPPDA rescinded its provision that members who exhibited films lacking PCA approval would be subject to a $25,000 fine. The Association had been advised by counsel that the fine was in restraint of trade. Although the change substantially weakened the Code Authority's enforcement mechanism, the oligarchical character of the movie industry assured continued adherence to the Code.

Howard Hughes and "The Outlaw"

The right of the Motion Picture Association of America to bestow, withhold or revoke its seal of approval was challenged in the courts by multi-millionaire Howard Hughes. Hughes produced a film entitled "The Outlaw," starring Jane Russell, which was denied Code approval. The primary objection to the film concerned the partial exposure of Ms. Russell's widely publicized bosom. Hughes had designed a special bra for Ms. Russell to emphasize her unusual contours. The film received the seal of approval after Hughes agreed to minimize Ms. Russell's exposure by making over a hundred changes in the movie. On February 5, 1943, the first public exhibition of "The Outlaw" began at a single theatre in San Francisco. Revealing pictures of Ms. Russell were displayed on billboards throughout the San Francisco area. The advertising for the film's debut created an uproar and resulted in a flood of public protest. Arrests were threatened and the offensive posters were withdrawn. After a short run the picture closed, and Hughes concerned himself with the war effort.

Early in 1946, Hughes released "The Outlaw" throughout the country and launched a massive advertising campaign using newspapers, magazines, billboards, and even sky writing. An airplane wrote the words "The Outlaw" in the sky over Pasadena, and then made two enormous circles with a dot in the middle of each. Newspaper advertisements for the movie included such questions as "What are the two great reasons for Jane Russell's rise to stardom?" Some of Hughes' advertisements had not been submitted to the Code Authority for approval or had been rejected after being submitted.

On September 6, 1946, while Hughes was recovering from a very serious airplane accident, the Production Code Administration revoked its seal of approval for the movie. Hughes Productions initiated a suit against the Motion Picture Association in the United States District Court in New York City, charging the Association with violation of the antitrust laws. The Court upheld the right of the Code Authority to deny approval because of unacceptable advertising practices and found no evidence that the policies of the MPPDA tended to reduce or destroy competition in the production, distribution, or exhibition of motion pictures. Nor did the Court find that the organization's practices were aimed or designed to achieve such an effect.

Changing of the Guard

Eric Johnston, president of the U.S. Chamber of Commerce, replaced Will Hays as president of the MPPDA in 1945, and changed its name to the Motion Picture Association of America (MPAA). After Johnston's death in 1963, Ralph Hetzel served as acting president for three years. Jack Valenti, former assistant to the late President Johnson, has been head of the MPAA since 1966. When Valenti accepted the MPAA presidency, he was given a seven-year contract at an annual salary of $150,000, plus expenses. His contract was renewed for another five years in 1973.

Geoffrey Shurlock, who had served on the Production Code staff since 1932, succeeded Joseph Breen as head of the PCA in 1954, a position he maintained for 14 years. In 1968, the PCA's name was changed to the Code and Rating Administration (CARA). Eugene Dougherty held the top post from the end of 1968 to the summer of 1971. He was succeeded by Dr. Aaron Stern, a psychiatrist, who resigned in April 1974. The current head is Richard Heffner, a communications consultant and an adjunct professor at Rutgers University.

The power of the original Code stemmed primarily from the studios' agreement to bar from their theatres any film that did not carry the PCA's seal of approval. The Code Authority could virtually guarantee the failure of any picture it deemed unacceptable. The 1930 Production Code, with minor revisions, lasted for two-and-a-half decades.

The Decline of the Production Code

In an effort to combat television, motion pictures became more naturalistic and sexually explicit. As early as 1953, movies successfully defied the Production Code and explored controversial themes. In that year, Otto Preminger, backed by United Artists, produced the first major film to be released without the Code's seal of approval. The film, "The Moon is Blue," dealt with a proposed adultery which never took place. In 1956, another Preminger film, also released through United Artists, entitled "The Man with the Golden Arm," failed to receive Code approval because it concerned drug addiction. Both films were highly profitable. The prevailing belief that a major production was financially doomed without the PCA's seal of approval was shattered. In 1956, the Production Code was modified to permit stories involving drug addiction, kidnapping, prostitution and, even abortion. Although changes in the Code were not dramatic, interpretation was greatly liberalized. An important factor in the erosion of the Code's authority was the Supreme Court's antitrust decision. Divorcement of theatres made it virtually impossible for the major studios to enforce the Code. Five years later, the Code was amended again to allow homosexuality and other sexual aberrations to be presented "with care, discretion, and restraint."

During the 1960s American society underwent dramatic social and political upheaval. The rigid restrictions of the Production Code Administration seemed particularly antiquated at a time when there were riots in the streets, insurrections on the college campuses, rising doubts about the institutions of marriage and the church, and a general disintegration of social traditions. Film-makers, reflecting the national scene, became more frank and open in their treatment of subject matter. In 1966, four months after Jack Valenti took office, the original Code was replaced by a more streamlined version which authorized the labeling of certain approved films as ''suggested for mature audiences.'' Whereas the 1930 Code had forbidden even the mention of certain sexual matters, the 1966 Code said simply that ''restraint and care shall be exercised in presentations dealing with sex aberrations.'' The revised Code reflected a growing awareness in the movie industry that the drafting of narrowly defined standards sufficient to ensure films which reflect the tastes and sensibilities of an increasingly sophisticated viewing audience was extremely difficult if not virtually impossible to accomplish.

Jack Valenti decided that the MPAA should exert every effort to promote the revised Code. He assumed a considerable amount of the responsibility for explaining, and selling, the new Code to the nation. Trailers were run in movie houses with Julie Andrews telling audiences to watch for the Code seal. And theatre managers hung special plaques outside their box offices to show that they upheld and believed in the principles of the Code. What was not announced was that they were not prevented from playing films that did not carry the Code seal.

Motion Picture Rating System

A new attempt at self-regulation began on November 1, 1968, when the motion picture industry instituted the Motion Picture Rating System. The Motion Picture Association of America (MPAA) now requires that each film produced or distributed by its members be submitted to MPAA's Code and Rating Administration (CARA) for rating prior to commercial release. The Motion Picture Rating System is operated under the joint auspices of the MPAA, the International Film Importers and Distributors of America (IFIDA), and the National Association of Theatre Owners (NATO). Producers and distributors who are not members of any of these organizations are invited to participate on a voluntary basis. Non-participation results in an automatic X rating by most theatres around the country. CARA classifies each film submitted into one of four designations:

G—General Audiences. All ages admitted.

PG *—Parental Guidance Suggested. Some material may not be suitable for pre-teenagers.

R—Restricted. Under 17 requires accompanying parent or adult guardian.

X—No one under 17 admitted.

The seven-member Rating Board is comprised of a chairperson, selected by the president of the Motion Picture Association, and six other persons, who are in turn selected exclusively by the chairperson. This procedure is designed to insulate the Rating Board from industry pressure. The members serve on CARA for an indeterminate period of time. The president of the Motion Picture Association does not participate in, nor may he overrule, the Board's decisions. The MPAA estimates that about 99 per cent of the producers of "responsible films" submit their films to CARA for a rating. Most producers of "pornographic movies," according to Jack Valenti, avoid the formal rating procedure and simply self-apply an "X" rating. The other symbols, "G," "PG," and "R" may not be self-applied since they are registered with the U.S. Patent and Trademark Office.

In determining a film's rating, CARA evaluates thematic content, visual treatment, and use of language. If a film company desires a less restrictive rating, CARA will indicate specific changes which must be made. Frank Perry's "Last Summer," for example, was re-rated "R" after one Anglo-Saxon expletive and a brief incident from a rape scene were deleted. Stanley Kubrick's "A Clockwork Orange" was originally released by Warner Brothers in 1971 with an "X" rating. The film won critical acclaim and numerous awards. But the stigma of its "X" rating did not permit widespread distribution, thus substantially reducing the film's potential box office gross. Several newspapers declined to accept advertising for the film because of its "X" rating. Kubrick agreed to delete a total of 30 seconds from a sex orgy and a gang-rape sequence. The film's rating was subsequently changed from "X" to "R" and it was re-released.

* This designation has undergone a series of changes. Originally the symbol was "M—suggested for mature audiences." Early in 1970, "M" was changed to "GP—General Audiences—parental guidance suggested." Two years later, "GP" was changed to the current "PG" designation.

A film company unwilling to make the suggested changes may appeal to the Code and Rating Appeals Board for a change in rating. The Appeals Board, comprised of 22 members, gathers as a quasi-judicial body with the MPAA president acting as chairman. After the film in question is reviewed, the chairman calls on a representative of the company appealing the rating and a representative of the Rating Board. When the presentations are completed, members of the Appeals Board question the two opposing representatives. Following this, they are both asked to leave the room while the Board discusses the appeal, and a secret ballot is taken. The decision of the Appeals Board cannot be appealed; however, the Appeals Board has the authority to grant a producer a rehearing. Originally, a two-thirds vote was required to *sustain* a Rating Board decision. MGM's $10 million production, "Ryan's Daughter" needed a widespread distribution just to break even. But, because of the picture's adultery theme and a nude scene it received an "R" rating. MGM threatened to relinquish its MPAA membership unless the rating was changed to "PG." The Appeals Board convened and the rating change was granted. "Drive, He Said," a Columbia Pictures release, was rated "X" because of nudity, excessive profanity, various forms of sexual activity. Columbia appealed the rating and engaged Ramsey Clark, the former U.S. Attorney General, to present its case before the Appeals Board. Clark's basic argument was that the "X" rating was prejudicial since the picture was moral and serious in intent. Clark further held that the only rightful censor is the parent refusing to allow a child to see a film. When the vote was taken only 20 members of the Appeals Board were present. The vote was 12 to sustain the "X" and 8 to change the rating to "R." Since a two-thirds vote was necessary to sustain the "X" rating, the minority vote prevailed and a rating of "R" was granted. The bylaws have since been changed and now a two-thirds vote is necessary to *change* a Rating Board decision. The MPAA reports that from November 1968 through August 1975, the Appeals Board heard 65 appeals; it upheld 44 ratings, changed 18, and 3 cases were not decided.

The present classification system has its share of critics. The *New York Times* film critic, Vincent Canby, among others, has characterized the rating system as "ineffective and confusing." The National

Catholic Office for Motion Pictures and the Film Commission of the National Council of Churches have also withdrawn their endorsement of the rating system. The Code and Rating Administration is in the untenable position of having to strike a balance between the conflicting demands for totally unrestrained expression and outright censorship.

7

Development of American Broadcasting

IN THE UNIVERSE OF mass communications, the broadcasting media—radio and television—are by far the most powerful and pervasive. Simple informational statistics reveal, more than any rhetorical utterance, the unbelievable scope, reach, and potential power of the broadcast media. There are over 353 million working radios in the United States. The invention of the transistor has made radio astonishingly portable. There are floating radios for the pool or bathtub, clock radios, radio flashlights, radio pendants, all of which come in a wide assortment of colors, shapes and sizes. Some 98 per cent of all American homes have at least one working radio.

The figures for television are equally impressive. Television has a 97 per cent saturation. Over 45 million American households are equipped with color television. More people watch even the lowest-rated primetime television programs than could fill a Broadway theatre in 20 or more years—even if it was filled to capacity every night of the week. Popular programs are watched by 40, 50 or even 60 million people. Only one country rivals the United States in the popularity of television—Japan.

Early Radio Pioneers

The miracle of broadcasting is the result of a long prelude of electronic and other technical achievements which made the whole concept of mass communications possible.

The broadcast media use that form of electromagnetic energy called "radio." The nature and existence of radio energy was first demonstrated by Heinrich Hertz during the late 1880s. Nathan Stubblefield, an eccentric inventor from the backwoods of Kentucky, claimed to have transmitted the human voice from one point to another without the use of wires in the early 1890s. He is reported to have publicly demonstrated the transmission of voice and music via radio waves in January 1, 1902, in his home town of Murray, Kentucky. His contributions, however, went unrecognized and on March 30, 1928 he was found dead in a tiny shack, the apparent victim of starvation. Other and more prominent scientists were also experimenting with radio waves during the 1890s, including Oliver Lodge in England, Alexander Popov in Russia, Adolphus Slaby in Germany, and Edouard Branly in France.

Incorporating the ideas of these European scientists a young Italian, Guglielmo Marconi, was able to accomplish what the scientific giants of Europe could not. In 1895 he demonstrated that through the use of a Morse key, dots and dashes could be transmitted via radio waves. The Italian Minister of Post and Telegraph expressed no interest in Marconi's invention so, accompanied by his Irish-born mother, he sailed for England in February 1896. Unlike so many inventors who were technical geniuses but inept in industry, Marconi demonstrated an astute mind for the business world. In 1897, at 23 years of age, he joined with a small powerful group of businessmen and formed the Wireless Telegraph and Signal Company, Ltd. (British Marconi).

Accepting an invitation from the *New York Herald* to provide radio (then called "wireless") coverage of America's Cup races, Marconi soon established an American subsidiary of his British company. On November 22, 1899, the Marconi Wireless Telegraph Company of America (American Marconi) was incorporated under the laws of New Jersey. Marconi, a man of modest ambition, wanted total control of world communications.

Although he never fully achieved his goal, Marconi built a powerful communications empire. He developed a policy paralleling that of the telephone companies—the Marconi organization did not sell equipment, but communication. He would install radio equipment on a ship and furnish a man to maintain and operate it. The equipment would remain Marconi property, and the man a Marconi employee. He built shore stations which were directed to communicate only with Marconi-equipped ships, except in emergencies. The United States Navy, indignant about Marconi's policies, built its own shore stations and contracted with other experimenters.

Around 1905, John Ambrose Fleming, a Marconi employee, utilizing the work of Thomas Edison, developed a glassbulb vacuum tube which detected radio waves. One year later, a Yale-educated minister's son named Lee De Forest, expanding on Fleming's work, developed what he called the "Audion," a three-element vacuum tube. The Audion functioned as both a detector and an amplifier of radio waves. Among other things, the Audion was a key factor in the development of long-distance telephony, sound movies and television.

Reginald Fessenden, a Canadian, was one of the first inventors to experiment with voice transmission. Whereas Marconi had broken up the radio wave, Fessenden superimposed voice as modulations or variations on a continuous wave. With the help of Ernst Alexanderson, a General Electric Company engineer, he was able to transmit voice and music on Christmas Eve, 1906, to the ships at sea equipped with radio receiving equipment. Alexanderson had built a high-frequency alternator at Brant Rock, 11 miles from Plymouth, Massachusetts to produce the electromagnetic radiation necessary for the voice transmissions.

For many experimenters, including Marconi, the objective was not voice, but distance. By 1901 Marconi had transmitted the letter "S" across the Atlantic Ocean. Subsequently, transatlantic stations were constructed. The Marconi interests acquired the patents of many other inventors. As radio became increasingly complex, the number of patents multiplied into the thousands. Many competing companies were formed and years of patent disputes ensued. A patent conveys the exclusive right to make, use, refrain from using, or vend an invention throughout the United States and its territories. Patent rights are limited to 17 years to prevent a monopoly in perpetuity.

United Wireless, a company which resulted from the business union of Lee De Forest and an entrepreneur named Abraham White, was the major competitor to Marconi. Through unsavory manipulations, White cheated De Forest out of his assets. In 1912, Marconi won a patent infringement suit against White and United Wireless went into bankruptcy. Marconi quickly acquired the company's ship installations and land stations, thereby gaining almost total dominance of radio communication in the United States.

The sinking of the Titanic in April 1912 dramatized the importance of radio communication and provided a boon for the Marconi Company by bringing radio to the public's attention. Another ship was only a short distance away from the Titanic, but its radio operator had gone off duty about a quarter of an hour before the Titanic had sent out its distress signals. Over 1,500 lives were lost. A 21-year-old Marconi telegrapher, David Sarnoff, was on duty at the radio station atop the Wanamaker Building in New York City at the time the disaster occurred. He established faint communications with a ship which was in contact with the rescue ship Carpathia. President Taft ordered all other radio communication on the eastern seaboard to cease while young Sarnoff remained at the telegraph key for 72 consecutive hours recording the names of more than 700 survivors. The Titanic disaster awakened the public and the Congress to the potential uses of radio, then still called wireless. Sarnoff became nationally known, and radio attained the status of big business.

David Sarnoff, the eldest of five children, had arrived in America in 1900 at the age of nine from his native Russian province of Minsk. He settled in the tenements of Manhattan's lower east side with his impoverished family. His father, Abraham, who had arrived in the United States six years earlier to work as a house painter in order to secure money for his family's passage, soon succumbed to illness and took to his bed, an invalid until death. David assisted his family by selling newspapers, running errands for a butcher, and singing soprano in a synagogue choir for $1.50 a week. In 1906, young Sarnoff quit school to support his mother, three brothers and sister. He was hired as a $5.00-a-week messenger-boy by the Commercial Cable Company, located in the *New York Herald* Building. He earned 10¢ an hour in overtime. In his spare moments he learned Morse code. He applied for a job as a telegrapher with American Marconi, but was hired as an office boy instead. His base salary was elevated to $5.50 a week. Within a short time he became a telegraph operator. David Sarnoff, an immigrant slum dweller, had entered the world of electronics.

Lee De Forest was one of the most imaginative and creative inventors in the early development of radio. As early as 1910, he broadcast the tenor voice of Enrico Caruso from the stage of the Metropolitan Opera. In his lifetime he patented over 300 inventions. Unfortunately, unlike Marconi, he lacked business acumen. As Marconi's business flourished, De Forest approached the brink of bankruptcy. After being cheated by White, he formed another radio company, utilizing the Audion patents which he had maintained. A fraudulent stock promotion perpetuated by officers in his new company caused its demise. Financially destitute, he sold the amplification rights under the Audion patents to AT&T for a mere $50,000. AT&T needed an efficient amplifier to establish long-distance telephone circuits and reportedly was prepared to pay as much as $500,000 for the amplification rights. Eventually, De Forest sold all his radio patent rights to the telephone company for an estimated quarter of a million dollars. Marconi challenged the Audion patents in the Courts and in 1916 the U.S. District Court ruled that, as a detector, the Audion infringed on Fleming's original invention which was owned by Marconi. A stalemate resulted.

Radio Goes to War

After the United States' entry into World War I, the U.S. Navy took control of all radio communications and effected a temporary moratorium on patent disputes. Several companies, including AT&T, General Electric, Westinghouse, and American Marconi, manufactured radio equipment according to government specifications. The development of radio greatly accelerated during the war years. General Electric expanded its high-powered Alexanderson alternator to 200,000 watts. A "feedback" circuit developed in the pre-war years by a Columbia University undergraduate, Edwin Armstrong, significantly improved the effectiveness of the Audion as a detector. During the war Armstrong developed an even more effective amplifier called the "superheterodyne" circuit which enormously increased the sensitivity of radio receivers. By the close of the war, transatlantic voice transmission into Europe had become a reality.

After the war terminated, the U.S. Navy did not immediately relinquish control over private radio facilities. A bill was introduced in the House of Representatives to give the Navy peacetime jurisdiction over radio. Relations with Great Britain were strained, and a return to the pre-war status would mean domination of American radio service by the Marconi interests. Something had to be done about Guglielmo Marconi.

Owen Young of General Electric offered a solution. Young, working in conjunction with Navy officials, proposed the establishment of a new corporation which would acquire the assets and operations of American Marconi. The plan called for individual stockholders in the Marconi Company to receive comparable shares in the new company and for General Electric to purchase Guglielmo Marconi's stock holdings. Marconi was in an untenable position. The Navy controlled all of his land stations and, even if they were returned, the likelihood of securing government contracts seemed remote. On October 17, 1919 the new corporation was formed and given the patriotic name, Radio Corporation of America (RCA). One month later it took over American Marconi's operating organization and assets. General Electric became the principal stockholder in the new company. Almost all of the American Marconi employees stayed on to work for RCA, including David Sarnoff who became commercial manager for the new company. Only U.S. citizens were permitted to serve as RCA directors and officers and not more than 20 per cent of the stock could be held by foreigners. Within a few months AT&T, which controlled the De Forest patents, established cross-licensing agreements with GE and RCA. Each was permitted to use the others' patents. AT&T became an RCA stockholder. The GE-RCA-AT&T alliance dominated the radio industry.

Westinghouse initially appeared to be disenfranchised from the burgeoning business of radio. War contracts ceased, and it did not have the necessary patents to engage in peacetime production. However, the company managed to gain a foothold in radio by acquiring the patents of Reginald Fessenden and Edwin Armstrong. In June 1921, Westinghouse was invited to join the RCA consortium. Under the cross-licensing agreements which were established, GE and Westinghouse manufactured receivers and parts, RCA sold the radio equipment under its trademark, and AT&T was granted control over commercial telephony as well as the exclusive right to manufacture, sell, or lease radio transmitters. General Electric and Westinghouse were permitted to make transmitters for their own use, and all of the companies could fill government contracts in any area.

The Advent of Broadcasting

During its early development, radio was primarily a maritime instrument used for point-to-point communication. In 1920, the hobby of a Westinghouse engineer, Frank Conrad, transformed radio into a major new industry. Conrad built a radio transmitter in his garage and spent his Saturdays transmitting phonograph music via radio waves. He went on the air at regular times each week and asked anyone who heard him to send a postcard describing the reception. Not only did people respond but they requested that particular music be played. A Pittsburgh department store decided to capitalize on Conrad's hobby by running an advertisement in the *Pittsburgh Sun* which described the radio activities and encouraged people to purchase earphone-type home receiving sets.

Westinghouse executives quickly grasped the merchandising potential of providing radio entertainment to stimulate the sales of receiving sets. Westinghouse had made radio receivers during the war, and now saw a new market for its products. The company constructed a transmitter on the roof of the Westinghouse factory in East Pittsburgh and applied to the Department of Commerce for a special license to broadcast—to transmit radio signals *intended* for the general public. On November 2, 1920, Westinghouse, using the assigned call letters KDKA, broadcast the returns of the Harding-Cox Presidential election and inaugurated a regular daily program service. In 1921 the first Westinghouse home receivers were manufactured.

The Westinghouse broadcast venture precipitated widespread interest in the potential uses of radio as a broadcasting medium. Department stores, churches, newspapers, colleges and universities applied for broadcasting licenses.

Westinghouse opened stations in New Jersey, Chicago, Philadelphia and Boston. General Electric built the powerful WGY in Schenectady, New York, as well as stations in Denver and San Francisco. RCA purchased WJZ, the Westinghouse station in New Jersey, and established it as a New York City station in 1923. AT&T was at first reluctant to enter broadcasting because it could not produce or sell radio receivers under the patent agreements. However, it had exclusive control over commercial telephony and decided to rent the use of its broadcast facilities to the public. On August 28, 1922, WEAF, the AT&T owned-and-operated station in New York City, broadcast its first income-producing program—a 15-minute message from the Queensboro Corporation about the joys of owning a cooperative apartment in the Jackson Heights Section of New York. Queensboro paid $50 for the broadcast. The first efforts at radio advertising were tame compared to today's sophisticated approaches. Many sponsors merely attached their names to an orchestra or a singing group. WEAF's sponsored programs included the "A&P Gypsies," the "Ipana Troubadours," and the "Lucky Strike Orchestra." Hans von Kaltenborn, associate editor of the *Brooklyn Eagle,* did regular news broadcasts on WEAF. In 1924, Kaltenborn was taken off the air because he made critical comments regarding the Secretary of State's curt response to the Soviet Union's bid to establish diplomatic relations with the United States.

Radio was fast becoming a household fixture. By the end of 1922 radio receiver sales soared to $60 million. The primary beneficiaries of the broadcasting boom were GE, Westinghouse, and their selling agent, RCA. However, many radio manufacturing companies, in apparent violation of patent rights, shared the revenue. Radio programming during the early '20s consisted primarily of vocal and instrumental music. The advent of broadcasting badly hurt the phonograph industry, which survived the 1920s primarily through the sale of jazz recordings by black musicians who were denied access to the radio medium.

During the early '20s the operation of a broadcast station became increasingly more expensive. AT&T demanded compensation from stations using transmitters which infringed upon the telephone company's patent rights. A license fee was instituted by AT&T on the basis of a station's wattage. The American Society of Composers, Authors, and Publishers (ASCAP) also demanded a license fee in the form of annual royalties for the broadcast of copyrighted music. Early in 1923, ASCAP confronted WEAF, AT&T's New York station; AT&T acceded to ASCAP's demands and agreed to pay an annual fee. Other stations were not as conciliatory. In August 1923, a Federal District Court ruled that copyrighted music played on WOR, the Bamberger department store station, did not constitute an eleemosynary performance and therefore warranted royalty payment.

The Growth of Networks

The whole structure of commercial broadcasting as we know it today has its roots in the 1920s. Soon after its entry into broadcasting, AT&T began experimenting with the use of telephone lines for broadcast station interconnection. On January 4, 1923 WEAF was linked with WNAC, a Boston station owned by Shepard Stores, for a special broadcast. Later the same year, Colonel Edward Green, an eccentric New England millionaire who operated a station for his own amusement, arranged for his station, WMAF, to be interconnected with WEAF on a continuing basis. AT&T gradually added other stations and by the end of 1924 WEAF was interconnected with 25 stations in a coast-to-coast hookup.

RCA, GE and Westinghouse attempted to interconnect stations through the use of Western Union telegraph lines with WJZ as the flagship station, but the quality of the broadcast signal proved inferior. Nevertheless, by the end of 1925 WJZ was linked to over a dozen stations.

In 1926, in a renegotiation of the cross-licensing agreements, AT&T sold its broadcast assets, including WEAF, to RCA with the understanding that AT&T would lease its telephone long-lines for interconnection of RCA's broadcast outlets. AT&T was assured of a substantial income by providing station linkage without incurring any of the financial risks of broadcasting. RCA was given a free hand to engage in commercial network broadcasting. The same year, RCA established a central broadcasting subsidiary, the National Broadcasting Company (NBC) with RCA, GE, and Westinghouse holding 50, 30, and 20 per cent of the stock, respectively. With the acquisition of WEAF and AT&T's other broadcast assets, NBC had two outlets in New York and other locations. Rather than duplicate programming on two stations in the same broadcast area, NBC was organized as two semi independent organizations—the Red Network and the Blue Network. The color designations allegedly resulted from use of a red and blue pencil to outline on a map the locations of the interconnected stations within NBC's domain. The Red Network was comprised of those that were hooked up with WEAF, whereas the Blue Network consisted of the stations originally interconnected by telegraph lines to station WJZ.

In 1929, RCA acquired the Victor Talking Machine Company with its well-known trademark, the dog listening to "His Master's Voice." Under David Sarnoff, who, after serving in several positions had become a vice-president, the company began to manufacture, as well as distribute, receiving sets and tubes. RCA Communications, was incorporated to operate a world-wide radio telegraph system. RCA bought and developed Photophone, an early talking picture device, the rights to which it later traded for controlling stock in RKO Pictures.

David Sarnoff became president of RCA in 1930. That year, RCA took over the GE and Westinghouse interests in NBC. Two years later, government antitrust action forced GE and Westinghouse to relinquish their RCA holdings. RCA was left with substantial debts, but under Sarnoff's direction the company was able to pay its first dividend in 1937. At the 1939 World's Fair in New York City, RCA demonstrated its television system. RCA was forced to divest itself of the Blue Network in 1943. In 1947 David Sarnoff became board chairman and chief executive officer of RCA. In the early 1950s, RCA developed a compatible color television system. Over the past two decades RCA expanded into non-broadcast fields and has acquired Cushman & Wakefield, the real estate firm; Random House, the book publishers; the Hertz Corporation complex that rents and leases automobiles, trucks and other equipment, Coronet Industries, and Banquet Foods. Under the direction of board chairman Robert Sarnoff (his father, David, died on December 19, 1971), RCA employed over 130,000 people and is still one of the largest companies in the country. In a corporate shakeup in November 1975, Robert Sarnoff abruptly resigned his post at RCA.

Columbia Broadcasting System

Shortly after the formation of NBC, the Judson Radio Program Corporation was organized to supply talent and develop radio programs. NBC established its own artists bureau. Unable to place programs on NBC, Arthur Judson joined with three associates to form the United Independent Broadcasters (UIB) in January, 1927. UIB planned to develop a network by contracting for radio time on broadcast stations and providing programs to sell to advertisers. There were hundreds of stations around the country not affiliated with either of the

NBC networks which needed program material to fill out their schedules. UIB had difficulty securing AT&T interconnections and experienced severe financial difficulties. Judson and his associates were primarily interested in managing talent and sought financial and organizational assistance in establishing the network.

In April 1927, the Columbia Phonograph Record Company joined UIB and formed an organization called the Columbia Phonograph Broadcasting System. The network made its debut on September 18, 1927 over a 16-station hookup. Each of the affiliates was to be paid $500 per week for 10 hours of radio time. The Judson Radio Program Corporation provided programming. The new network had trouble securing sponsors and deficits mounted. The Columbia Phonograph Record Company withdrew from the venture. Isaac and Leon Levy of WCAU, Philadelphia, first affiliate to join the network, acquired stock. Jerome Louchheim, a subway builder, purchased controlling interest and the network was renamed the Columbia Broadcasting System (CBS). Louchheim became incapacitated from a hip injury and the Paley family, owners of the Congress Cigar Company, purchased control of the network in September 1928. William Paley, aged 27, became president of the Columbia Broadcasting System. A graduate of the Wharton School of Business at the University of Pennsylvania, he had been an executive in his family's cigar company. Young Paley proved to be an astute businessman and by the end of 1929 the company was showing a profit. In 1939, CBS entered the recording field with its purchase of the American Record Corporation (ARC) for $700,000. ARC's subsidiaries included the Columbia Phonograph Co., one-time owner of the network.

During the summer of 1934, a young Ohio State University Ph.D. candidate in psychology, named Frank Stanton, joined the CBS staff in the research department. In 1946, at the age of 38, Dr. Frank Stanton became president of CBS, prompting the *New Yorker* magazine to note that he was "one of the few men to achieve success despite the handicap of a Ph.D." Under Stanton's leadership, CBS began an extensive decentralization, and eventually diversification, program. In 1951, he subdivided the company into three divisions: radio, television, and the CBS laboratories. These divisions were later expanded into seven autonomous divisions, each with its own president and its own administrative system. Each division is viewed as a "profit center" with its own statement of profit and loss. CBS entered the manufacturing field in April 1951, with its purchase of Hytron Radio and Electronics Corporation, a tube manufacturer, and its set-making subsidiary, Air King Products Company. In 1964 CBS purchased an 80 per cent interest in the New York Yankees for $11.2 million. CBS sold its Yankees stock in 1973.

Today, CBS Inc. in addition to its broadcast division, is engaged in the production and distribution of records and phonographs, electronic research and development, publishing (Holt, Rinehart and Winston), the manufacture of musical instruments (Steinway and Sons) and a host of other activities. In 1972, Dr. Stanton was elevated to the position of vice-chairman and was succeeded in the presidency of CBS Inc. by Charles T. Ireland, an executive from the International Telephone and Telegraph Corporation. Mr. Ireland succumbed to a heart attack soon after, and in July 1972, 37-year-old Arthur R. Taylor was elected president of CBS Inc. and a member of CBS board of directors. Mr. Taylor has a B.A. in Renaissance history and an M.A. in American economic history from Brown University. After teaching for a brief period, he entered the business world in 1961 as a trainee at the First Boston Corporation. By 1964 he became an assistant vice-president in the underwriting department and in 1969 a director of the firm, responsible for new business development. He joined the International Paper Company in 1970, and at the time of his move to CBS he was executive vice-president and chief financial officer. His career has been nothing short of meteoric.

William S. Paley bypassed John A. Schneider, now head of the CBS Broadcast Group, and Richard Jencks, then CBS corporate vice-president in Washington, D.C., both of whom were thought to be serious contenders for the presidency, and went outside the company in an apparent effort to move CBS away from too much dependence on broadcasting for its income and into diversified fields.* Although CBS is best known for its television and radio interests, by the close of 1971 less than half of its net corporate sales came from broadcasting. This may be attributable, however, to the CBS owned-and-operated stations' failure to achieve maximum profit potential. Dr. Frank Stan-

---

* Mr. Jencks retired in April 1976 and was succeeded by Bill Leonard, former vice president for CBS News.

ton retired from CBS on March 31, 1973. Septuagenarian William Paley still maintains his position as board chairman of CBS Inc.

Mutual Broadcasting System

In 1934, WGN in Chicago, a subsidiary of the *Chicago Tribune,* WOR in New York, the Bamberger department store station, WLW in Cincinnati, owned by the Crosley Radio Corporation, and WXYZ in Detroit, owned by the Kunsky-Trendle Broadcasting Corporation, agreed to share the charges of telephone interconnection to provide simultaneous broadcasting of particular programs. Shortly thereafter, they incorporated as the Mutual Broadcasting System. Originally established as a cooperative programming venture, Mutual's primary program asset was "The Lone Ranger" which originated on WXYZ in 1933. Mutual's first programs were broadcast on October 2, 1934, and by the middle of the following year, an interchange of programming was arranged with the Canadian Broadcasting Corporation. WXYZ left Mutual in September 1935 to join the NBC network. Mutual, unlike CBS and NBC, did not maintain a programming division or originate programming. The primary function of the new network was to coordinate program exchanges between its affiliated stations. Mutual gradually expanded, primarily by adding low wattage stations in rural areas to its hookup.

There were 211 station affiliates in the MBS network on December 7, 1941 when programming was interrupted for a brief description by Welby Edwards in Honolulu of the Japanese attack on Pearl Harbor. On January 4, 1943, Miller McClintock, an advertising executive, assumed his duties as the first salaried MBS president. By the close of 1946, Mutual served 502 radio stations. When Mutual celebrated its 20th anniversary in 1954, the network was owned by RKO Teleradio Pictures, Inc., the General Tire and Rubber Company's subsidiary for the operation of its vast broadcasting and motion picture interests which soon included the ownership of six radio stations, four television outlets, RKO Radio Pictures, Inc., RKO Unique Records, and the RKO Recording Division. Within a few years, MBS was acquired by a syndicate headed by Armand Hammer. Several more changes in ownership occurred prior to April 1960, when Mutual became the wholly-owned subsidiary of Minnesota Mining and Manufacturing (3M) Company. Since 1966, the Mutual Broadcasting System, Inc., has been a wholly-owned subsidiary of the Mutual Broadcasting Corporation, an organization formed by John Fraim, former vice-president of the L. M. Berry Company of Dayton, Ohio. The Berry Company publishes the Yellow Pages telephone directories.

Today, MBS serves more than 685 radio stations in the United States, Canada, Mexico, Guam, and the Virgin Islands. Mutual also operates the Mutual Black Network adding an additional 95 stations to its transmission facilities. In addition to various news services, MBS's programming includes "Notre Dame Football," "NFL Monday Night Football," as well as major bowl games such as the Sugar Bowl, "Championship Baseball Playoffs" and "Wide Weekend of Sports," among others. On Sundays the network offers a block of sponsored religious programming which includes "The Lutheran Hour," the oldest continually sponsored program in radio history.

Radio Programs

Comedy was the favorite program type during the 1930s. Audiences were apparently delighted over the antics of Ed Wynn, Joe Penner, Burns and Allen, Eddie Cantor, and Jack Pearl. By 1935, former vaudeville star Jack Benny (né Benjamin Kebelsky), under the sponsorship of Jell-O, was emerging as "America's No. 1 Funnyman." NBC paid Jack Benny $10,000 a week, 39 weeks a year. Most commercial radio shows were produced by the sponsor's advertising agency. The network organization provided studio facilities and sold network time. The cost of sponsoring a top network radio show was approximately $38,000 a week, $20,000 for talent and about $18,000 for one-half hour of network time.

One of the most popular comedy shows on radio throughout the '30s was "Amos 'n' Andy" starring Freeman Gosden and Charles Correll. In the early years of the depression, "Amos 'n' Andy" was so popular that some movie theatres would stop the projector in mid-reel at 7 p.m. each weekday evening to broadcast the program to patrons who would otherwise have stayed home. Each episode of the program was 15 minutes long and was broadcast over the NBC Red Network from 7:00 to 7:15 p.m. five times a week. From March 1939 until February 1943 "Amos 'n' Andy" was presented on the CBS network. After going off the air for several months, the program returned on NBC in October 1943 in a once-a-week half-hour format on Friday evenings at 10 o'clock.

The radio show centered around the comic misadventures of two black men, Amos Jones and Andrew Brown. Other characters in the program included Lightinin', Algonquin J. Calhoun and George "Kingfish" Stevens. Much of the show's humor was based on malapropisms like "Is you mulsifyin' or revidin'?" Gosden and Correll (who were white) wrote the scripts and for several years played all the characters, virtually all of whom were black. NBC paid Gosden and Correll an annual salary of $50,000 apiece for their services. The program during the '30s was sponsored by Pepsodent toothpaste which experienced a 76 per cent increase in sales after the first year of sponsorship.

A radio program which rivaled "Amos 'n' Andy" in listener popularity was the "Chase and Sanborn Hour," starring ventriloquist Edgar Bergen and his top-hatted, monocled, tuxedo-attired wooden dummy, Charlie McCarthy. The show's announcer was Don Ameche, and a regular guest on the program between the years 1937–39 was the comic genius, W. C. Fields. Irreverent and cynical on the surface, Fields projected an underlying sentimentality. In most of Field's appearances on the show, he engaged in verbal duels with Charlie McCarthy. Although Fields had a nice rapport with Bergen, he sometimes had to be restrained from damaging the wooden dummy. Indeed, many members of the listening audience thought of the sassy-tongued Charlie as a separate, living human being. On the December 12, 1937 broadcast of the program over the NBC-Red Network, guest Mae West caused a public furor when she traded innuendoes with Charlie (Bergen) in a sketch about Adam and Eve. Mae West as Eve delivered such lines as: "I like a man that takes his time. Why don't you come home with me? I'll let you play in my woodpile . . . You're all wood and a yard long." The lines themselves, of course, cannot account for Ms. West's unique delivery. Everything she said sounded suggestive. The broadcast provoked an official Federal Communications Commission investigation and demands for congressional hearings. Letters from irate listeners appeared in the *Congressional Record*.

Other popular radio programs included "Major Bowes' Amateur Hour," "Royal Gelatine Hour" starring Rudy Vallee, "Kraft Music

Hall'' starring Bing Crosby, and the ''Lux Radio Theatre.'' The latter show ran for 21 consecutive years. The program, which was sponsored by Lever Brothers, the makers of Lux soap, featured Cecil B. DeMille from 1935 to 1945 as producer-host. DeMille developed the idea of presenting radio adaptations of successful Hollywood movies, using the original stars. Performers such as Don Ameche, Claudette Colbert, Ronald Colman, Bob Hope, Walter Pidgeon, William Powell, and Loretta Young frequently appeared on the program. DeMille left radio in January 1945 after failing in his court fight to prevent his suspension by the American Federation of Radio because he refused to pay a one-dollar union assessment to oppose a so-called ''right to work'' proposition on the previous November's ballot. Unionism had become firmly entrenched in the broadcast media.

Radio News

Radio grew slowly as a major source of news. In December, 1932, the board of directors of the American Newspaper Publishers Association (ANPA) recommended that the broadcasting of news should be confined to brief bulletins designed to encourage newspaper readership. Other recommendations included the treatment of radio program schedules as paid advertising and a prohibition against providing news in advance of its publication in the newspapers. Soon after, the Associated Press (AP) voted to provide no more news to networks. The United Press (UP) and the International News Service (INS) also stopped their sale of news to radio stations. A two-year battle ensued to eliminate radio news competition. The radio networks were compelled to establish their own news organizations. A. A. Schechter became virtually a one-man news department at NBC. His news gathering for Lowell Thomas' evening newscast over NBC-Blue consisted primarily of making telephone calls. CBS set up a more extensive news organization, the Columbia News Service, under the direction of Paul White, former United Press newsman. By the Fall of 1933, H. V. Kaltenborn and Boake Carter were doing daily CBS newscasts. In December 1933, representatives of the broadcast and newspaper industries met at the Hotel Biltmore in New York City and arrived at a ''peace treaty.'' CBS agreed to disband its news service. NBC also agreed to withdraw completely from gathering its own news. The representation of news on the networks would be confined to two five-minute periods daily, one in the morning after 9:30 and one at night after 9:00. The major wire services (AP, UP, INS) would supply the news free to a Press-Radio Bureau which was formed at network expense to defray the cost of individual news collection. Commercial sponsorship of Press-Radio Bureau bulletins was *verboten*.

Newspaper efforts to curtail radio news collapsed in 1935 when UP and INS obtained releases from the Press-Radio Bureau agreement, in order to sell full news reports to stations. UP offered a wire report especially written for radio. Radio coverage of Bruno Richard Hauptmann's 1935 trial in Flemington, New Jersey for the kidnap-murder of aviation hero Charles Lindbergh's baby son over the CBS Network elevated mellow-voiced announcer Boake Carter to a position of prominence. Gabriel Heatter, an MBS commentator, was also catapulted to fame for his ad-lib radio coverage on the night of Hauptmann's death in Trenton's electric chair. He moved from the ranks of minor newsmen to a $3,500-a-week commentator. His opening motto: "Ah, there's good news tonight!" became familiar to millions of Americans.

The dean of American radio commentators was unquestionably, H. V. Kaltenborn. A Wisconsin-born Harvard-educated scion of German nobility, his high-pitched, precisely accentuated tones captivated radio listeners. Kaltenborn broadcast via short-wave the sounds of the Spanish Civil War. An accomplished linguist, he was constantly on the air during the "Munich Crisis" instantly translating German and French. Between September 12–29, 1938, he made about 85 separate broadcasts—some lasting two hours.

In 1937, Edward R. Murrow, then unknown, was sent by CBS to London as European news chief. In building his foreign news staff, Murrow sought reporters, not announcers. His first recruit was William L. Shirer, a veteran of European reporting. Shirer, of course, went on to achieve fame as the author of the best-selling history of Nazi Germany, *The Rise and Fall of the Third Reich*. During the summer of 1939, a young journalism graduate from the University of Minnesota named Eric Sevareid joined Murrow's news staff. In August 1940, Edward R. Murrow began his memorable "This is London" broadcasts which poignantly chronicled the devastation heaped on the English people by German bombers.

Radio in Wartime

Shortly after the beginning of World War II, an Office of Censorship was created under the direction of Byron Price, then executive news director of the Associated Press. Its primary function was to exercise supervision over information published or broadcast that had any relationship to war conditions. Censorship was to be "voluntary." The Office of Censorship exercised only the right to "suggest" what materials were unsuitable for broadcast or publication. A "Code of Wartime Practices" was issued in January 1942, which prohibited the broadcast or publication of information concerning weather conditions in any part of the United States. Also banned was news about troop, ship or plane movements, the location of military bases or fortifications, and all but the most general information concerning damage from enemy attacks or casualties incurred by American or Allied forces in combat with the enemy.

J. Harold Ryan, who later became president of the National Association of Broadcasters (NAB), was put in charge of the Office of Censorship's radio division. Radio scripts could be submitted for evaluation before broadcast, but it was not a requirement. In an effort to avoid dissemination of possible coded material, broadcasters were asked to eliminate any "man-on-the-street" or other interview programs in which people other than station employees or well known local citizens could have access to the microphone. Quizzes, telephone request programs, notices of club meetings, and amateur hours tended to disappear from the air. The voluntary code proved to be successful. Byron Price was awarded a special Pulitzer Prize for his wartime work.

Other special war agencies included the Foreign Broadcast Intelligence Service, a division of the FCC which was set up to listen to and analyze foreign short-wave broadcasts. The Office of War Information (OWI) was established in June, 1942 to coordinate the government's news and propaganda efforts under the direction of veteran newsman Elmer Davis. At the time of his appointment, Davis was a nationally known news commentator on the CBS Network. Playwright Robert Sherwood headed OWI's foreign information section which utilized short-wave radio stations to carry out its propaganda function. Propaganda broadcasts to the American people involved several agencies, including the public relations division of the War Department.

Throughout the first half of the 1940s, the war dominated every phase of American life. In 1943 CBS president William S. Paley accepted an overseas psychological warfare assignment with the Office of War Information. Paley, who achieved the rank of colonel, aided in the preparation of recordings, intended to give guidance to resistance groups in occupied lands, which were broadcast to the European continent on D-Day. RCA's David Sarnoff also went on active duty as a colonel serving the Pentagon in the capacity of communications consultant and later at the headquarters of General of the Army Dwight D. Eisenhower in Europe. RCA's wartime production included radar, the proximity fuse and the sniperscope. David Sarnoff was elevated to the rank of brigadier general in 1944. For the remainder of his life even his sons referred to him as "General."

The potential impact of radio on mass behavior was reinforced by the enormous sale of war bonds resulting from singer Kate Smith's radio appeals. On February 1, 1944, she made 57 separate appeals during an 18½-hour period over the CBS network. She stimulated an estimated $108 million sale of war bonds.

In the post-war years, radio profits helped the networks to defray the cost of experimentation in the emerging medium of television. Bing Crosby broke network radio's taboo against recorded programming when he switched from NBC to the American Broadcasting Company in 1946. Crosby signed a $30,000-a-week contract with Philco to do a program transcribed in advance for broadcast over the ABC Radio Network. NBC had been reluctant to permit recorded programs, fearing that the practice would eliminate the economic advantages of networking.

In 1948, one of radio's highest paid personalities was veteran performer Arthur Godfrey, whose affiliation with CBS dated back to 1930 when he was a disc jockey on the company's Washington, D.C. station. CBS paid him an annual salary of $258,400, not including an additional $185,000 paid by CBS to Arthur Godfrey Productions for program and record services. The popular redhead became a major television star by 1950 with his Monday evening half-hour program "Arthur Godfrey's Talent Scouts" and "Arthur Godfrey and His Friends," an hour-long Wednesday evening variety show. His cracker-barrel informality lasted on network television until 1959.

Godfrey continued on CBS network radio seven days a week until 1972.

CBS scored a major competitive coup in 1948 when William Paley "raided" NBC's top comedy talent. In negotiations between CBS and MCA, the leading talent agency, a plan was worked out whereby talent would be sold as "properties" and therefore be eligible for the low capital gains income tax rate. In the post-war years those in high income brackets paid taxes ranging up to 91 per cent. The financial gain from the sale of property was taxed at much lower rates ranging up to only 25 per cent. In October 1948, CBS purchased "Amos 'n' Andy" outright for $2 million. Within a month CBS also acquired Jack Benny's Amusement Enterprises, which owned "The Jack Benny Show," for a reported $3.2 million. Burns and Allen, Edgar Bergen and Red Skelton soon followed. The switch took place in the middle of the radio season. With Jack Benny and "Amos 'n' Andy" in its Sunday night line-up, CBS topped NBC in the ratings on January 10, 1949. During the same month CBS acquired the services of Bing Crosby for both radio and television. The network entered the television era with a large reservoir of important talent.

Early Rating Services

By 1928, radio was becoming a medium for mass advertising. Radio's economic posture dictated that sponsored programs attract the largest possible audience. Programs were viewed as vehicles designed to deliver people to the sponsor's commericals. At first, fan mail was the prime determinant of program popularity. Then in March 1930, the Cooperative Analysis of Broadcasting (CAB) was organized under the direction of Archibald Crossley, a market research specialist, to provide a more accurate measurement of audience size. Crossley's method of estimating program popularity was primitive in comparison with today's scientific application of statistical theory to audience measurement. He called people in the early evening, finding their names in public phone books. Individuals having unlisted numbers or without phones were excluded from the sample. Crossley limited his survey to residents in 33 cities who were asked to recall what programs they had heard during the preceding 24-hour period. The method relied solely on the *recall* ability of the individuals questioned. Reports were issued twice monthly and were only available to subscribers. Radio performers became concerned about their "Crossley."

A second rating service was initiated by Claude E. Hooper in the Fall of 1935. Hooperatings, as the service was called, employed the telephone *coincidental* method whereby an individual phoned would be asked to supply only information about the program he was listening to at the time of the call. Hooper's sample covered 103 urban districts, with no rural residences included. National ratings were established on the basis of a statistical analysis of the sample. Hooper also provided ratings for programs in individual cities. Hooperatings soon superseded CAB as the dominant rating system. The CAB abandoned its recall method for coincidental telephone calls after 1941, but was unable to compete against Hooper and discontinued its service within five years.

A. C. Nielsen, a retail surveyor for food and drug companies, launched a new rating service in 1942. Nielsen used an Audimeter to estimate audience size. The Audimeter initially was a metering device attached to the radio receiver which recorded on paper tape whether the radio was turned on and to what station it was tuned. The paper tapes were collected by Nielsen field representatives bi-weekly. The tape was eventually replaced by 16mm film which households included in the sample were asked to mail to the Nielsen home office for tabulation. Nielsen's radio sample included 1,100 homes across the country. In 1950, the A. C. Nielsen Company purchased Hooper's national radio and television services.

By the early 1950s, the "disc jockey" was gaining a position of prominence on the radio medium. Within a few years, television surpassed radio as the primary source of entertainment during the evening hours. By the second half of the 1950s, network radio functioned as little more than a news service. CBS offered some network programming but radio had become essentially local in character. Few network programs survived the 1960s. The once all-powerful radio networks were relegated to minor programming roles.

In 1967 ABC received a special dispensation from the FCC to operate four separate radio network services: Contemporary, Entertainment, Information, and FM. Each network offers a program schedule tailored to specific audiences. For example, the Contemporary Network is intended for pop music and rock-and-roll outlets, and provides brisk news reports and interviews with musical luminaries who appeal to the younger generation. Within five years, the number of ABC radio affiliates more than quadrupled to over 1,200.

MBS formed the Mutual Black Network (MBN) in May, 1972 to provide black-oriented stations with live radio network news and sports from the "black perspective." All of MBN's material is written, produced and delivered by blacks. In addition to hourly five-minute newscasts, MBN features such programs as "Dr. Martin Luther King Speaks," a program dealing with black lifestyle and the contributions of the late Dr. King. Guests like Jesse Jackson, Julian Bond, and FCC Commissioner Ben Hooks have appeared frequently on this program. Other MBN programs include "In Focus," a five-minute commentary provided to the network by *Encore* magazine. Ms. Ida Lewis, editor and publisher of *Encore,* is the commentator. Four-hundred stations carried MBN's account of the Muhammad Ali/George Foreman fight from Zaire, Africa. Thirty-one of MBN's affiliates are owned, or completely operated, by black people.

8

Broadcasting Law

ALL COMMUNICATIONS LAW is based on constitutional authority. Congress asserts control over radio communication by virtue of Article I Section 8 Paragraph 3 of the U.S. Constitution: "The Congress shall have power . . . to regulate commerce with foreign nations, and among the several states, and with the Indian tribes. . . ." The Supreme Court has consistently held that modern judges should reason by analogy to the kinds of activities the framers of the Constitution knew. Hence, radio communication constitutes "commerce . . . among the several states."

Since its infancy, radio has been under some form of government regulation. In 1910, Congress amended the Interstate Commerce Act to incorporate interstate and foreign radio communication under Federal jurisdiction. In the same year it enacted the Wireless Ship Act which required vessels of specified types to carry radio equipment. The first comprehensive radio legislation in the United States was the Radio Act of 1912 which authorized the Secretary of Commerce and Labor (Secretary of Commerce after 1913) to require and issue licenses for radio transmission. However, the law did not clarify the Secretary's authority to determine frequency, power, or hours of transmission. This same legislation governed broadcasting during its early years. During the years 1922–25, the then Secretary of Commerce, Herbert Hoover, held four national radio conferences with the leaders of broadcasting in the hope that the industry could govern itself. With each conference, however, Hoover assumed more control over broadcasting.

In 1926, Eugene McDonald of the Zenith Corporation, which owned WJAZ, Chicago, challenged the Secretary of Commerce's power to regulate broadcast hours, limit power, and assign frequencies.* Without authorization Zenith moved to a Canadian wavelength and changed its hours of broadcast operation. The federal government initiated legal action against Zenith and the U.S. District Court ruled that the Commerce Secretary did not have the authority to restrict frequency, power, or hours of operation. The Attorney General of the United States concurred with the court's decision. The result was that new stations went on the air, using any frequencies they desired. Existing stations changed their frequencies and increased their power. Confusion and chaos resulted, and even the most dubious were now convinced that governmental control of broadcasting was imperative if the chaotic conditions that existed were to be eliminated.

In February 1927, Congress, exercising its constitutional prerogative, passed the Radio Act of 1927. The Act, which was derived primarily from legislation proposed at the 1925 National Radio Conference, reflected, to a large extent, the work of Representative Wallace White of Maine.

In many ways, the 1927 Radio Act was already obsolete at the time it was passed. Nothing in the Act, for example, accounted for the rise of networks as the dominant force in broadcasting. Congress apparently operated on the premise that the American system of broadcasting was characterized by local, autonomous stations, providing programs specifically for the communities they served. In so assuming, the Congress made an egregious error.

The Act established a five-member Federal Radio Commission, to be appointed by the President, with the advice and consent of the Senate. One Commissioner was to be appointed from each of five geographical districts across the United States. The districts were selected with the idea that each Commissioner would become a specialist in the problems of his area.

* In a case involving the Intercity Radio Co., Inc., which was decided in 1923, a court found that the Secretary of Commerce could not deny a license to any applicant; however, the Commerce Secretary interpreted the court's decision as giving him the power to assign frequencies to prevent interference.

While the Radio Act was imperfect in many ways, it established several important basic assumptions and conditions. Concern for the use of national resources was reflected in Section I of the Act which provided for the use, but not the ownership, of frequencies. Section 13 stated that any company found guilty of monopolistic practices after the Act went into effect was to be denied a license. Eugene Lyons, in his RCA-approved biography of David Sarnoff, casually notes that RCA by 1927 established a system of liberal licensing under which virtually all patents became accessible to nearly all those interested in return for "modest" royalties. Actually, each licensee was required to pay 7.5 per cent of total sales. In 1927, RCA derived a substantial portion of its net revenue from licensee royalties.

An inherent conflict existed between Sections 11 and 29 of the Act. On one hand, Section 29 specified that nothing in the Act should be interpreted as giving the regulatory Commission power to interfere with the right of free expression. On the other hand, in consideration of applications for the renewal of licenses, Section 11 required the regulatory Commission to consider the "public interest, convenience and necessity." In determining a licensee's public service, the Commission seemed compelled to take into account the content and character of its broadcasts.

The ambiguity of the law was somewhat clarified in the 1931 U.S. Court of Appeals affirmation of the FRC's refusal to renew the broadcast license of "Dr." John R. Brinkley. Brinkley, who had obtained his medical license from a Kansas diploma mill for $100, used his radio station, KFKB, Milford, Kansas, to advertise an operation involving the use of goat glands to restore sexual vigor. He also diagnosed and prescribed medicines for his listeners solely on the basis of letters he had received from them. In affirming the Commission's decision, the U.S. Court of Appeals cited the FRC's *Second Annual Report* (1928) which warned broadcasters against using uninteresting or distasteful material of a private nature. The Court considered the decision to be an application of this guideline, and charged the FRC with consideration of the "character and quality" of the past service of the licensee. Further, the Court judged this action to be the right and responsibility of the Commission and not censorship as proscribed by the Radio Act of 1927. The FRC was given the ticklish task of regulating program content without engaging in censorship. In an effort to clarify its requirements and standards the FRC promulgated "Rules and Regulations" in 1932.

The refusal to renew a license on the basis of past programming would seem to be a violation of the prohibition of censorship. Broadcasters, anticipating that certain content would be found objectionable by the Commission, might be reluctant to broadcast the material for fear that their licenses would not be renewed. The courts, nevertheless, have limited the definition of censorship to prior restraint.

Despite its ambiguities and obsolescence, the Radio Act of 1927 was incorporated, with minor revisions, into the Communications Act of 1934 which is the legislation under which broadcasting in America operates today. Thus, the basic law governing broadcasting in the latter half of the 1970s was conceived in the middle '20s.

The Communications Act of 1934

Prior to 1934, no single agency was charged with broad authority over communication. Wire and radio communications were partially regulated by several agencies, chiefly the Interstate Commerce Commission, the Postmaster General, and the Federal Radio Commission.

The laws governing communications were consolidated and broadened in the Communications Act of 1934 and their administration was placed under control of one regulatory agency, the seven-member Federal Communications Commission (FCC). The Commissioners, who hold staggered seven-year terms, are appointed by the President with the advice and consent of the Senate. One of the Commissioners is designated by the President to serve as chairperson, or chief executive officer of the Commission. The President determines the duration of the chairperson's tenure. The salary of a Commissioner is about $43,000 a year. The Chairperson receives an additional $2,000. No Commissioner may have a financial interest in any Commission-regulated enterprise and no more than four Commissioners may be members of the same political party.

The Commission operates on an annual budget of about $51 million, and has a staff of approximately 2,000 people who supervise the activities of over 8,000 broadcast stations and 80 common carriers. Common carriers offer their facilities and service for "common" or general use to all comers. Public utilities, such as the telephone, are generally common carriers. The FCC staff is subdivided into five operating bureaus—Broadcast, Cable Television, Common Carriers, Field Engineering, and Safety and Special Radio Services. With few exceptions, FCC personnel are under Civil Service.

In the regulation of *inter*state telephone and telegraph, the Commission has the power to determine reasonable rates, prescribe standards of service, control mergers and expansion or curtailment of service, and to undertake other activities to insure the best possible service. The FCC does not regulate purely *intra*state wire services; these are under the jurisdiction of their respective state utility commissions.

Government Communication

Regulation of radio operations by the federal government does not fall within the province of the FCC. The utilization of the radio spectrum is divided into two compartments, one private and the other governmental. Section 305 of the Communications Act gives the President the power to regulate governmental communications. The sharing of government allocations is coordinated through the Interdepartment Radio Advisory Committee (IRAC) which was formed in 1922. IRAC is composed of representatives from those government departments and agencies making extensive use of radio. The Department of Defense, for example, has its own communication satellite network, telephone system, and data transmission system.

In 1970, President Nixon issued an Executive Order creating the Office of Telecommunications Policy (OTP). The primary function of OTP is to serve as the President's principal advisor on telecommunications. The director of OTP is appointed by the President subject to confirmation by the Senate. OTP oversees the activities of IRAC. The IRAC Frequency Assignment Subcommittee (FAS) considers each proposed government application for frequency assignments and submits its recommendations to OTP. The assistant director of OTP serves as chairman of IRAC.

About 25 per cent of the useable radio frequencies are allocated for exclusive federal governmental use and the government shares an additional 45 per cent with the private sector. Section 606 of the Communications Act gives the President the power to take control of all frequencies and facilities in time of national emergency.

Network/Affiliate Relationships

In the late 1930s, the FCC took an increasingly active interest in the relationship of the network to its affiliated stations. NBC and CBS dominated American broadcasting. Together they controlled 85 per cent of the nighttime wattage. In 1938 the FCC initiated an investigation into network (or *chain* as they were once called) practices. Three years later, the Commission issued the "Report on Chain Broadcasting." The FCC expressed dismay over NBC's dual radio network. The Report stated that NBC's control over two networks was monopolistic in effect. Since the FCC has little direct control over networks, divorcement was encouraged in a roundabout way. The Commission held that no license shall be issued to a standard broadcast station affiliated with an organization that maintains more than one network.

Under a practice called "option time," stations relinquished large blocks of broadcast time to be programmed by the network, in a manner somewhat analogous to the control exercised by movie companies over exhibitors. CBS's affiliation contract gave it the right to take over any period in an affiliate's schedule. The Commission ruled that network contracts may not require affiliated stations to option more than three hours in each of four day-parts, or to make option time available on less than 56-day's notice. Affiliation contracts were limited to two years. Contracts could not prevent an affiliate from accepting programs made available to it by another source. Stations were free to reject "clearance" of network programs which they believed to be unsatisfactory or unsuitable. Networks were prohibited from owning more than one station of the same kind (AM, FM, TV) in the same market. Stations could not enter into contracts which prevented them from changing their time-rates for non-network programs.

Both NBC and CBS were in the talent management field. The Commission saw a conflict in the networks representing talent which they also employed. Within two months after the FCC issued its Report, CBS withdrew as a talent manager, selling its Columbia Artists Bureau for $250,000 to Music Corporation of America (MCA), a company which was founded in 1924 by a Chicago ophthalmologist, Dr. Jules C. Stein, with a capital of $1,000. MCA, through its wholly-owned subsidary, Revue, also produced programs. Ironically, Justice Department intervention eventually forced MCA to withdraw from the talent-representation business. The CBS-controlled Columbia Concerts Corp. was sold to a group of its own management headed by Arthur Judson, founder of United Independent Broadcasters, the progenitor of CBS. Judson retained stock interests in CBS and became a multi-millionaire. When he died in January 1975 at the age of 93, his CBS holdings were second only to those of William S. Paley. The NBC Artist Bureau was also established as a separate agency, National Concerts and Artists.

Meanwhile, CBS and NBC challenged the FCC's authority in the courts, and in 1943 the U.S. Supreme Court upheld the right of the Commission to regulate broadcasting practices and compel compliance to its network monopoly rules. NBC's Blue Network was sold to Edward Noble, the Lifesaver tycoon, who changed its name to the American Broadcasting Company (ABC). ABC began with only two stations and partial ownership of a third. In 1953, ABC merged with United Paramount Theatres and Leonard H. Goldenson, who had been president of the theatre operation, assumed the presidency of the newly formed American Broadcasting-Paramount Theatres, Inc. In July of 1965, the parent company's name was changed to American Broadcasting Companies, Inc. Under the direction of Mr. Goldenson, who has a law degree from Harvard Law School, the company expanded rapidly. By 1966, ABC owned 399 theatres in 34 states, five VHF television stations, six AM and six FM radio stations, one of the three major television networks, as well as one of the four major radio networks in the world. Its 137 television affiliates could reach 93 per cent of the then 50 million television households in the United States. Its radio network was capable of reaching 97 per cent of the then 55 million homes with radio.

Today, ABC's varied interests include one of the nation's leading motion picture theatre chains, with more than 260 theatres in the Southern United States; a commercial and office complex in Century City Los Angeles; a major recording division with 14 labels of its own; farm publications and leisure magazines; and scenic and wildlife attractions in several states.

In 1966, ABC entered into a merger agreement with the International Telephone and Telegraph Company (ITT). By the time of the proposed merger, ITT had become a giant international conglomerate with 433 separate boards of directors and derived about 60 per cent of its income from holdings in over 40 foreign countries. It is currently one of the 10 largest industrial corporations in the world, with interests in electronics manufacturing, telephone systems, consumer finance, life insurance, investment funds, loan companies, car rentals (Avis), and book publishing. About half of its domestic income comes from U.S. government defense and space contracts. The masterful manager of this enormous complex of men and companies is Harold Sydney Geneen, whose annual salary approaches a million dollars. He is one of the two or three highest paid corporate executives in the United States.

Since the ABC/ITT merger involved the assignments and transfer of the licenses of 17 broadcast stations, it required the approval of the Federal Communications Commission. Section 310(b) of the Communications Act of 1934 requires that the transfer of control of any corporation holding broadcast licenses must be approved by the FCC to assure that "the public interest, convenience and necessity will be served thereby." * The ABC/ITT merger was approved by the Federal Communications Commission, but the Justice Department appealed the merger to the U.S. Court of Appeals. In January 1968, while the Justice Department's appeal was pending, ITT abandoned its attempt to merge with ABC.

A major objection to the proposed merger came from Commissioner Nicholas Johnson. He declared that the FCC majority's treatment of the case made "a mockery of the public responsibility of a regulatory commission that is perhaps unparalleled in the history of American administrative processes." In his 72-page dissent he presented in simple language the economic truths of the merger and pointed out the vagaries and ambiguities of the financial jargon and figures offered by ITT. He cautioned against the far-reaching pyramiding of information control that was occurring, noting that ITT's economic interests are constantly affected by news events at home and abroad. ABC's journalistic integrity seemed likely to be compromised by the structure of the proposed new organization. Johnson reasoned

* For a brief period in the late 1940s, the FCC's "Avco Rule" required licensees to solicit competitive bids for stations offered for sale. The rule was rescinded in 1949. Congress amended Section 310(b) of the Communications Act in 1952, forbidding the FCC from considering whether the public interest might better be served by someone other than the proposed transferee to whom the licensee wishes to sell. In so doing, the Congress seemed to encourage trafficking in licenses.

that RCA's ownership of NBC should not be cited as an excuse for allowing a second network to come under the control of a similar company. He wrote, "I, for one, can see great virtue in having only one-third rather than two-thirds of the major networks owned by corporations heavily engaged in domestic defense and space work and in foreign countries. Perhaps we should consider requiring RCA to divest itself of NBC. . . ."

Nicholas Johnson's tenure on the FCC expired on July 1, 1973. He remained several months afterward, until Congress confirmed his successor. In a large percentage of the decisions reached by the FCC, Johnson voted with the majority. His articulately reasoned dissents, however, were nationally headlined. In the lead article of the July 1973 *Yale Law Journal,* entitled "A Day in the Life: The Federal Communications Commission," Nicholas Johnson and his former legal assistant, John Jay Dystel, present a scathing report of the inadequacies of the FCC. They state that the Commission frequently lacks sufficient data, relies heavily on information provided by interested parties, considers broad questions piece-meal, often decides cases it does not understand, and fails to anticipate major problems before they arise.

Prime Time Access Rules

On May 7, 1970, the Commission adopted new rules concerning network practices. These rules, known as the "Prime Time Access Rules," prohibit television stations in the top 50 markets in which there are three operating commercial stations from broadcasting more than three hours of network programming between 7:00 and 11:00 p.m. EST. The limitation on network programming took effect in October 1971. Effective the following year, stations were not permitted to fill the non-network hour with off-network or feature film reruns. The rules also prohibit television networks from engaging in domestic syndication (the sale of programs on a station-by-station basis) and restrict the networks' foreign distribution to the sale of their own programs. In addition, the new regulations prohibit networks from acquiring syndication or other subsidiary broadcast rights in television programs produced by independent producers. The Commission's primary aim in promulgating these rules was to strengthen station licensee autonomy and increase program diversity by expanding the potential number of program sources. Even the current FCC Chairman, Richard Wiley, concedes that the Prime Time Access Rule has been less than successful in achieving its objectives.

There have been several attempts to modify the Prime Time Access Rule since its inception. The current version of the Rule, which took effect on September 8, 1975, still bars top 50 market affiliates from airing more than three hours of network or off-network programming in prime time. However, children's, public affairs, and documentary programs are exempt from the Rule.

Regulation of Program Content

In the period immediately following World War II, the Commission expressed concern over broadcast program content. On March 7, 1946, the FCC issued a report entitled "Public Service Responsibility of Broadcast Licenses." The report which was mimeographed and had a blue cover became known as the "Blue Book." The "Blue Book" was not part of the FCC's *Rules and Regulations,* but an expression of the Commission's philosophy on program matters. The report cited glaring disparities between station promise and performance and emphasized the need for more sustaining (non-sponsored) programs. Facts and figures were given to document advertising excesses. The Commission noted the dearth of controversial programs and called for greater discussion of public issues.

The "Blue Book" caused considerable controversy within the ranks of the broadcasting industry. *Broadcasting* magazine, a traditional supporter of the industry, equated the report with out-and-out censorship. Judge Justin Miller, then president of the National Association of Broadcasters, condemned the "Blue Book," as a violation of freedom of expression guaranteed under the Communications Act. Nevertheless, it stood for many years as the most comprehensive FCC interpretation of the public interest. But despite the furor surrounding its release, the "Blue Book" was never really enforced by the FCC. Nor, to this day, has the Commission clearly and succinctly defined its "public interest" standards.

In July 1960, the FCC issued a "Programming Policy Statement" which established guidelines that were less restrictive than its 1946 counterpart. For example, the FCC decided that there was, in fact, no valid basis for distinguishing between sustaining and commercially sponsored programs from a public interest standpoint. The Commission listed 14 major elements of programming usually necessary to meet the public interest. These elements included: (1) Opportunity for Local Self-Expression; (2) The Development and Use of Local Talent; (3) Programs for Children; (4) Religious Programs; (5) Educational Programs; (6) Public Affairs Programs; (7) Editorialization by Licensees; (8) Political Broadcasts; (9) Agricultural Programs; (10) News Programs; (11) Weather and Market Reports; (12) Sports Programs; (13) Service to Minority Groups; (14) Entertainment Programming.

The FCC qualified its statement by noting the above elements were neither constant nor all-embracing and were not intended to serve as a rigid mold or formula for station operations. In its lack of clear delegation of responsibility, the 1960 "Programming Policy Statement" reflects the dichotomy between the Commission's desire to regulate programming in the public interest and its reluctance to engage in any action which may be interpreted as censorship. The ambiguity still prevails.

Political Broadcasting

The FCC has shown consistent concern that the broadcast licensee exercise responsibility in the execution of his obligation in the area of political broadcasting. Section 315 of the Communications Act of 1934 as amended, is the principal section relative to political broadcasts. Section 315 mandates that if a licensee permits a legally qualified candidate for any public office to use its broadcast facilities, it must afford equal opportunities to all other candidates for that office to use the broadcast station. A legally qualified candidate is defined as any person who meets the qualifications prescribed by the law of the state in which he is a candidate.

Section 315 as amended in 1959, exempts candidates who appear in any:

(1) bona fide newscast;
(2) bona fide news interview;
(3) bona fide news documentary (if the appearance of the candidate is incidental to the presentation of the subject of subjects covered by the news documentary);
(4) on-the-spot coverage of bona fide news events (including, but not limited to, political conventions and activities incidental thereto).

Under Section 315, no obligation is imposed on the licensee to make its station available to any political candidate. However, once a candidate does appear, all other candidates for the same office, if they apply to the station within seven days, must be given an opportunity to appear on the station. Once a station has agreed to, or is obligated to, provide a candidate with broadcast time, it cannot censor or refuse to carry the candidate's message. For example, in August of 1972, the FCC refused to allow Atlanta broadcasting stations to reject a political message from J. B. Stoner, a candidate for U.S. Senator on the National States Rights party ticket. Mr. Stoner's advertisement stated that "The main reason why niggers want integration is because the niggers want our white women. I'm for law and order with the knowledge that you cannot have law and order and niggers too." The Atlanta chapters of the NAACP and the ADL complained to the FCC. The Commission ruled that Stoner's presentation was permissible, since it did not contain any direct incitement to violence.

In late September 1975, the Federal Communications Commission ruled that news conferences and political debates by candidates for any public office may be treated as bona fide news events and therefore are exempt from Section 315's requirement that all legally qualified candidates be given equal opportunity for broadcast coverage. The broadcaster now has the discretion to determine whether the debate or news conference is newsworthy. Some critics of the Commission's ruling argue that it lacks statutory authority since neither a debate nor a news conference is the type of spontaneous, apolitical occurrence Congress regarded as a conventional news event.

Fairness Doctrine

Considerations of fairness in the presentation of controversial issues invokes the FCC's "Fairness Doctrine." The Fairness Doctrine has its roots in the FCC's June 1949 policy statement on editorializing in which the Commission stated that stations might editorialize providing they offered opportunities for opposing points of view.* The Doc-

---

* A prohibition against editorializing was thought to be in effect between 1941 and 1949. The supposed ban on editorials arose from the interpretation of a short dictum extracted from the FCC's 1941 *Mayflower* decision which stated that the broadcaster cannot be an advocate. However, nowhere in the 13-page majority statement of 1949 is there any mention of a ban, nor does it suggest in any way that a ban is being lifted.

trine has since been expanded to include all areas of controversy concerning issues of public importance. When a licensee permits his facilities to be used to air a controversial issue of public importance, he must afford reasonable opportunity for the presentation of contrasting points of view. A broadcaster is not required to provide a forum of opposing views within the same program or series of programs. He is merely expected to make a provision for opposing views in his overall programming, either by providing time to spokesmen for contrasting views or presenting his own programming on the issue.

The Fairness Doctrine appeared to receive Congressional support in the 1959 amendment to Section 315 which formally imposed the obligation on the broadcaster "to afford reasonable opportunity for the discussion of conflicting views on issues of public importance."

Despite attempts by the Commission, the Congress and the Courts to clarify the Fairness Doctrine, it continues to be fraught with uncertainties. The Fairness Doctrine deals with the broad question of affording "reasonable opportunity" for the presentation of contrasting viewpoints on controversial issues in a station's overall programming. Appearances by candidates involve the precise formula of "equal opportunities." When a candidate appears on a station, equal opportunity is mandatory. When *issues* are treated the licensee is permitted much wider discretion.

In 1967 the Commission promulgated special fairness rules on personal attack and candidate endorsement. If, during the presentation of views on a controversial issue of public importance, an attack is made upon the honesty, character or integrity of an identifiable person or group, the station must notify the person or group attacked within one week and provide a script or tape or, if these are not available, an accurate summary, and offer time for reply. When a licensee endorses or opposes candidates for political office, similar steps must be taken within 24 hours.

The Commission further extended the Fairness Doctrine in its so-called "Zapple" ruling of 1970, which requires that when a licensee sells time to supporters or spokesmen of a candidate during an election campaign who urge the candidate's election, discuss the campaign issues, or criticize an opponent, then the licensee must afford comparable time to the spokesmen for the opponents.

Several interesting cases illustrate the operational and philosophical problems inherent in the Fairness Doctrine. In 1968, for example, John Banzhaf decided to test the Fairness Doctrine provision for covering controversial issues of public importance. Banzhaf requested that WCBS-TV in New York be instructed by the FCC to counterbalance its cigarette commercials with information indicating that cigarettes might be dangerous to health. In a stunning surprise decision, as far as the broadcasting industry was concerned, the FCC did precisely what Banzhaf and his organization (Action on Smoking and Health) had demanded. Stations henceforth had to include anti-smoking spots, many by the American Cancer Society, and this move led eventually to the banning of all cigarette commercials from the air—the ban, however, does not extend to print. In a 1974 policy statement, the Commission excluded product commercials from Fairness Doctrine applicability.

Another instance, invoking the Fairness Doctrine personal attack rule, is particularly interesting because of the expressed opinion by the Supreme Court that the critically important group to consider is the public. A rabble-rousing preacher, the Rev. Billy James Hargis, had given vent to a bitter personal attack on a newsman, Fred J. Cook, accusing him of being a Communist. When the Red Lion Broadcasting Co., station WGGB AM-FM, in Pennsylvania, refused to offer Cook time for rebuttal, Cook petitioned the FCC and was turned down. The case reached the Supreme Court where, in overruling the Commission, the Court noted very significantly that what was paramount was "the right of the viewers and listeners, not the right of the broadcasters." This was a portentous decision as far as the broadcasters were concerned.

The Commission refused to renew the license of WXUR, a Media, Pa. radio station licensed to the Rev. Carl McIntire's Faith Theological Seminary. McIntire, claimed the Commission, did not permit views in opposition to his "right-wing" politics to be presented on the station. The court, in upholding the FCC's decision, skirted the fairness issue by ruling on the basis of the licensee's misrepresentation of programming intentions in the license application.

Still a fourth Fairness Doctrine matter was the Accuracy in Media petition to the Commission for right of reply to an NBC program on pension systems—the claim being that NBC violated the Fairness Doctrine and failed to present all sides of the pension issue. The FCC upheld AIM, but was reversed by the U.S. Court of Appeals. The case did not end there, apparently, for Accuracy in Media has announced its intention of pursuing the matter to the highest court.

Thus, the Fairness Doctrine itself has become one of the most controversial of issues confronting both broadcasting and the government. Senator William Proxmire (D. Wis.) submitted legislation providing that the Doctrine be eliminated, but it is doubtful whether the issue will reach actual consideration on the floor of Congress. Meanwhile, beset by argument and counter-argument from broadcasters and from public access advocates, the FCC continues to weigh the problem, but the Fairness Doctrine is still very much in evidence.

The Broadcast License: A Case Study

The most valuable commodity a station owner possesses is his broadcast license. The value of the license far exceeds that of the tangible broadcast facilities. The economic stability of the entire broadcast industry rests on the assumption that licenses will be routinely renewed every three years.

Consequently, few Federal Communication Commission decisions have caused as much alarm in the broadcast industry as the *WHDH* case. The Commission, for the first time in its history in applying comparative criteria in a renewal proceeding, ruled against the incumbent license holder and awarded the frequency to a challenger.

WHDH-TV, owned by the publishers of the Boston *Herald Traveler,* was granted a construction permit for Channel 5 in the Boston area in April 1957, following a comparative hearing involving four applicants. Two of the losing applicants challenged the award in federal courts. Charges were also made in a hearing of the Legislative Oversight Committee of the House Interstate and Foreign Commerce Committee that both WHDH and one other applicant for the Boston channel, the Massachusetts Bay Telecasters, had attempted to influence the then chairman of the Federal Communications Commission, George C. McConnaughey, at various luncheon meetings outside the regular processes of adjudication. The U.S. Court of Appeals in July 1958 remanded the Channel 5 case back to the FCC with instructions to investigate the matter of *ex parte* contacts. After an almost six-month delay the Commission, now under the chairmanship of John C.

Doerfer, finally ordered the case reopened and a new hearing was held. The special hearing examiner, Horace Stern, concluded that the luncheons had not been improper. The then Attorney General of the United States, William P. Rogers, who had been participating as a Friend of the Court, stated in a very strongly worded brief that the luncheons were clearly improper and that both applicants should be disqualified. He recommended that a new comparative hearing should be initiated by the FCC. Meanwhile the Legislative Oversight Committee had disclosed that FCC Chairman Doerfer had been padding his expense account, and taking vacations as a guest of major broadcast groups who had cases pending before the Commission. President Eisenhower, just before retiring from office, requested Doerfer's resignation. Newton Minow, an appointee of the late President John F. Kennedy, succeeded Doerfer as Chairman. The Commission requested that the Court of Appeals, which had retained jurisdiction in the Channel 5 case, remand the entire case to the FCC for reconsideration and final action. The court accepted the recommendation, and remanded the case to the Commission; the FCC thereafter set aside the grant to WHDH and announced that all four parties to the original application would be given the opportunity to file new briefs and to present oral argument.

In September 1962, the Commission found that, while the comparative position of WHDH had been weakened by the evidence of the questionable luncheons, WHDH nevertheless made the strongest showing and remained the most desirable of the applicants. WHDH, after five years of operating under various temporary authorizations, was granted a regular license. However, the license was issued for a period of only four months, with the understanding that at the end of that period the Commission would consider other applications for the Channel 5 license. At the time of renewal, three applicants accepted the Commission's invitation and challenged WHDH's license—Charles River Civic Television, Boston Broadcasters, Inc., and Greater Boston TV Co. Inc. (one of the original applicants).

After one of the longest comparative hearings in the history of U.S. regulatory agencies, the hearing examiner concluded that WHDH was still the best qualified applicant for the Channel and recommended renewal of its license. The case had been further complicated by the death of Robert Choate, who had been president of both the Boston

Herald Traveler Corp. and WHDH, Inc. It was Choate who had parta-ken of lunch with FCC Chairman McConnaughey. One of the appli-cants, Boston Broadcasters Inc., appealed to the Commission in an oral argument to reverse the hearing examiner's decision.

In January of 1969 the FCC in a 3 to 1 vote, the barest of quorums, failed to renew WHDH's license and awarded Channel 5 to the challenger, Boston Broadcasters, Inc. The majority seemingly ig-nored the old issue of the luncheons and ruled on the basis of diver-sification and integration of management. The hearing examiner had recommended that the WHDH license be renewed on the basis of its past performance. The Commission, in reaching its decision, strictly applied the criteria set forth in its 1965 "Policy Statement on Compar-ative Broadcast Hearings," particularly in relation to past performance and media diversification. Consequently, the Commission found that the examiner had placed an extraordinary and improper burden upon the new applicants since the "Policy Statement" notes that a past record within the bounds of average performance should be disre-garded. The Commission found, for example, that WHDH had never editorialized. WHDH's past performance, while not inadequate, certainly was not above average. On the issue of diversification of ownership, the "Policy Statement" considers it a primary objective in the Com-mission's licensing scheme. The FCC found that a grant to either Charles River or BBI would result in far greater diffusion of control of the media of mass communications as compared with WHDH, whose owners also controlled a powerful standard broadcast station, an FM station, and a major newspaper in the city of Boston. Between Charles River and BBI, the Commission found that BBI merited slight prefer-ence on the diversification factor.

In his concurring statement, Commissioner Nicholas Johnson saw the decision as a major step away from concentrated ownership toward local control. "The door is thus opened," said Commissioner John-son, "for local citizens to challenge media giants in their local com-munity at renewal time with some hope of success. . . ." After sev-eral unsuccessful appeals by WHDH, BBI finally went on the air on March 19, 1972 with its call letters WCVB-TV.

Meanwhile, the broadcast industry, fearful that the WHDH case would establish a dangerous precedent by creating a rash of license challengers ("strike applicants"), urged Congress to enact protective legislation. Senator John Pastore of Rhode Island, Chairman of the Commerce Sub-Committee on Communications introduced S.2004, a bill which would require the FCC to ignore competing applications for licenses until it had decided that the present licensee should be denied renewal. Citizen opposition measurably slowed the progress of the "Pastore bill." Then, without any formal rule-making proceedings, the FCC, on January 15, 1970, issued its own licensee renewal "Policy Statement."

The 1970 "Policy Statement" provides that the renewal issue must be determined first in a proceeding in which challengers are permitted to appear only for the limited purpose of calling attention to the incumbent's failings. The Commission stated that it would give preference to the existing licensee over a competitior if the licensee can demonstrate that his programming has substantially met the needs and interests of his audience. The Senate bill was thereafter deferred in favor of the Commission's "compromise."

The Commission's "Policy Statement" was challenged by the Citizens Communications Center in the U.S. Court of Appeals (D.C. Cir.). On January 11, 1971 the Court repudiated the Commission's 1970 "Policy Statement" finding it unreasonably weighted in favor of the licensee it is meant to regulate, to the detriment of the listening and viewing public.

The FCC and the Public Morality

Under the Communications Act of 1934, as amended, the Federal Communications Commission has broad and extensive powers—it may issue cease and desist orders, impose monetary forfeitures, deny license renewals, and even revoke licenses in mid-term. The Commission's actions, however, must be reconciled with constitutional and statutory limitations. The First Amendment to the U.S. Constitution denies the federal government the power to limit expression and Section 326 of the Communications Act provides that the FCC shall not "interfere with the right of free speech by radio communication." The courts, however, have always assumed that certain kinds of expression are not constitutionally protected, and this is reflected in Section 1464 of the U.S. Code which states:

> Whoever utters any obscene, indecent, or profane language by means of radio communication shall be fined not more than $10,000 or imprisoned not more than two years or both.

During the past 15 years, the Commission has increasingly exercised its powers to curtail the dissemination of allegedly obscene and indecent broadcast matter. In 1962, the Commission denied renewal of a Kingstree, South Carolina radio station's license because of "coarse, vulgar, and suggestive" material broadcast by a disc jockey, Charlie Walker. Walker had worked at the station for eight years and was generally on the air for four hours a day. His shows included, "Rise and Shine," "Grits and Gravy," "Mountain Jamboree," and "Sundown Hoedown." The following is fairly typical of Walker's rustic broadcast humor:

> I've always been a gentleman, I sure don't go beating up my women before I love 'em. . . . Tell me, would you go around bruising your groceries before you eat 'em? Well, that's the way I feel about them gals.

The station's licensee, Edward G. Robinson Jr., claimed First Amendment protection for the Walker broadcasts. The Commission contended that broadcast material is subject to tighter strictures than other media, since it is available at the flick of a switch to young and old alike. Walker's principal appeal, said the Commission, lay in his smut and that "smut signalized, characterized, and was in fact the dominant note of his broadcasts." The Commission's decision not to renew the station's license was upheld by the U.S. Court of Appeals because the licensee misrepresented facts in its presentation to the FCC. The Supreme Court refused to review the case. Thus, the determination as to whether the Commission acted within the bounds of the prevailing constitutional standards was unresolved.

Two years later, in a strongly worded statement defending the right of a station to air provocative programs, the FCC attempted to clarify the obscenity issue as applied to broadcasting. The case involved the Pacifica Foundation's three non-commercial, listener-supported FM radio stations: WBAI-FM, New York, KPFA-FM, Berkeley, and KPFK-FM, Los Angeles. Pacifica had encountered licensing difficulties with the FCC over a period of several years. Its applications for the license renewal of KPFA-FM and for a license to cover a construction permit for KPFK-FM had been pending before the FCC since 1959. The renewal application of the WBAI-FM license had been pending since 1960. Throughout this period the Commission permitted the stations to broadcast on a temporary permit.

In determining Pacifica's license renewal requests, five programs were given serious consideration by the Commission because of listener complaints: Edward Albee's "The Zoo Story"; "Live and Let Live," a discussion of the problems of eight homosexuals; readings by Lawrence Ferlinghetti of some of his poetry; a reading of the poem, "Ballad of the Despairing Husband," by its author, Robert Creeley; and an Edward Pomerantz program of readings from his unfinished novel, *The Kid*. The Commission found nothing contradictory to the public interest in the broadcasts of the programs, "The Zoo Story," "Live and Let Live" and the readings from *The Kid*. It found the Ferlinghetti and Creeley programs were "two isolated errors in the licensee's application of its own standards—one in 1959 and the other in 1963." In granting Pacifica's request for license renewal, the Commission set forth a major policy statement concerning regulation of program content:

> . . . such provocative programming as here involved may offend some listeners. But this does not mean that those offended have the right, through the Commission's licensing power, to rule such programming off the air waves. Were this the case, only the wholly inoffensive, the bland, could gain access to the radio microphone or TV camera.

In April 1970, the Commission attempted to clarify its authority under Section 1464 of the United States Code. The FCC selected as its test case WUHY-FM, a non-commercial radio station licensed to Eastern Education Radio, Philadelphia, Pennsylvania. The Commission focused its attention on a one-hour, weekly program titled "Cycle II," which was designed to reach a young listening audience. The licensee described the program, which was broadcast from 10 p.m. to 11 p.m., as "underground" in its orientation and concerned with "avant garde" forms of social and artistic expression. During a 50-minute pre-recorded interview which was broadcast on January 4, 1970, Jerry Garcia, leader of a California rock-and-roll group "The Grateful Dead," frequently interspersed his views with such expletive phrases as:

> S--t man.
> I must answer the phone 900 f----n' times a day, man.
> Right, and it s---s it right f-----g out of ya, man.
> That kind of s--t.
> It's f----n' rotten man. Every f----n' year.

Neither the licensee nor the Commission received any complaints with respect to this specific broadcast. However, the Commission had received several complaints about a program entitled "Feed," the predecessor to "Cycle II" in the 10 p.m. time slot. The Commission monitored the January 4th program and requested comments from WUHY concerning the broadcast. The licensee contended that the program could not be labeled obscene because it did not appeal to prurient interest. The FCC held that the expletives used by Garcia were "indecent" in that they were "patently offensive by contemporary community standards, and utterly without redeeming social value." The Commission imposed a minimal forfeiture of $100 and invited the licensee to test the decision in the courts. WUHY-FM elected to pay the forfeiture, and consequently the constitutional issues were once again left unresolved. In a sharp dissent, Commissioner Nicholas Johnson criticized the majority of the Commission for ignoring decades of First Amendment law by punishing a broadcaster for indecent speech "without so much as *attempting* a definition of that uncertain term."

The Commission followed its *WUHY* decision by invoking a $2,000 forfeiture against Sonderling Broadcasting Corporation, licensee of WGLD-FM, Oak Park, Illinois, for broadcasting obscene material on its "Femme Forum" programs of February 21, and February 23, 1973. "Femme Forum" employed a format in which an announcer engaged in telephone discussion with callers from the listening audience that dealt primarily with explicit sex talk. A number of other broadcast stations throughout the country were using a similar format, which is sometimes referred to as "topless radio." The topic of WGLD's February 23rd program was "oral sex." Some of the remarks broadcast that day included colloquial expressions for various forms of sexual contact. The discussion was very explicit. The Commission ruled that the material broadcast by WGLD met the prevailing definition of obscenity in that it appealed to a prurient interest in sex and was patently offensive to contemporary community standards. Commissioner Nicholas Johnson, in his lengthy dissent, concluded that the FCC has no competency in the area of obscenity and that the decision imposed a "chilling effect" on the various forms of broadcast expression.

Although Sonderling chose to pay the fine, the Illinois Citizen

Committee for Broadcasting, along with the Illinois Division of the American Civil Liberties Union appealed the Commission's ruling to the U.S. Court of Appeals. In November 1974, the court upheld the Commission noting that the probable presence of children in the audience is relevant to a determination of obscenity.

On February 12, 1975, the Federal Communications Commission issued a declaratory order holding that language broadcast by WBAI (FM), New York, the owned-and-operated station of the Pacifica Foundation, in a recorded comedy monologue by George Carlin was indecent and prohibited by Section 1464 of the U.S. Code.

Carlin's monologue consisted of a comedy routine that was almost wholly devoted to the use of four-letter expletives. The following is an excerpt from the broadcast:

> It's a great word, f--k, nice word, easy word, cute word, kind of. Easy word to say. One syllable, short u. fuh ends with a kuh. Right? A little something for everyone. F--k. Good word. Kind of a proud word, too. Who are you? I am F--K. F--K OF THE MOUNTAIN. Tune in again next week to F--K OF THE MOUNTAIN.

In addition, Carlin used several other expletives. The monologue was played at approximately 2 p.m. on October 30, 1973. The FCC received a complaint from a man in New York City who heard the broadcast on his car radio. The man noted that his young son was with him when he heard the broadcast and that "Any child could have been turning the dial and tuned in to that garbage. . . ."

The Federal Communications Commission ruled that Carlin's monologue was "indecent," since it depicted sexual and excretory activities and organs in a manner patently offensive by contemporary community standards for the broadcast media at a time when there was a reasonable risk children might be in the audience. "Obnoxious, gutter language describing these matters," noted the Commission, "has the effect of debasing and brutalizing human beings by reducing them to mere bodily functions." The Commission qualified its ruling by adding that during the late evening hours, when the number of children in the audience is reduced to a minimum, it would consider whether the work could be redeemed by a claim that it has literary, artistic, political or scientific value. The Commission has apparently shifted from a concern based solely on the quality of content to a position which incorporates the context of the presentation. In terms of indecency, at least, it has developed a variable standard. The Commission's declaratory order actually appears to widen the latitude of expression permissible for adults on the broadcast media in that it allows for more divergent and controversial discussions and presentations. If a broadcaster exercises reasonable control over scheduling, promotion, and the general context of the presentation of material which may be thought to be offensive by some members of the audience, that material is not necessarily proscribed. Thus, employment of the ancient Anglo-Saxon expletive for the sex act may be permissible on the broadcast media under certain circumstances.

Pacifica argued that immediately prior to the broadcast, listeners were advised that it included language they might regard as offensive and those who might be offended should tune out and return later. In addition, Pacifica noted that Carlin was not mouthing obscenities "but using words to satirize as harmless and essentially silly our attitudes towards those words." Pacifica is appealing the Commission's ruling in the U.S. Court of Appeals.

Ultimately, the U.S. Supreme Court must determine whether the FCC, through its administrative judgments, has inhibited the dissemination of constitutionally protected expression. Several questions need to be resolved: Is the FCC's regulation of broadcast content consistent with the prevailing constitutional standards regarding obscene and indecent material? Do FCC programming standards restrict adults to broadcast expression deemed appropriate for children or easily offended adults? Does the FCC employ rigorous safeguards to ensure that constitutionally protected expression is not curtailed?

9

Commercial Television

THE DEVELOPMENT OF electronic television as a successful and powerful medium of mass communications resulted from the contributions of many diverse individuals. Patents for a device to send pictures via wire were issued in Germany as early as 1884. In 1923, Vladimir Zworykin, who began his communications career in the Czarist army, obtained a patent on the iconoscope tube, the progenitor of today's image orthicon television camera. Zworykin, who emigrated from Russia in 1919, was employed as a researcher with Westinghouse. In 1930, Westinghouse, General Electric and RCA merged their television research programs at the RCA laboratories in Camden, New Jersey. NBC began doing experimental telecasts from the Empire State Building in 1932. Early attempts to develop television were based on the use of a spinning disk that scanned electrical impulses and gave a motion picture effect. The picture was less than satisfactory.

Television experimenters during the 1930s included young Philo Farnsworth who had outlined a scheme of electronic television in 1922 to his high school science teacher in Rigby, Idaho. Beginning in 1927 Farnsworth, with the financial backing of a group of California bankers, began acquiring patents for his "image-dissector" system. Farnsworth and his backers incorporated as Television Laboratories, Inc. Farnsworth held more than 165 patents, including the fundamental patents covering scanning, synchronizing, focusing, contrast, controls, and power. The Farnsworth organization established cross-licensing agreements with RCA, and in September, 1939, RCA reluc-

146

tantly agreed to pay substantial royalties for the Farnsworth patents. CBS also began television experiments. Dr. Allen B. DuMont, who had become interested in television while working for the DeForest Company in the late 1920s, engaged in television research during the mid-'30s. Working in a garage laboratory at his home, Dr. DuMont developed a relatively inexpensive long-life cathode-ray tube which allowed for scanning by an electronic beam that formed a picture by speeding back and forth across a fluorescent screen placed at the end of the tube. In 1939, his company was the first to offer eletronic television sets for sale to the public. DuMont received financial backing for his television venture from the Paramount Pictures Corporation. Television research culminated in RCA's public demonstration of a 441-line electronic system at the 1939 New York World's Fair. An early telecast presented Freeman Gosden and Charles Correll as "Amos and Andy" in blackface make-up. At the official opening of the Fair in April, 1939, David Sarnoff and Franklin Delano Roosevelt stood before the television camera.

In 1940, the Federal Communications Commission held hearings on proposals for the adoption of television standards in an effort to establish full scale commercial operation of the medium. The Commission, aided by the Radio Manufacturers Association, established the National Television System Committee (NTSC) to draw up transmission specifications acceptable to all sectors of the industry. On the basis of the NTSC's recommendations, the Commission approved commercial operation of television stations effective July 1, 1941. Eighteen channels, each 6 megacycles wide, were authorized in the Very High Frequency (VHF) portion of the radio spectrum. The line standard was charged from 441 to 525, and Frequency Modulation (FM) was adopted for the audio component of the television signal.

Frequency Modulation

FM was developed by Edwin Armstrong in the mid-'30s. In 1939, Armstrong's experimental 50,000-watt FM radio station at Alpine, New Jersey transmitted a regular schedule of programs. In May 1940, the FCC authorized commercial operation of FM radio, and followed this with its decision that television should use FM sound. Channel 1 was removed from the television band and assigned to FM radio. FM and AM-FM combination sets went on sale to the public.

Early in 1940, RCA demonstrated an electronic dot sequential color television system to the FCC. Dr. Peter Goldmark of CBS experimented with a field sequential color system. A wartime freeze was imposed on all station construction and set production. Edwin Armstrong made his FM patents available to the military, royalty-free. Near the end of the war, the FCC moved the FM band up the spectrum to 88–108 megacycles. All existing FM receivers became obsolete.

Post-War Television Growth

CBS filed a petition with the FCC on September 27, 1946 requesting approval for commercial operation of its color system in the Ultra High Frequency (UHF) band. But CBS met opposition for its proposal from RCA and DuMont, among others. CBS's color system was incompatible with black-and-white and therefore would result in the obsolescence of sets in operation. RCA advanced the view that color television should come at a later date when a high quality compatible color system could be developed. In March 1947, the FCC denied CBS's petition for color standards and decreed a go-ahead under the existing black-and white system. Within less than a year, in a move some viewed as suspicious, FCC Chairman Charles R. Denny Jr. resigned to join NBC as vice-president and general counsel.

A major breakthrough in electronics research came in 1948, when the Bell Laboratories announced the invention of the transistor—a small, inexpensive amplifier which revolutionized communications technology. Prior to the advent of the transistor, amplification had been accomplished by bulky, fragile glass vacuum tubes. The transistor, which was developed by a Bell research group led by William Shockley, Walter Brattain, and R. B. Gibney, works on the principle that the movement of electrons in semiconductors, such as germanium and silicon, can be controlled by adding very small amounts of impurities.

The number of applications and authorizations for television stations mushroomed after the end of the war, and the FCC soon began to realize that the 12 channels then allocated for television use were inadequate. The Commission also became concerned that the mileage separations it had proposed for television stations were insufficient to prevent interference. On September 29, 1948, the Commission declared a temporary "freeze" on all new television stations. At the time of the freeze there were 108 television stations authorized to go on the air. During the freeze period 11 cities in the top 50 markets were without any television service. Major cities like Houston, Kansas City, Milwaukee, Pittsburgh and St. Louis had only one station each. New York and Los Angeles, however, each enjoyed seven television stations. On April 14, 1952, the FCC, in its historic, albeit unimaginatively titled, "Sixth Report and Order," terminated its nearly four-year freeze on television applications and authorized 70 Ultra High Frequency (UHF) channels for television in addition to the 12 Very High Frequency (VHF) channels which were already in use. The VHF channels retained the numbers 2–13, and the UHF channels were assigned the numbers 14–38. The new table of assignments made more than 2,000 television channels available throughout the United States, of which 242 were exclusively for educational television. Each station would be separated by a minimum distance of 155 miles. There is a mathematical limit to the number of signals that can be put on the radio spectrum.

On July 11, 1952, the FCC issued its first group of Construction Permits (CP) to 18 of the 716 applicants who had applied for television licenses.* One of the fortunate recipients of a CP was Lady Byrd Johnson, wife of the then Senate Democratic Whip, Lyndon Baines Johnson. By October 1952, the Johnson family's channel 7 station, KTBC-TV, was transmitting pictures through the airwaves in Austin, Texas. For many years, the Johnson station enjoyed a virtual monopoly in the Austin area since the two competing outlets assigned by the FCC were on the UHF band.

The Johnson family fortune was built primarily from broadcasting interests. Early in 1943, the Johnsons used Lady Byrd's modest inheritance to acquire radio station KTBC in Austin, Texas. FCC records indicate that the Johnsons purchased the outlet for $17,500, with the understanding that Mrs. Johnson would pay off the station's debts, which had amounted to almost $50,000. The stock was in Lady Byrd's name, but Lyndon Johnson maintained a keen interest in the operating and financial details of the station. At the time Mrs. Johnson pur-

---

* The actual license is not issued until after a station has been constructed and tested to determine if its signal conforms to the terms, conditions, and obligations set forth in the application. Therefore, the first step toward acquiring a license is to obtain a Construction Permit.

chased KTBC, the station was limited to daytime operation and did not have a network affiliation. She applied to the FCC for unlimited broadcasting hours and for authorization to quadruple the station's 250-watt transmitting power. The first request required allocation of an entirely different wave length. The regulatory body seemed most accommodating. Both requests were granted to the wife of the influential Senator. The station soon gained affiliation with CBS. Network affiliation meant more advertising and more profits. A young time-salesman with the station after World War II was John Connally, who went on to become Governor of Texas, and, to his later chagrin, advisor and confidant to Richard M. Nixon. The Johnson family's initial investment catapulted into a vast broadcasting empire. Mrs. Johnson placed her stocks in trust after Lyndon Johnson became President in 1963 and removed them when he left office in 1969.

Color Television

Meanwhile, the FCC had approved CBS's somewhat improved color system on October 16, 1950, effective on November 20th of the same year. Within days after the decision was announced, RCA petitioned the U.S. District Court in Chicago to enjoin the Commission's order. The Federal District Court ruled against RCA and an appeal was carried to the U.S. Supreme Court which sustained the lower court decision on May 28, 1951. David Sarnoff set his scientists to a grinding 18-hour-a-day pace in an effort to perfect a compatible color system. In mid-1953, the National Television System Committee petitioned the FCC to reconsider its support of the CBS system. The NTSC favored the compatible, all-electronic system advocated by RCA and others. On December 17, 1953, the FCC reversed itself on the CBS system and ordered industrywide standards for color television based largely, though not entirely, on the RCA dot sequential system. The CBS field sequential color system was junked. Ironically, the CBS system, which adapts easily to computer processing techniques, was revived in 1970 to provide color pictures from the moon.

Television Networks

The technical development of television led inevitably to the formation of television networks. Network organizations integrate stations into a nationwide interconnected system, utilizing the facilities of

AT&T, so that programs may be broadcast simultaneously to a substantial portion of the nation's population. AT&T's first intercity coaxial cable television relay link became available in 1948. In September 1951, Harry S Truman, the last President to be elected without extensive use of the television medium, addressed the Japanese Peace Treaty Convention in San Francisco on the first coast-to-coast telecast. The major television networks emerged out of the radio organizations of ABC, CBS, and NBC. The Mutual Broadcasting System did not attempt to develop a television network. A fourth television network, the DuMont Network, was in operation until September 1955. Popular DuMont performers included Bishop Fulton Sheen and Jackie Gleason. DuMont covered the unprecedented Senate Army-McCarthy hearings in 1954, a remarkable demonstration of the sheer informational power of the new medium. The demise of the DuMont Network was, in large part, attributable to the FCC's failure to provide an adequate number of VHF outlets in large cities. During the freeze period, DuMont urged the Commission to assign at least four VHF stations in major markets. DuMont foresaw that unless its proposal was implemented, the network would be relegated to relying on UHF affiliations. Since the UHF signal is higher in the spectrum, it does not travel as far as a VHF signal and consequently reaches a potentially smaller audience. Moreover, most television sets manufactured in the 1950s were not equipped to receive UHF signals. Since set manufacturers, such as RCA, owned VHF stations, they were understandably not anxious to encourage competition by providing a multiplicity of the UHF channels. The economics-of-scarcity keep VHF television profits high. The FCC was convinced that healthy economic competition would exist within the framework of its master plan. After an unsuccessful attempt to establish a viable fourth network, DuMont gave up network operation and sold its television stations. DuMont's Pittsburgh station became KDKA-TV, a Westinghouse station. The Metropolitan Broadcasting Company (Metromedia) acquired DuMont's New York City station and other television outlets. Today, television stations are dominated by an oligarchic television network industry.

Television Programming

Popular early network television shows included the "Texaco Star Theatre" starring Milton Berle, whose zany antics earned him the title of "Mr. Television"; "Your Show of Shows" featuring Sid Caesar and Imogene Coca, who offered subtle pantomimes and often hilarious character sketches; and Ed Sullivan's "Toast of the Town," a variety hour which survived on CBS for almost a quarter of a century. Mystery offerings such as "Lights Out," "Suspense," "Danger," and "The Clock" caused the hearts of TV viewers to palpitate. Most television programs in the early 1950s were live, which initially caused problems in gauging time. The William Esty advertising agency which produced "Man Against Crime," starring Ralph Bellamy, included a search scene near the end of most episodes, the length of which was determined by the amount of time remaining to the close of the show.

One of the most colossal financial successes in television was the "I Love Lucy" series, starring Lucille Ball and her then husband, Desi Arnaz. Each half-hour episode was filmed in one session before a studio audience at a production cost of about $38,000. When Lucy became pregnant, her pregnancy was written into the show and, as the blessed event grew near, an episode was filmed in which she gave birth to a boy, since Desi reportedly always wanted a son. On January 19, 1953, at Cedars of Lebanon Hospital in Los Angeles, Lucy gave birth to Desiderio Alberto IV, an 8½ pound boy. That evening the Lucy-has-a-son episode was telecast. The event rated newspaper headlines only slightly smaller than the inauguration of Dwight D. Eisenhower as President of the United States, which occurred on the same day. Some 179 "I Love Lucy" episodes were filmed. Lucy and Desi bought the RKO movie studios and renamed them Desilu, a contraction using parts of their first names. Desilu produced and packaged a number of successful television shows. Their $20 million television empire was later sold to Gulf and Western Industries. Other Lucille Ball vehicles include "The Lucy Show" and "Here's Lucy" with 156 and 144 episodes, respectively. Lucille Ball may be seen in some markets around the country five different times during a given day. She has been seen on television more often than any human being who ever lived. After a spectacularly successful career Ms. Ball announced her retirement from weekly television and her show went off the air in 1974, but she continues to do occasional "specials." In syndication, the Lucille Ball programs are undoubtedly the most watched comedies in the entire history of television.

The television version of "Amos 'n' Andy" went on the CBS Network the first week of July, 1951 under the sponsorship of the Blatz Brewery, Milwaukee, Wisconsin, the makers of Blatz beer. Tim Moore was cast in the role of George "Kingfish" Stevens, the principal character in the television series. At the annual convention of the NAACP, which met in Atlanta, Georgia, during the last week of June, 1951, a resolution was passed against "The Amos 'n' Andy Show" stating that it depicted "the Negro and other minority groups in (a) stereotyped and derogatory manner. . . ." Despite the NAACP resolution, the series began on schedule. In New York City, a group of black actors organized to protest the NAACP's actions concerning the show. They asserted that the organization's position would jeopardize the employment opportunities for black actors on television. On the other hand, the committee for the Negro in the Arts protested that the show was a "flagrant revival of stereotypes." The NAACP, joined by several other organizations, continued its campaign against "Amos 'n' Andy." Finally, after two seasons, the Blatz Brewing Company discontinued its sponsorship and the series was dropped from the CBS television network in 1953. Local television stations in various parts of the country continued to telecast syndicated reruns of the original series. CBS, which owns all rights to "The Amos 'n' Andy Show," recently stated that there are no plans to make the show available for any purpose. It is doubtful, to say the least, that any program even faintly resembling the tone of "Amos 'n' Andy" could possibly be shown on television today when networks are making an effort to present minorities realistically and without stereotyping.

Television News

Early television news efforts were modest. The networks relied primarily on the newsreel organizations for pictorial content. Both CBS and NBC offered regularly scheduled 15-minute early-evening newscasts. NBC-TV's "Camel News Caravan," which was shown at 7:45 p.m., featured suave, boutonniered John Cameron Swayze, who went on to later fame selling Timex watches. CBS-TV presented "Television News with Douglas Edwards" at 7:30 p.m. The news gathering facilities of both networks were woefully inadequate, and it was not uncommon for the news shows to rely exclusively on government-supplied footage for their coverage of world events. When

ABC in 1955 countered both CBS and NBC News with entertainment programming beginning at 7:30 p.m., the move cut sharply into the audience of the news shows. CBS and NBC were eventually forced to reschedule their news programs adjacent to the primetime period. The two networks expanded their nightly news shows to a half-hour in 1963. ABC did not follow suit until 1967.

Today, the expense of operating a network news organization is prodigious. NBC, for example, maintains about 50 domestic camera crews for its news, sports, special events and documentary coverage. CBS has 20 full-time network news crews and ABC has 16. In addition, each of the networks has camera crews in nine cities overseas. News camera crews cost about a $100,000 a year each to maintain. These crews generate an estimated 20 times as much news footage as is actually used in the final stories—all of which has to be transported, processed and edited. Television coverage of events occurring in "remote" areas around the world is particularly expensive. The economic structure of the network news organizations compels producers to concentrate their filmed stories in a limited number of locations. Whether or not an event is covered often depends on where it occurs and the availability of network crews.

A regularly scheduled news program, unlike newspapers, is restricted by time. The average half-hour news program, excluding commercial announcements, presents less than 20 minutes of news. Consequently, television news rarely treats any event in depth; it is primarily a headline medium. All of the words presented in the average news program would not fill even one page of the *New York Times*. Many newsmen, including Walter Cronkite, believe that the nightly network news feed would benefit greatly by being extended to an hour.

Only a tiny fraction of the world's actual events are transmitted by television each day and those events are shaped by selection, emphasis and suggested inferences. Since television is a visual medium, it tends to concentrate on visually realizable occurrences. Television uses close-ups for what it deems important and leaves the apparently unimportant in the background. Segmented happenings can become an artificially exciting, unified continuous event. News stories often take on the attributes of fiction or drama, with their own structure and conflict, problem and denouement. The television medium itself helps to shape the events that it reports.

See It Now

A controversial news documentary titled "See It Now," which combined the talents of Edward R. Murrow and Fred Friendly, made its debut on November 18, 1951 over the CBS Television Network, sponsored by the Aluminum Company of America. In the first show, Murrow noted in his introductory remarks that he and Friendly were "an old team trying to learn a new trade." Murrow and Friendly had collaborated on a record album, "I Can Hear It Now," and a radio program, "Hear It Now." The premiere telecast featured a live, simultaneous showing of the Golden Gate Bridge and the Brooklyn Bridge. The creative team soon turned to more substantive topics, and the program gradually became controversial, establishing a definite point of view. In October 1953, "See It Now" presented "The Case Against Milo Radulovich, A0589839," the incredible tale of a young Michigan University student and Air Force reservist who had been asked to resign his commission because unidentified accusers had charged that his sister and father had radical leanings. When Radulovich refused to resign, an Air Force board at Selfridge Field ordered his separation from the military on security grounds. He had not been allowed to face his accusers, or even to read the specific allegations against him. The Air Force refused to participate in the "See It Now" telecast of these happenings.

Murrow and Friendly devoted the entire half-hour of the show to the Radulovich story. In a filmed statement Radulovich noted: "The actual charge against me is that I had maintained a close and continuing relationship with my dad and my sister over the years." Another filmed segment showed Radulovich's father, a Serbian immigrant, reading a letter he had written to President Eisenhower, which concluded: "Mr. President . . . they are doing a bad thing to Milo. They are wrong . . . He has given all his growing years to his country . . . I ask nothing for myself. All I ask is justice for my boy. Mr. President, I ask your help." Murrow in his conclusion stated: "Whatever happens in the whole area of the relationship between the individual and the state, we will do it ourselves—it cannot be blamed upon

Malenkov, or Mao Tse-Tung, or even our allies. And it seems to us that—that is, to Fred Friendly and myself—that that is a subject that should be argued about endlessly.''

It was a bold statement to make in the era of McCarthyism. The program was more than an exposé of unjust military procedures. Through the use of an individual case, Murrow and Friendly were repudiating the outrages of the whole phenomenon of McCarthyism.

It was inevitable that the team would eventually tackle the Senator himself. On March 9, 1954, "See It Now" did a special report on Senator Joseph R. McCarthy. The program consisted primarily of juxtaposed McCarthy film footage which highlighted the Senator's inconsistencies, and his wild, unsubstantiated accusations. Adding very little commentary, Murrow allowed the Wisconsin demagogue to destroy himself. A key sequence involved the testimony of Reed Harris, of the State Department's information agency, who appeared before McCarthy's Senate Permanent Subcommittee on Investigations to answer questions about, among other things, a book he had written in 1932 while an undergraduate student at Columbia University. McCarthy singled out a passage from the book which advocated that marriage "should be cast out of our civilization as antiquated and stupid religious phenomenon." Harris had been suspended from his Columbia classes as a result of the book and McCarthy established that the American Civil Liberties Union had supplied him with an attorney. He asked if Harris was aware that the ACLU "has been listed as a front for and doing the work of the Communist Party." Murrow later pointed out that neither the Attorney General, the FBI, nor any other federal government agency has ever listed the ACLU as subversive. McCarthy's accusatory tactics were dramatically shown up during the telecast.

Reaction to the program, as might be expected, was immediate and polarized. Gilbert Seldes, the distinguished critic of the *Saturday Review,* criticized Murrow for purposely portraying Senator McCarthy in the most unfavorable light possible. Surprisingly, Sol Taishoff, the publisher of the generally conservative *Broadcasting* magazine, exclaimed, "No greater feat of journalistic enterprise has occurred in modern times than that performed by Ed Murrow last Tuesday on 'See It Now'." The favorable comments far outweighed the unfavorable. However, columnists like Jack O'Brian, George Sokolsky, Walter

Winchell and Westbrook Pegler repeatedly lashed out at Murrow. A second McCarthy program was presented the following week which showed the Senator interrogating a suspected Communist, Annie Lee Moss. McCarthy's reliance on hearsay, without collaboration, as well as his badgering, bullying tactics were readily apparent. Ironically, four years later, the Subversive Activities Control Board reported that Annie Lee Moss had indeed been a member of the Communist Party.

On the April 6th show, McCarthy, accepting an offer of free time, responded to Murrow's broadcasts in a presentation written for him by Hearst columnist, George Sokolsky. He characterized Murrow as "the cleverest of the jackal pack which is always found at the throat of anyone who dares to expose individual communists and traitors." The Murrow-McCarthy encounter became a national spectacle. Murrow was regarded in some circles as "that traitor." Some months after the McCarthy broadcasts, Murrow was the principal speaker at the annual Junior Chamber of Commerce ceremony to honor the year's "ten outstanding young men." As Murrow rose to speak, one of the young men walked out in protest. He was Robert F. Kennedy, who had served as counsel for several months to Senator McCarthy's Subcommittee.

Red Channels

The socio-political climate of the early 1950s was particularly conducive to evangelical patriotism. The United States was involved in a military conflict against Communist forces in Korea. Hollywood was in a state of turmoil over the HUAC investigations. Those of liberal persuasion in the highly visible and carefully scrutinized entertainment industry were particularly vulnerable to the over-zealous protectors of the national security.

In April 1947, three ex-FBI men, John G. Keenan, Theodore Kirkpatrick, and Kenneth Bierly, founded the American Business Consultants, Inc. in New York City. One month later, the organization began publishing a four-page newsletter "Counterattack: The Newsletter of Facts on Communism." None of the publishers was considered to be experts on Communism, but they were spurred on by a desire to "expose the Red Menace."

Subscribers to "Counterattack" were entitled to the Special Reports which the newsletter published irregularly. The most controversial of these reports was "Red Channels: The Report of Communist Influence in Radio and Television." "Red Channels" listed the names of 151 persons in the radio-television industry who were linked either in the past or present with a variety of alleged Communist causes.* Its publication in June 1950 marked the formal beginning of blacklisting in the radio-television industry. Ed Sullivan, host of a television show launched in 1948 called the "Toast of the Town," praised "Red Channels" and worked closely with Theodore Kirkpatrick to insure the loyalty of guests appearing on his show. "Red Channels" soon became known as "the Bible of Madison Avenue."

The publishers of "Red Channels" never held that everyone listed was actually a subversive or a Communist, but they did believe that those whose names appeared should explain their affiliations, and the industry accepted the proposition. The publication of "Red Channels" coincided directly with the first reports of the Korean conflict. Network officials rushed to rid programs of persons who might cause embarrassment. "Counterattack" subscribers bombarded the networks with letters, protesting the appearance of listees. Many of those listed were required to endure long clearance procedures before they found themselves employable again. Philip Loeb, who played Jake in the CBS television version of the popular radio show, "The Goldbergs," was a "Red Channel" listee. The sponsor, Sanka coffee, a General Foods product, received a flood of protests concerning his appearance on the program. The show was dropped by General Foods at the end of the 1951 season and moved over to NBC under a new sponsor. When it returned to the air, Loeb was no longer playing Jake. He was reported to have received a settlement. His radio and television career ceased. In 1955 Philip Loeb committed suicide.

By 1952, blacklisting was generally accepted in the entertainment industry. The unfortunate circumstance was that the practice was carried on, for the most part, by people who were personally and privately opposed to it. Opponents were often reluctant to participate in any public defiance, understandably fearful that any resistance to blacklisting might be interpreted as an attempt to help the Communists. Once blacklisting was institutionalized, it expanded and soon went far beyond the names in "Red Channels." The practice was also

* Included on the list were Leonard Bernstein, Howard Duff, John Garfield, Lillian Hellman, Burl Ives, Zero Mostel, Orson Welles, and a host of other notables.

complicated by the unique structure of the radio-television industry. In Hollywood, most hiring was concentrated in the major studios. But, in radio and television during the 1950s, advertising agencies, networks, program packagers, and sponsors all had a voice in deciding who was to be employed. The result was a multiplicity of lists and procedures, different policies on different networks, all adding to confusion. Thus, it often happened that a television personality might be acceptable to the agency and network, but not to the sponsor. Because facts were hard to come by, decisions tended to be capricious and often unfortunate.

Lucille Ball suddenly became highly controversial in 1953 when newspapers carried stories that in the mid-'30s, Communist meetings had been held at her home. She was also accused of signing Communist Party petitions and being listed as a member of the Communist Party's Central Committee of California. Ms. Ball appeared before the House Committee on Un-American Activities and explained that she had registered as a Communist in 1936 to please her Socialist grandfather. She swore that she was never active in the Communist Party, nor had she ever voted Communist. The Committee apparently was satisfied with her explanation.

Not unexpectedly, the Federal Communications Commission also acquiesced to the anti-Communist pressure groups. On April 9, 1952, the issue of blacklisting was placed before the FCC by the American Civil Liberties Union. The ACLU asked for an investigation of the blacklisting and for FCC regulation designed to terminate the practice. The ACLU claimed that blacklisting was against the public interest because it denied the public the right to see or hear artists due to irrelevant considerations. The FCC could not take direct action against the networks themselves, but voted to grant only temporary renewal of licenses to the stations involved. As a result of pressure from anti-Communistic forces, however, the Commission reversed its action on June 11, 1953.

Aware, Inc. was another organization formed to combat the alleged Communist conspiracy in entertainment industry. Aware's position was that a performer wanting to clear himself should not only prove he is not a Communist or Communist sympathizer, but give ample evidence that he was "actively" anti-Communistic. Neutralism was not condoned. Americans had to "stand up and be counted."

Aware issued bulletins listing people it regarded as suspect. Again, however, irrevocable proof was hard to obtain.

Members of the American Federation of Television and Radio Artists (AFTRA), threatened by blacklisting, turned to their union for help. The New York chapter set up a committee headed by chapter president Vinton Hayworth to deal with this problem. Hayworth was also an officer in Aware, Inc. This committee did not take any positive action in regard to blacklisting, and opposition to the Aware-dominated board of directors grew. The dissenters attempted to elect a new board, but lost the December 9, 1954 election. After that, Aware, Inc. issued a special bulletin in which the losing candidates were listed along with their past associations.

Aware's tactics initially tended to unify the opposition rather than destroy it. In March 1955, a majority of the local membership adopted a resolution condemning the blacklisting activities of Aware. It was submitted by referendum to the entire membership, and despite Aware's threats, passed by a 2 to 1 vote. After the vote to condemn Aware, a new slate of liberals were put up for election. To keep the issue against blacklisting clear, it was essential that the new ticket should be rigorously anti-Communist, but just as determinedly against Aware's activities. The "middle of the road" slate included Charles Collingwood, Gary Moore, Orson Bean, John Henry Faulk, Janice Rule, Faye Emerson, and others. They issued a "declaration of independence" opposing Communism as well as the "denial of employment by discriminatory and intimidating practices, especially by outside organizations."

The slate won 27 of the 35 board places in the December 15, 1955 election. Collingwood became president; Faulk and Bean, vice presidents. John Henry Faulk, a WCBS talk show host and disc jockey, received the highest number of votes and it was toward him that Aware planned its attack. It responded by distributing 2,000 copies of a bulletin which denounced Faulk by listing past associations and links in the "Red Channels" style to influential individuals and organizations. Laurence Johnson, a supermarket executive in Syracuse, New York who was very active in anti-Communist causes, deluged Faulk's sponsors with protestations. Another leader in the anti-Faulk campaign was Vincent Hartnett, who had written the introduction to "Red Channels." He worked as a consultant investigating alleged subversive activities. Faulk sued Aware, Inc., Hartnett, and Johnson for libel in June 1956. Sponsors quickly deserted Faulk, and CBS fired him. Faulk became unemployable for the next six years. Finally in June 1962 he won his case. A State Supreme Court jury in Manhattan awarded him the unprecedented amount of $1 million compensatory damages, and $2.5 million in punitive damages. The Appellate Division of the New York Supreme Court affirmed the verdict, but reduced the damages to $550,000. Lawrence Johnson died during the trial, and Faulk received $175,000 from Johnson's estate before the appeal was heard. Of this, Faulk's lawyer Louis Nizer received $100,000. Aware Inc. disbanded without assets and the entire $550,000 judgment fell to Vincent Hartnett who pays 10 per cent of his salary every year to Faulk and Nizer. The whole Faulk episode was clearly not one of broadcasting's finer hours.

As blacklisting acquired notoriety, its effectiveness diminished as an institution. Many artists, controversial a year or two earlier, were now welcomed. Still, isolated incidents continued to occur. In 1962, the folk-singing Weavers with Pete Seeger were dropped from their appearance on "The Jack Paar Show" because they refused to sign a loyalty oath just prior to the performance. The American Civil Liberties Union protested to the FCC, but the Commission declared that it could not direct stations to carry or not to carry particular programs. On September 10, 1967, Pete Seeger appeared on "The Smothers Brothers Show;" commercial television had been closed to him for 17 years. The era of blacklisting appeared to have come to an end, but industry attempts to control controversial content continued unabated. One of Seeger's songs entitled "Waist Deep in the Big Muddy," which was obliquely critical of President Johnson and the Vietnam War, was cut from the videotaped program despite Tom Smothers' heated protests. As a result of public outcry, Seeger was invited a few months later for a return engagement in which he sang the song in its entirety. The practice of blacklisting presumably passed from existence.

Television Movies

A major staple of television since its inception has been the theatrical feature film. One of television's earliest stars was William Boyd, star of the "Hopalong Cassidy" series, low-budgeted theatrical releases which were first produced beginning in 1935. When Paramount terminated the series because of rising costs, Boyd bought the movie rights and started making the films himself. In a far-sighted move, he also secured the television rights. The films became the television sensation of 1948, and William Boyd who had been in movies since 1919, became one of the TV medium's first major stars.

Other western stars who galloped into television in their old movies included Gene Autry and Roy Rogers. Both had achieved initial fame as the stars of innumerable minor westerns made by Republic Pictures Corporation, a small Hollywood production and distribution company founded in 1935 by a former tobacco executive named Herbert J. Yates. In February 1967, CBS purchased the old Republic Studio, which consisted of 70 acres with 17 sound stages, for $9.5 million and renamed it CBS Studio Center.

The Pennsylvania State Board of Film Censorship adopted a regulation in 1949 requiring all films which were to be exhibited by Pennsylvania television stations to be submitted first to the Board for review. The five television stations then operating in Pennsylvania filed suit in the Federal District Court to determine the legality of the Board's requirement. The court ruled that state censorship was illegal because television was interstate in its nature and therefore subject only to federal regulation. The U.S. Court of Appeals upheld the lower court ruling, and the U.S. Supreme Court, in February 1951, refused to review the case.

In January 1956, RKO Teleradio Pictures, the General Tire and Rubber Company subsidiary for the old RKO Pictures, sold 740 feature films and 1,000 short subjects to C&C Super Corp., who later released them to television. It was a point of major breakthrough. Until then, Republic had been the only other company of significance to sell its film assets to the rival medium. The same month, Columbia Pictures released 104 features to television through its subsidiary, Screen Gems. By March 1956, a $21 million deal between PRM, an investment firm, and Warner Bros. was announced, involving the sale of 850 Warner features and 1,500 shorts for distribution to television. A few months later came an estimated $16–$20 million deal for 725 MGM features. In November 1956, National Telefilm Associates acquired the television rights to the 20th Century-Fox film library of 390 feature films in exchange for half-interest in the NTA Film Network.

Paramount also succumbed to the lure of television in a $50 million deal. Within a three-year period, an estimated 9,000 pre-1948 Hollywood features were released to television stations. The pre-1948 films were owned outright by the studios and involved no payment of residuals to artists. In the early 1960s, the majors began selling their post-1948 films which required negotiations with the various unions for residual payments.

A federal district court ruled in 1960 that six distributors of pre-1948 features were engaging in "block booking" which forced television stations to take many unwanted films distributed by a given company in order to obtain the features they wished to show. The distributors involved were Loew's (MGM film), Associated Artists (Warner Bros.), Screen Gems (Columbia), National Telefilm Associates (20th Century-Fox), C&C Super (RKO), and United Artists, the distributor for various independent producers. The lower court's decision that the distributing companies violated the Sherman Anti-Trust Act was appealed to the U.S. Supreme Court. In November 1962, the High Court ruled, in a unanimous decision, that the six defendants violated the antitrust act when they forced television stations to take packages of films containing pictures they did not want. The Court's decision did not preclude the sale of film packages per se, provided that there was not an unreasonable price differential between what is charged for individual films and what is charged for the same film when included in a package. *Loew's, Inc. et al* v. *United States,* 371 U.S. 38 (1962).

Few theatrical features appeared on network television during the 1950s. Indeed, the release of over a $100 million worth of feature motion pictures to television stations was thought to be a threat to network dominance. Network program fare consisted primarily of situation comedies, detective dramas, westerns, and quiz shows. The latter format created a major scandal when it was revealed that the contests were rigged. Hints of quiz "fixing" began to surface as early as 1957. Articles concerning alleged collusion appeared in *Look* and *Time*. The New York District Attorney began an investigation in the fall of 1958. Popular quiz shows included "The $64,000 Question," and "Twenty-One." On the latter program, an instructor of English at Columbia University named Charles Van Doren, from a distinguished family of scholars and writers, made 14 appearances and won $129,000. In

1959, Mr. Van Doren explained to the Legislative Oversight Committee of the House Commerce Committee that the show's producer had given him the questions, and sometimes the answers, before his appearance. He admitted that he had even been coached to feign nervousness during the questioning. Other quiz programs were also found to be rigged. Revlon, the sponsor of "The $64,000 Question" and "The $64,000 Challenge" apparently had instructed production personnel as to which contestants should lose and which should be allowed to continue. The scandals resulted in the networks taking over production control from the sponsor.

Commercial Announcements

The Federal Communications Commission proposed rules, in May 1963, that would have placed definite limits on the time devoted to commercial announcements by radio and television stations. The maximum limits proposed were identical to those provided in the self-regulatory codes of the National Association of Broadcasters (NAB), and were far from restrictive.

The broadcast industry adamantly objected to the Commission's attempt to regulate the business practices of stations and exerted strong pressure on Congress. A measure was introduced in the House of Representatives, which passed by an overwhelming vote, to prohibit the FCC from attempting to interfere with the business operations of the broadcast industry. The bill was not taken up in the Senate during that session of Congress. Nevertheless, the House action was apparently sufficient indication to the FCC as to the sentiments of the nation's lawmakers. In January 1964, the FCC stated that it had "found adoption of specific rules limiting the commercial content of broadcasters not appropriate at this time." However, the Commission emphasized that it would still concern itself with problems of over-commercialization in its overall evaluation of station performance. There are to this day no specific government regulations limiting the amount of television time devoted to commercial announcements. Stations are subject only to the voluntary limitations imposed by the National Association of Broadcasters.

Network Entertainment Programming

In network program departments, there's an aversion to amateurs. The emphasis is on slick professionalism. There is little latitude for experimentation and innovation. As Paul Klein, former director of research at NBC, recently commented, the networks want innovative, unconventional programming—with a track record. Most primetime network shows are produced by the television subsidiaries of the major Hollywood film studios and the 10 or so firmly established independent television producers.

The middle 1960s saw the advent of a rash of network "spy" programs, precipitated, perhaps, by the revelations of clandestine CIA activities throughout the world. Television programs such as "The Man From U.N.C.L.E.," "Get Smart," "I Spy," and "Mission Impossible" helped to minimize and rationalize the impact of alleged CIA skullduggery abroad. Robert Lewis Shayon, then critic for the *Saturday Review,* singled out "Mission Impossible" as the most harmful program on the air. He noted that the heroes of the program interfered in the affairs of foreign nations with whom the United States was at peace and broke their laws under the guise of impeccable morality. Shayon wrote, "the program series tends to legitimatize unilateral force for solving international problems at a time when our nation recognizes, or at least verbalizes, the desperate urgency of collaborative efforts among nations for world order." The program still enjoys great popularity in syndication.

The sensation of the latter half of the 1960s was "Laugh-In," which became part of NBC's mid-season replacement schedule in 1968. The show's rapid-fire kaleidoscopic segments apparently compelled audience attention. Comedians Dan Rowan and Dick Martin gave a sense of continuity to the visually and conceptually complex collage. Much of the humor was of a sexually suggestive nature. Catchphrases like "sock it to me" and "look that up in your Funk and Wagnalls" were oft repeated. A measure of the show's popularity is evidenced in the reported statement that Funk and Wagnalls had to go into extra printings of its dictionary in order to satisfy a 20 per cent rise in sales.

One of the most innovative and convention-shattering series to appear on television has been "All in the Family," which made its debut on January 21, 1971 over the CBS Network as a mid-season replacement. The show is adapted from the hit BBC series "Till Death Do Us Part," a John Speight creation in which the central character is a Cockney hatemonger. The American version is produced by Norman Lear and Alan (Bud) Yorkin's Tandem Productions, Inc. ABC had first expressed interest in the series and commissioned two pilot episodes starring Carroll O'Connor and Jean Stapleton. After spending over $250,000, ABC executives decided not to deviate from television's traditional pusillanimity. CBS's newly installed network executives, president Robert D. Wood and then programming vice-president Fred Silverman, revived the project in 1970.* The pilots were well received by members of the public, who were randomly selected along New York City's Avenue of the Americas to view them in CBS's theatre-laboratory located in the company's granite monolith at 51 West 52nd Street, popularly known as "Black Rock."

Before the show made it to the airwaves, Lear, who wrote most of the first year's scripts, was said to have had several confrontations with the then Hollywood head of CBS's program practices department, William Tankersley. The series, of course, centers around the family life of a bigot named Archie Bunker, who openly professes his disdain for racial and ethnic groups with such epithets as "kike," "wop," and "jungle bunny." Lear conceded to the deletion of "smart-ass" and "goddammit" from the dialogue of the first episode, but he made few other concessions to the CBS hierarchy. Anticipating a public furor, the network hired extra telephone operators for the premiere telecast to receive protest calls and ran a voice-over disclaimer with the credits noting that the program presented "a humorous spotlight on our frailties, prejudices, and concerns." Reaction to the show was surprisingly slight and, for the most part, favorable. In its first few months on the air, the program was a marginal performer in the ratings. In a new time slot the following fall, "All in the Family" became the most popular show on television, rivaling "Lucy" and "The Beverly Hillbillies" in all-time audience appeal. Each show is taped twice before live audiences, with the elements of both tapings edited together for presentation to the television audience. The series' controversial themes have included sexual impotency, menstruation, menopause, wife-swapping, homosexuality, and rape. Archie's bigotry is an inherent part of almost every episode. In addition to its network earnings, Tandem Productions also gets a percentage on the

* Fred Silverman left CBS in 1975 to become president of ABC Entertainment at a reported annual salary of $250,000 plus substantial stock in the company. Within a week of the announcement of his move, ABC's stock increased in value by more than $80 million.

sale of such merchandise as Archie Bunker T-shirts, beer mugs, and the like.

Lear and Yorkin scored with another BBC adaptation, "Sanford and Son," starring Redd Foxx and Demond Wilson. This series generally eschews controversy, camouflaging its blandness with an occasional, mildly militant remark by Foxx, such as "Just because he's white doesn't mean he's stupid." The show serves primarily as a vehicle for Foxx's brilliantly delivered one-liners.

"All in the Family" generated several spin-offs. Edith Bunker's brassy, liberal-minded cousin, "Maude," quickly soared in the ratings. In a two-part episode during the 1972–73 season, the much-married Maude, played by Bea Arthur, decided to have an abortion when she learned that she was pregnant at the age of 47. Nothing quite like this had ever been done on television before. Two decades earlier, Desi Arnaz had to obtain the support of a rabbi, a minister, and a priest in order to convince CBS that there was no reason why pregnancy could not be portrayed tastefully on a telecast.

Maude's black maid, Florida, played by Esther Rolle, also graduated into her own program, "Good Times." Archie's black neighbors, "The Jeffersons," spun-off into a series by moving into a fashionable white neighborhood. Tandem's situation comedies consistently rank among the top 10 television shows. The company's only television failure to date has been "Hot l Baltimore," adapted from a successful off-Broadway play.

Prime time shows are not always profitable for the producer during their initial network run. Producers of filmed shows, in particular, often lose money and go into deficit financing in the hope of eventual profit from foreign and domestic syndication. Grant Tinker, the president of MTM Enterprises (and the husband of Mary Tyler Moore), claims that his company sustains losses week-in and week-out. MTM productions are filmed with three cameras simultaneously before a live studio audience. This method allows for many changes to be made in the cutting room since there are three different angles for each scene. The shows would be cheaper to do in videotape, but MTM producers feel that the high-key lighting required for tape results in a harsh, hard-edged quality. However, the skyrocketing cost of shooting with film may force MTM to shift to tape. During the 1975–76 season MTM had six weekly series on primetime television totalling three-

and-a half hours, making it the leading independent supplier of network programming.

The average primetime filmed television program costs the network about $275,000 an hour to present. The network generally sells six minutes of commercial time during a one-hour program for an average of $80,000 a minute, bringing in a theoretical gross of $480,000. Each network-affiliated station must be compensated for carrying the program. A network-affiliated station is usually paid about 30 per cent of its hourly "Class A" rate—the price per hour that the station normally charges advertisers for the time in which they carry network programs and commercials. Affiliates receive a set amount of compensation per hour from the network, regardless of what amount the network is able to secure for the sale of time. This practice proves very profitable to the network with a show like "Sanford and Son" which sells for as much as $60,000 for a single 30-second commercial. However, most programs in a network's prime-time inventory do not fetch anywhere near that amount. Advertising rates are computed on the basis of cost-per-thousand (CPM) people reached. A primetime audience costs an advertiser about $5.00 per thousand bulk. The networks claim that they barely break even on the first showing of many primetime television programs.

Until about 1960, nearly every network television series consisted of 39 original episodes, and 13 reruns usually played during the summer months. Then the average half-hour show cost less than $50,000 to produce; an hour segment rarely ran more than $100,000. Over the past decade and a half TV production costs have soared and networks have compensated for the rising prices by increasing the number of reruns. Today, summer begins in March. Before the winter snows have melted, some episodes have been repeated twice. An exhaustive study conducted by Dr. Clay Whitehead of the White House Office of Telecommunications Policy (OTP) in 1972, showed that the average network series aired no more than 22 to 24 original programs each year. Reruns, according to the Whitehead report, accounted for 51.8 per cent of all prime time programming.

Those most adamantly opposed to the practice of reruns are, of course, the various broadcast unions whose membership is heavily unemployed. Others, such as Robert D. Wood, president of the CBS Television Network, argue that reruns are a benefit rather than a blight because only 14 per cent of the public sees a given show during its first broadcast. Reruns, says Mr. Wood, give the public the opportunity to catch a show they missed first time round. If the networks are sincere, they should schedule and advertise repeated shows well in advance. Indeed, public television stations often repeat a show two or three times in the same week, a practice that has proven to be popular with many viewers. Reruns are very profitable for the network. When the videotape or film of a show which initially cost $275,000 to present is repeated, the cost is reduced to about $30,000. Although advertisers pay less for commercial time on reruns, a profit of about $100,000 is realized.

Shows outside the primetime period are sometimes enormously profitable for the network. The spectacularly successful "Tonight Show" on NBC realizes between $10 and $15 million a year in net income in spite of Johnny Carson's colossal $61,538.46 salary per week, 52 weeks a year. Carson's current contract, which he signed in April 1972, calls for salary increases to $65,384.62 per week effective April 10, 1977. He is required to work only 4 days per week and receives 15-weeks annual vacation.

The "Tonight Show's" weekly budget, including Johnny Carson's salary, is about $200,000. The program carries approximately 20 minutes of commercial time because the NAB limit on commercials is more permissive after 11 p.m. NBC affiliated-stations receive 12 minutes to sell locally. The network sells its eight minutes at a rate of about $23,800 per minute which brings the network a theoretical gross of $190,400 per night, $952,000 per week, and $49,504,000 per year. The gross is theoretical, since the rate for commercial minutes is not firmly fixed. The network sales department offers frequency discounts and various other advertising plans.

The network also derives income from the sale of commercial time on its owned-and-operated stations. WNBC in New York City, for example, charges approximately $1,800 for a commercial minute on the "Tonight Show," or $21,600 per night, $108,000 per week, and $5,616,000 per year. Again, the gross is theoretical, since the local station offers reduced rates to large advertisers, as well as sundry combination plans.

The "Tonight Show" format was the brainchild of Sylvester "Pat" Weaver, who joined NBC in 1949 as vice-president in charge of television. Another Weaver creation is the "Today Show" which went on the air in 1952. This show, too, continues to be extraordinarily profitable for NBC. Its total weekly operating budget is about $135,500. Expenditures, on the daily two-hour early morning program, break down roughly into $88,695 for above-the-line expenses and $46,805 for below-the-line costs. The above-the-line costs include such things as talent, directors, writers, picture and sound labs, editing, and still rentals. The weekly cost of talent for the basic show, which includes the salaries of Barbara Walters and Jim Hartz, is about $18,769. Ms. Walters receives $7,000 per week, fifty two weeks a year. Below-the-line costs include stagehands, scenery construction, wardrobe, studio facilities, special effects and the like. NBC offers dividend participation plans whereby an advertiser may purchase commercial time in "packages" which include "Today," "Tonight" and "Saturday-Sunday Tonight." The package price for "Today" is about $11,400 per 60-second participation on NBC's full-station lineup.

Television Ratings

The success or failure of any television program is determined by the estimated number and kinds of people watching. The only company which continuously provides national ratings for network shows is A.C. Nielsen. Nearly every program decision made by the networks is based on the Nielsen numbers. Nielsen meters in 1,200 households across the country are connected via telephone lines to the Nielsen computer center at Dunedin, Florida to produce audience estimates within 36 hours.

The Audimeter monitors tuning activities at 30-second intervals throughout the day. The rating for a given program is computed by determining the percentage of households tuned to the program out of the total number of households owning television sets. A rating of 10.0 would indicate that 10 per cent of America's 70 million television households, or 7.0 million homes are tuned to a particular program. The Audimeter, however, only indicates if a set is turned on and to what channel it is tuned, not whether any one is watching. The set may be serving as a romantic night light or amusing the family dog. This factor has resulted in some people challenging the usefulness of the rating service.

In addition to the rating, Nielsen also provides the share-of-audience. The *share* is a competitive evaluation which gives the percentage of homes actually using television which are tuned to a particular program. If 40 million television households were using television and 10 million were tuned to "Sanford and Son," the program would have a 25 share. The share allows a network to evaluate how it is competing against other programs on the air at the same time. Generally, to remain on the network, a program must maintain a 30 share. A new show will be kept on the air even when its share falls below 30 if the audience appears to be building. On the other hand, a program with a 30-plus share may be dropped if its audience has been slipping over a period of time. A show with a "40 share" is a solid hit.

The Audimeter sample simply provides a tally of the estimated number of households using television. It does not give any information about the kinds of people, if anyone, who are watching. Demographic data such as the age and sex of those actually watching the home screen is provided by diaries. Nielsen systematically places diaries in three groups of approximately 750 households each across the country. Each group provides detailed data about their viewing behavior every third week on a rotating basis. The rotation of diary homes is done to minimize "diary fatigue." One diary is provided for each set in the household. The diary information is collated with the meter results and is published bi-weekly. Demographic data have become increasingly important to advertisers who are more concerned with people who will *buy*, rather than with gross head counts.

Nielsen does not seek qualitative responses to the programs viewed. Ratings indicate the estimated number and kinds of people who are watching television, and the stations to which they are tuned. They do not provide critical reaction to a particular program. The viewer may be merely selecting what Paul Klein, former director of research at NBC, has called the "least objectionable program."

Nielsen homes receive a few dollars each month to compensate for the 5 to 7 watts of electricity used by the meter. Nielsen also pays about 50 per cent of their normal television repair bills excluding work on the TV antenna. Nielsen households are changed at the planned rate of 20 per cent each year. An additional 10 to 12 per cent change primarily as a result of household movement. No home has an Audimeter for more than five years. Nielsen draws its national sample from the U.S. Census, plus interim census updates. The seemingly small samples used by Nielsen to estimate the viewing habits of over 200 million people are statistically sound, provided that the sample is random—each and every member of the population being measured has an equal chance of being included in the sample. An estimated 30 per cent of the homes asked by Nielsen refuse to allow the Audimeter to be installed. Many diaries are unuseable because they are filled out incorrectly, or not returned. The unresolved question is whether or not people who refuse to have a meter on their sets or neglect to return the diaries have viewing habits different from those who effectively participate in the sample. This offers a fertile area for further investigation.

Since many local stations cannot afford to pay for a rating service on a regular basis, Nielsen conducts three ''sweeps'' each year in which ratings are computed simultaneously for virtually every station in the nation. Local stations use the data from each sweep to establish advertising rates for the following quarter. NBC provided an advertising boom for its affiliated stations by scheduling ''The Godfather'' in two segments during the November 1974 sweep period. Local samples are drawn from telephone directories.

Although the Nielsen company receives an estimated $20 million a year income for its various rating services, audience measurement constitutes only about 10 per cent of its overall business. The A.C. Nielsen Company's primary business is auditing the inventories of supermarkets and drugstores to provide manufacturers with information as to how fast their goods are moving out to the public.

Nielsen's major competitor in the arena of local television ratings is the American Research Bureau (ARB), which, like Nielsen, simultaneously measures all local markets in the fall, late winter and spring. The scope and methods of the two companies are nearly identical— both use diaries which cover one week and draw their samples from telephone directories. Each company also offers specialized services. Nielsen uses its Audimeter in New York, Los Angeles, and Chicago to produce ''overnight'' ratings in these areas. ARB offers telephone coincidental and recall services for telecasts not covered by the ''sweep periods.''

Several other research firms produce television ratings on a ''custom'' basis. C. E. Hooper, Inc., Trendex, Inc., and Statistical Research Inc. are the most prominent. They all use the telephone coincidental interview as their primary technique to measure viewing habits.

An advertiser generally seeks programs which appeal to the most economically active viewers—people with money, people with changeable buying habits, people who need the product. As a result, most prime time television shows are aimed at people in the 18 to 49 age range, since presumably they spend the most money. Shows that fail to attract the 18 to 49 year olds are generally dropped even if their overall rating is high. Robert D. Wood, president of the CBS Television Network, decided not to renew the Red Skelton and Jackie Gleason shows after the 1969–70 season because they skewed young and old, attracting insufficient numbers in the middle-age range. Advertisers considered the two comedians overpriced for the "quality" of audience they delivered. "Gunsmoke," starring James Arness, was cancelled after 20 years, despite an estimated audience of nearly 36 million people, because the show tended to appeal to rural audiences and older people. Older, poorer and rural people are much less important to the network program planners than young-to-middle-aged urban and surburban middle-class people. In the land of television, all viewers are not created equal. Profit maximization takes priority over the public interest, and business is so good that the networks are unlikely to change voluntarily.

10

Self-Regulation
of Broadcasting

CONTROL OF CONTENT in the broadcast media rests primarily with the industry itself since the government has been extremely reluctant to intrude on the programming process. Despite the broad statutory powers of the Federal Communications Commission, it has not been a very effective regulatory organization. The most conspicuous failure of the Commission has been its inability to raise the quality of programming on commercial television. One critic has aptly characterized the FCC as a "tower of Jell-O." Yet, the Commission is restricted to the extent that it has little legislative or judicial power.

The program content of television is determined, in large part, by the three major networks since they provide about 85 per cent of evening primetime programming. Some 87 per cent of all commercial television stations in the United States are affiliated with either CBS, NBC, or ABC, and 60 per cent of all programming on affiliated stations originates from these networks. Each of the three major television networks has formulated its own standards and expectations for broadcast content which spell out network policy in specific situations. These standards are administered by what are euphemistically called Standards and Practices, Continuity Acceptance or Program-Practices departments.

ABC's policies and standards, for example, are implemented by its Department of Broadcast Standards and Practices, which in theory, operates independently of the ABC Television Network so that there is, in effect, a system of "checks and balances" in determining the acceptability of program material. Each entertainment program is reviewed at all phases, from script stage through final production and editing. Where a particular television program or series or made-for-television movie is expected to include sensitive or controversial subject matter, discussions are held with the producer to ensure that the final product will conform to ABC program policies.

Television Movies

Feature films, initially produced for theatrical release, cause particular problems to network program-practices departments. A film is generally screened prior to acquisition by the network to determine whether it will require major or minor deletions. In some instances, the film is not acceptable at all. If for example a film was originally rated "R," ABC generally requires that it be re-edited and resubmitted to the Motion Picture Association of America for reclassification. ABC requires an MPAA rating of "PG" before a film is acceptable for telecast. NBC and CBS rely on their own judgments in presenting theatrical films. Before CBS presented Luchino. Visconti's "The Damned," an X-rated movie about the pre-World War II decadence among the German aristocracy, Warner Studios, the distributor of the film, cut 25 minutes of potentially offensive material from the original 154 minutes. CBS cut an additional 11 minutes before the movie was presented in the late evening hours. Despite these massive cuts, the network received a large number of protests and several affiliates refused to carry the film. It is interesting to note that some of the refusals to "clear" the program were effected *before* the station had even seen the edited version. With the exception of ABC's presentation of a re-edited version of "Midnight Cowboy," there have been no other showings of X-rated films by the major networks. Films containing sensitive subject matter are generally accompanied by an audio and video advisory to afford parents the opportunity to exercise discretion in regard to younger viewers in the household. In addition, the so-called family viewing hours (7–9 p.m. EST) are intended to eliminate programming in early evening primetime which may not be suitable for children.

Network program-practices departments also examine commercial material in an effort to prevent the presentation of false, misleading, or deceptive advertising. An advertiser must provide the network with substantiation or documentation for affirmative claims made for a particular product or service. The economic considerations and objectives of the network's Sales Department, according to CBS's program-practices vice-president, Tom Swafford, are considered irrelevant in the clearance process.

Network Program-Practices: A Case Study

The enormous power that the networks wield over television content is rarely evidenced, since their self-regulatory policies are generally implemented quietly and effectively, achieving little or no publicity. However, on occasion an internal conflict will reach the outside world through the medium of the newspaper. The most publicized confrontation between a network's guardians of public taste (some would call them ''censors'') and its creative talent involved Tom and Dick Smothers and CBS's program-practices department. ''The Smothers Brothers Comedy Hour'' began on CBS as a mid-season replacement in February 1967 on Sunday evenings at 9 o'clock opposite of NBC's highly successful ''Bonanza.'' The variety-comedy show quickly managed to tumble the unbeatable western from its longtime number one spot in the Nielsen ratings.

Almost from the show's inception, however, the Smothers brothers were at odds with the program-practices people over program material on such issues as politics, religion, narcotics, movie censorship, sex, and social protest. By today's standards, the programs, if rebroadcast, might seem tame. But in the more timid television world of the mid-1960s they were considered ''strong social comment.''

The first major confrontation with the program-practices department came in April 1967 when the brothers attempted to present a short skit with Tommy Smothers and commedienne Elaine May criticizing movie censorship. Such words as ''breast'' and ''heterosexual'' were used. The entire skit was cut. As the show achieved higher ratings and attracted a young audience, the brothers were permitted greater latitude in the discussion of social issues. The network faced the problem of holding to standards in the face of an enormously popular primetime program.

Nevertheless, the conflict between the brothers and the network continued. The stations, too, were said to have complained about some of the program's political satire and sexual permissiveness. CBS's program-practices department was particularly concerned about material which might offend religious viewers. The following exchange between Tom and Dick Smothers was deleted early in 1968:

> Dick: Do you know what Easter is actually all about?
> Tom: Sure, It's the day Jesus Christ rose from his tomb . . .
> Dick: That's right. I'm proud of you.
> Tom: . . . and if He sees His shadow, He has to go back in again for six weeks.

There were many subsequent deletions. A segment in which Harry Belafonte sang "Lord, Lord, Don't Stop the Carnival" against a background of film clips showing non-violent demonstrators at the 1968 Democratic National Convention was cut. CBS replaced the Belafonte song with a paid commercial for Richard Nixon, the 1968 Republican presidential candidate. A reference to Christ in a comedy monologue was cut from an October, 1968, program. The Smothers brothers had been told in advance of taping that the line was unacceptable, but they included it in the program anyway so that the program-practices department could see it in context. But CBS ordered the line cut without seeing the tape and turned down a personal request from the brothers to look at the show and reconsider the decision.

CBS soon required that each Smothers' show be previewed by the network's affiliated stations in a closed-circuit screening prior to broadcast. This is standard practice in any program that might create social or political problems, with the exception of news programs. The conflict heightened in March 1969, when after a prolonged dispute over some remarks by folk singer Joan Baez and comedian Jackie Mason, CBS replaced the program in which they appeared with a two-month old rerun. The network claimed that the rerun was shown because the revised tape of the originally scheduled program was submitted too late for Sunday broadcast. The Smothers brothers charged that CBS dropped the show because of Joan Baez's remarks about her husband's draft resistance. They further claimed that CBS demanded so many changes in the show that they could not possibly complete it on schedule. According to Tom Smothers, the program-practices department requested that several lines be deleted less than half-hour before the scheduled closed-circuit showing. CBS, in turn, noted that Tom Smothers had barred West Coast program-practices man, Sam Taylor, from the control room during rehearsals and taping. The show was later rescheduled but Ms. Baez was permitted to say only that her then husband, David Harris, was going to jail. CBS deleted her explanation that Harris had resisted military service and cut her comment, "Anybody who lays it out front like that generally gets busted, especially if you organize, which he did." The two brothers threatened to leave CBS unless the network eased up on its "censorship."

The program scheduled for April 6, 1969 included a "sermonette" by comedian David Steinberg which CBS's program-practices department wanted deleted. Steinberg had created a public furor the previous October when he delivered a monologue on the show about "the exciting personality of Moses . . . who had a wonderful rapport with God." CBS was overwhelmed with mail condemning the telecast. The Smothers agreed to delete the four-minute Steinberg piece, but, according to CBS officials, they did not deliver the revised tape at the agreed time on Thursday, April 2, 1969.

The following day, amid much controversy and debate, CBS announced that "The Smothers Brothers Comedy Hour" had been cancelled for the fall 1969 season. Robert D. Wood, CBS-TV network president, in announcing the show's cancellation, said that the brothers had failed consistently to deliver tapes of the program to the network in time for review by network executives and station affiliates. The Smothers brothers, on the other hand, asserted that the cancellation was merely the culmination of a continuing campaign of harassment. The outcome was, of course, inevitable. Network program offerings are not independent entities, rather they are integral parts of the corporate enterprise, and as such they must adhere to corporate expectations. In television's oligarchic structure there's little latitude for dissension or deviation from network policy. From the network viewpoint, it should be pointed out that it was CBS and its stations which assumed ultimate responsibility for what was aired and not the Smothers brothers.

National Association of Broadcasters

In addition to adhering to their own program requirements, all three television networks subscribe to the program and advertising standards of the National Association of Broadcasters (NAB), the broadcast industry's trade association and one of the most influential and effective groups in the capital. The NAB was organized in 1923 to thwart ASCAP's efforts to collect royalties for the use of copyrighted music by broadcast stations. The NAB's initial attempts to regulate radio content were aimed at eliminating such practices as direct advertising and the use of phonograph records without identifying them as such. In 1927, the NAB offered its first "Code of Ethics," a brief, simply worded document which outlined rather general admonitions to the broadcast industry.

In the 1929 Code, the NAB extended and revised its "Code of Ethics" to include prohibitions against the broadcasting of offensive material, the use of radio by dishonest or fraudulent persons or firms, the advertising of products which would be injurious to health, and the use of exaggerated or deceptive advertising claims. In addition, a "Standards of Commercial Practice" was added which, among other things, proscribed commercial announcements between 7:00 and 11:00 p.m. Since this was a time for recreation and relaxation, the NAB reasoned, any commercial programs should be of the "good-will type." In 1933, the NAB Code was incorporated under the National Industrial Recovery Act (NIRA). Within two years, the NIRA was declared unconstitutional by the U.S. Supreme Court and the broadcasting industry temporarily was without a code of self-regulation. A revised 10-point Code of Ethics was adopted in 1935. In 1937, the NAB was reorganized to deal with various business-wide problems such as unions and music licensing. Two years later, the Code was revised again to include recommendations about the length of commercials, children's programs, controversial issues, education, news, and religion. Commercial time was limited to 10 per cent of the program in the evening hours and the advertising of hard liquor was prohibited. The Code also ruled out the sale of time for controversial issues. The latter provision was changed in 1945 when the FCC ruled on the basis of a complaint filed by the United Automobile Workers against WHKC, Columbus, Ohio, that stations could not refuse to sell time for the presentation of controversial issues. The Radio Code has undergone several revisions over the years.

The NAB adopted a "Television Code of Good Practices" and set up a code compliance agency in 1952. The TV Code was based principally on the Radio Code, but contained elements of the existing Motion Picture Code. A television "Seal of Good Practice" was inaugurated as an enforcement device. Adherence to the Codes has only recently become a condition of NAB membership. Until April 1976, NAB members were not required to subscribe to the Codes. Many provisions in the Codes are incorporated as tactical maneuvers to avoid government regulation. For example, when toy advertising came under attack in the early 1960s the NAB instituted new guidelines including a central clearing system. When various consumer groups started attacking the growing use of "men in white" in television commercials, the TV Code banned such use in 1963. That same year, limitations were placed on advertising for arthritis and rheumatism aids. The recently instituted family viewing hour was established in response to criticism from members of the Congress.

Advertisements for "personal" products have caused the Code Authority particular problems. The NAB has reluctantly succumbed to industry pressure and rescinded its ban against advertisements for such products as Preparation H, a hemorrhoid remedy, and the various feminine deodorant sprays and hygiene products. Several TV stations around the country have begun carrying contraceptive ads, although the NAB still refuses to permit such advertising on television. The power of the NAB to punish a recalcitrant Code subscriber is limited to suspending or revoking his right to display the "Seal of Good Practice." Thus, responsibility in essence inheres in the network and stations.

In the past few years, television stations have come under increasing attack for excesses in sex and violence. In April 1975, the television board of the NAB adopted "family viewing" standards. Entertainment programming inappropriate for viewing by a general family audience may not be broadcast during the first hour of network entertainment programming in primetime, nor should such programming be presented by stations in the immediately preceding hour. Warnings or advisories are required when programs contain "material that might be disturbing to significant segments of the audience." The television board waived the family viewing time restrictions for programs under contract to a station as of April 8, 1975, the day the Code amendment was adopted. The waiver will extend to September 1, 1977. The family viewing standards are included in the NAB's Television Code at the end of the section headed "Principles Governing Program Content." This has resulted in considerable dislocation of many of the most popular network programs.

The NAB's Television Code is concerned with three distinct subject areas: The content of programs, the content of commercials and the amount of time permitted for advertising. Here in full is the eighteenth edition of the NAB's Television Code.

THE TELEVISION CODE

PREAMBLE

Television is seen and heard in nearly every American home. These homes include children and adults of all ages, embrace all races and all varieties of philosophic or religious conviction and reach those of every educational background. Television broadcasters must take this pluralistic audience into account in programming their stations. They are obligated to bring their positive responsibility for professionalism and reasoned judgment to bear upon all those involved in the development, production and selection of programs.

The free, competitive American system of broadcasting which offers programs of entertainment, news, general information, education and culture is supported and made possible by revenues from advertising. While television broadcasters are responsible for the programming and advertising on their stations, the advertisers who use television to convey their commercial messages also have a responsibility to the viewing audience. Their advertising messages should be presented in an honest, responsible and tasteful manner. Advertisers should also support the endeavors of broadcasters to offer a diversity of programs that meet the needs and expectations of the total viewing audience.

The viewer also has a responsibility to help broadcasters serve the public. All viewers should make their criticisms and positive suggestions about programming and advertising known to the broadcast licensee. Parents particularly should oversee the viewing habits of their children, encouraging them to watch programs that will enrich their experience and broaden their intellectual horizons.

PROGRAM STANDARDS

I. Principles governing program content

It is in the interest of television as a vital medium to encourage programs that are innovative, reflect a high degree of creative skill, deal with significant moral and social issues and present challenging concepts and other subject matter that relate to the world in which the viewer lives.

Television programs should not only reflect the influence of the established institutions that shape our values and culture, but also expose the dynamics of social change which bear upon our lives.

To achieve these goals, television broadcasters should be conversant with the general and specific needs, interests and aspirations of all the segments of the communities they serve. They should affirmatively seek out responsible representatives of all parts of their communities so that they may structure a broad range of programs that will inform, enlighten, and entertain the total audience.

Broadcasters should also develop programs directed toward advancing the cultural and educational aspects of their communities.

To assure that broadcasters have the freedom to program fully and responsibly, none of the provisions of this Code should be construed as preventing or impeding broadcast of the broad range of material necessary to help broadcasters fulfill their obligations to operate in the public interest.

The challenge to the broadcaster is to determine how suitably to present the complexities of human behavior. For television, this requires exceptional awareness of considerations peculiar to the medium.

Accordingly, in selecting program subjects and themes, great care must be exercised to be sure that treatment and presentation are made in good faith and not for the purpose of sensationalism or to shock or exploit the audience or appeal to prurient interests or morbid curiosity.

Additionally, entertainment programming inappropriate for viewing by a general family audience should not be broadcast during the first hour of network entertainment programming in prime time and in the immediately preceding hour. In the occasional case when an entertainment program in this time period is deemed to be inappropriate for such an audience, advisories should be used to alert viewers. Advisories should also be used when programs in later prime time periods contain material that might be disturbing to significant segments of the audience.*

These advisories should be presented in audio and video form at the beginning of the program and when deemed appropriate at a later point in the program. Advisories should also be used responsibly in

* Effective September 1975.

promotional material in advance of the program. When using an advisory, the broadcaster should attempt to notify publishers of television program listings.*

Special care should be taken with respect to the content and treatment of audience advisories so that they do not disserve their intended purpose by containing material that is promotional, sensational or exploitative. Promotional announcements for programs that include advisories should be scheduled on a basis consistent with the purpose of the advisory.* (*See Television Code Interpretation No. 5*)

II. Responsibility toward children

Broadcasters have a special responsibility to children. Programs designed primarily for children should take into account the range of interests and needs of children from instructional and cultural material to a wide variety of entertainment material. In their totality, programs should contribute to the sound, balanced development of children to help them achieve a sense of the world at large and informed adjustments to their society.

In the course of a child's development, numerous social factors and forces, including television, affect the ability of the child to make the transition to adult society.

The child's training and experience during the formative years should include positive sets of values which will allow the child to become a responsible adult, capable of coping with the challenges of maturity.

Children should also be exposed, at the appropriate times, to a reasonable range of the realities which exist in the world sufficient to help them make the transition to adulthood.

Because children are allowed to watch programs designed primarily for adults, broadcasters should take this practice into account in the presentation of material in such programs when children may constitute a substantial segment of the audience.

All the standards set forth in this section apply to both program and commercial material designed and intended for viewing by children.

III. Community responsibility

1. Television broadcasters and their staffs occupy positions of unique responsibility in their communities and should conscientiously endeavor to be acquainted fully with the community's needs and characteristics in order better to serve the welfare of its citizens.
2. Requests for time for the placement of public service announcements or programs should be carefully reviewed with respect to the

character and reputation of the group, campaign or organization involved, the public interest content of the message, and the manner
of its presentation.

IV. Special program standards

1. Violence, physical or psychological, may only be projected in
   responsibly handled contexts, not used exploitatively. Programs involving violence should present the consequences of it to its victims and perpetrators.

   Presentation of the details of violence should avoid the excessive, the gratuitous and the instructional.

   The use of violence for its own sake and the detailed dwelling
   upon brutality or physical agony, by sight or by sound, are not permissible.

   The depiction of conflict, when presented in programs designed primarily for children, should be handled with sensitivity.

2. The treatment of criminal activities should always convey their
   social and human effects.

   The presentation of techniques of crime in such detail as to be
   instructional or invite imitation shall be avoided.

3. Narcotic addiction shall not be presented except as a destructive
   habit. The use of illegal drugs or the abuse of legal drugs shall not
   be encouraged or shown as socially acceptable.

4. The use of gambling devices or scenes necessary to the development of plot or as appropriate background is acceptable only when
   presented with discretion and in moderation, and in a manner
   which would not excite interest in, or foster, betting nor be instructional in nature.

5. Telecasts of actual sports programs at which on-the-scene betting is
   permitted by law shall be presented in a manner in keeping with
   federal, state and local laws, and should concentrate on the subject
   as a public sporting event.

6. Special precautions must be taken to avoid demeaning or ridiculing
   members of the audience who suffer from physical or mental afflic-
   tions or deformities.

7. Special sensitivity is necessary in the use of material relating to
   sex, race, color, age, creed, religious functionaries or rites, or national or ethnic derivation.

8. Obscene, indecent or profane matter, as proscribed by law, is unacceptable.

9. The presentation of marriage, the family and similarly important
   human relationships, and material with sexual connotations, shall

not be treated exploitatively or irresponsibly, but with sensitivity. Costuming and movements of all performers shall be handled in a similar fashion.

10. The use of liquor and the depiction of smoking in program content shall be de-emphasized. When shown, they should be consistent with plot and character development.

11. The creation of a state of hypnosis by act or detailed demonstration on camera is prohibited, and hypnosis as a form of "parlor game" antics to create humorous situations within a comedy setting is forbidden.

12. Program material pertaining to fortune-telling, occultism, astrology, phrenology, palm-reading, numerology, mind-reading, character-reading, and the like is unacceptable if it encourages people to regard such fields as providing commonly accepted appraisals of life.

13. Professional advice, diagnosis and treatment will be presented in conformity with law and recognized professional standards.

14. Any technique whereby an attempt is made to convey information to the viewer by transmiting messages below the threshold of normal awareness is not permitted.

15. The use of animals, consistent with plot and character delineation, shall be in conformity with accepted standards of humane treatment.

16. Quiz and similar programs that are presented as contests of knowledge, information, skill or luck must, in fact, be genuine contests; and the results must not be controlled by collusion with or between contestants, or by any other action which will favor one contestant against any other.

17. The broadcaster shall be constantly alert to prevent inclusion of elements within a program dictated by factors other than the requirements of the program itself. The acceptance of cash payments or other considerations in return for including scenic properties, the choice and identification of prizes, the selection of music and other creative program elements and inclusion of any identification of commercial products or services, their trade names or advertising slogan within the program are prohibited except in accordance with Sections 317 and 508 of the Communications Act.

18. Contests may not constitute a lottery.

19. No program shall be presented in a manner which through artifice or simulation would mislead the audience as to any material fact. Each broadcaster must exercise reasonable judgment to determine

whether a particular method of presentation would constitute a material deception, or would be accepted by the audience as normal theatrical illusion.

20. A television broadcaster should not present fictional events or other non-news material as authentic news telecasts or announcements, nor should he permit dramatizations in any program which would give the false impression that the dramatized material constitutes news.

21. The standards of this Code covering program content are also understood to include, wherever applicable, the standards contained in the advertising section of the Code.

V. Treatment of news and public events

General

Television Code standards relating to the treatment of news and public events are, because of constitutional considerations, intended to be exhortatory. The standards set forth hereunder encourage high standards of professionalism in broadcast journalism. They are not to be interpreted as turning over to others the broadcaster's responsibility as to judgments necessary in news and public events programming.

News

1. A television station's news schedule should be adequate and well-balanced.

2. News reporting should be factual, fair and without bias.

3. A television broadcaster should exercise particular discrimination in the acceptance, placement and presentation of advertising in news programs so that such advertising should be clearly distinguishable from the news content.

4. At all times, pictorial and verbal material for both news and comment should conform to other sections of these standards, wherever such sections are reasonably applicable.

5. Good taste should prevail in the selection and handling of news:

    Morbid, sensational or alarming details not essential to the factual report, especially in connection with stories of crime or sex, should be avoided. News should be telecast in such a manner as to avoid panic and unnecessary alarm.

6. Commentary and analysis should be clearly identified as such.

7. Pictorial material should be chosen with care and not presented in a misleading manner.

8. All news interview programs should be governed by accepted standards of ethical journalism, under which the interviewer selects the questions to be asked. Where there is advance agreement materially

restricting an important or newsworthy area of questioning, the interviewer will state on the program that such limitation has been agreed upon. Such disclosure should be made if the person being interviewed requires that questions be submitted in advance or if he participates in editing a recording of the interview prior to its use on the air.

9. A television broadcaster should exercise due care in his supervision of content, format, and presentation of newscasts originated by his station, and in his selection of newscasters, commentators, and analysts.

Public Events

1. A television broadcaster has an affirmative responsibility at all times to be informed of public events, and to provide coverage consonant with the ends of an informed and enlightened citizenry.
2. The treatment of such events by a television broadcaster should provide adequate and informed coverage.

VI. Controversial public issues

1. Television provides a valuable forum for the expression of responsible views on public issues of a controversial nature. The television broadcaster should seek out and develop with accountable individuals, groups and organizations, programs relating to controversial public issues of import to his fellow citizens; and to give fair representation to opposing sides of issues which materially affect the life or welfare of a substantial segment of the public.

2. Requests by individuals, groups or organizations for time to discuss their views on controversial public issues should be considered on the basis of their individual merits, and in the light of the contribution which the use requested would make to the public interest, and to a well-balanced program structure.

3. Programs devoted to the discussion of controversial public issues should be identified as such. They should not be presented in a manner which would mislead listeners or viewers to believe that the program is purely of an entertainment, news, or other character.

4. Broadcasts in which stations express their own opinions about issues of general public interest should be clearly identified as editorials. They should be unmistakably identified as statements of station opinion and should be appropriately distinguished from news and other program material.

VII. Political telecasts

1. Political telecasts should be clearly identified as such. They should

not be presented by a television broadcaster in a manner which would mislead listeners or viewers to believe that the program is of any other character.

(Ref.: Communications Act of 1934, as amended, Secs. 315 and 317, and FCC Rules and Regulations, Secs. 3.654, 3.657, 3.663, as discussed in NAB's "Political Broadcast Catechism & The Fairness Doctrine.")

VIII. Religious programs

1. It is the responsibility of a television broadcaster to make available to the community appropriate opportunity for religious presentations.

2. Programs reach audiences of all creeds simultaneously. Therefore, both the advocates of broad or ecumenical religious precepts, and the exponents of specific doctrines, are urged to present their positions in a manner conducive to viewer enlightenment on the role of religion in society.

3. In the allocation of time for telecasts of religious programs the television station should use its best efforts to apportion such time fairly among responsible individuals, groups and organizations.

ADVERTISING STANDARDS

IX. General advertising standards

1. This Code establishes basic standards for all television broadcasting. The principles of acceptability and good taste within the Program Standards section govern the presentation of advertising where applicable. In addition, the Code establishes in this section special standards which apply to television advertising.

2. A commercial television broadcaster makes his facilities available for the advertising of products and services and accepts commercial presentations for such advertising. However, a television broadcaster should, in recognition of his responsibility to the public, refuse the facilities of his station to an advertiser where he has good reason to doubt the integrity of the advertiser, the truth of the advertising representations, or the compliance of the advertiser with the spirit and purpose of all applicable legal requirements.

3. Identification of sponsorship must be made in all sponsored programs in accordance with the requirements of the Communications Act of 1934, as amended, and the Rules and Regulations of the Federal Communications Commission.

4. Representations which disregard normal safety precautions shall be avoided.

    Children shall not be represented, except under proper adult supervision, as being in contact with or demonstrating a product recognized as potentially dangerous to them.

5. In consideration of the customs and attitudes of the communities served, each television broadcaster should refuse his facilities to the advertisement of products and services, or the use of advertising scripts, which the station has good reason to believe would be objectionable to a substantial and responsible segment of the community. These standards should be applied with judgment and flexibility, taking into consideration the characteristics of the medium, its home and family audience, and the form and content of the particular presentation.

6. The advertising of hard liquor (distilled spirits) is not acceptable.

7. The advertising of beer and wines is acceptable only when presented in the best of good taste and discretion, and is acceptable only subject to Federal and local laws (*See Television Code Interpretation No. 4*)

8. Advertising by institutions or enterprises which in their offers of instruction imply promises of employment or make exaggerated claims for the opportunities awaiting those who enroll for courses is generally unacceptable.

9. The advertising of firearms/ammunition is acceptable provided it promotes the product only as sporting equipment and conforms to recognized standards of safety as well as all applicable laws and regulations. Advertisements of firearms/ammunition by mail order are unacceptable. The advertising of fireworks is acceptable subject to all applicable laws.

10. The advertising of fortune-telling, occultism, astrology, phrenology, palm-reading, numerology, mind-reading, character-reading or subjects of a like nature is not permitted.

11. Because all products of a personal nature create special problems, acceptability of such products should be determined with especial emphasis on ethics and the canons of good taste. Such advertising of personal products as is accepted must be presented in a restrained and obviously inoffensive manner.

12. The advertising of tip sheets and other publications seeking to advertise for the purpose of giving odds or promoting betting is unacceptable.

    The lawful advertising of government organizations which

conduct legalized lotteries is acceptable provided such advertising does not unduly exhort the public to bet.

The advertising of private or governmental organizations which conduct legalized betting on sporting contests is acceptable provided such advertising is limited to institutional type announcements which do not exhort the public to bet.

13. An advertiser who markets more than one product should not be permitted to use advertising copy devoted to an acceptable product for purposes of publicizing the brand name or other identification of a product which is not acceptable.

14. "Bait-switch" advertising, whereby goods or services which the advertiser has no intention of selling are offered merely to lure the customer into purchasing higher-priced substitutes, is not acceptable.

15. Personal endorsements (testimonials) shall be genuine and reflect personal experience. They shall contain no statement that cannot be supported if presented in the advertiser's own words.

X. Presentation of advertising

1. Advertising messages should be presented with courtesy and good taste; disturbing or annoying material should be avoided; every effort should be made to keep the advertising message in harmony with the content and general tone of the program in which it appears.

2. The role and capability of television to market sponsors' products are well recognized. In turn, this fact dictates that great care be exercised by the broadcaster to prevent the presentation of false, misleading or deceptive advertising. While it is entirely appropriate to present a product in a favorable light and atmosphere, the presentation must not, by copy or demonstration, involve a material deception as to the characteristics, performance or appearance of the product.

   Broadcast advertisers are responsible for making available, at the request of the Code Authority, documentation adequate to support the validity and truthfulness of claims, demonstrations and testimonials contained in their commercial messages.

3. The broadcaster and the advertiser should exercise special caution with the content and presentation of television commercials placed in or near programs designed for children. Exploitation of children should be avoided. Commercials directed to children should in no way mislead as to the product's performance and usefulness.

   Commercials, whether live, film or tape, within programs initially designed primarily for children under 12 years of age shall be clearly separated from program material by an appropriate device.

Trade name identification or other merchandising practices involving the gratuitous naming of products is discouraged in programs designed primarily for children.

Appeals involving matters of health which should be determined by physicians should not be directed primarily to children.

4. No children's program personality or cartoon character shall be utilized to deliver commercial messages within or adjacent to the programs in which such a personality or cartoon character regularly appears. This provision shall also apply to lead-ins to commercials when such lead-ins contain sell copy or imply endorsement of the product by program personalities or cartoon characters. (Effective September 1975.)

5. Appeals to help fictitious characters in television programs by purchasing the advertiser's product or service or sending for a premium should not be permitted, and such fictitious characters should not be introduced into the advertising message for such purposes.

6. Commercials for services or over-the-counter products involving health considerations are of intimate and far-reaching importance to the consumer. The following principles should apply to such advertising:

   a. Physicians, dentists or nurses or actors representing physicians, dentists or nurses, shall not be employed directly or by implication. These restrictions also apply to persons professionally engaged in medical services (e.g., physical therapists, pharmacists, dental assistants, nurses' aides).

   b. Visual representations of laboratory settings may be employed, provided they bear a direct relationship to bona fide research which has been conducted for the product or service. (*See Television Code, X, 11*) In such cases, laboratory technicians shall be identified as such and shall not be employed as spokesmen or in any other way speak on behalf of the product.

   c. Institutional announcements not intended to sell a specific product or service to the consumer and public service announcements by non-profit organizations may be presented by accredited physicians, dentists or nurses, subject to approval by the broadcaster. An accredited professional is one who has met required qualifications and has been licensed in his resident state.

7. Advertising should offer a product or service on its positive merits

and refrain from discrediting, disparaging or unfairly attacking competitors, competing products, other industries, professions or institutions.

8. A sponsor's advertising messages should be confined within the framework of the sponsor's program structure. A television broadcaster should avoid the use of commercial announcements which are divorced from the program either by preceding the introduction of the program (as in the case of so-called "cow-catcher" announcements) or by following the apparent sign-off of the program (as in the case of so-called trailer or "hitch-hike" announcements). To this end, the program itself should be announced and clearly identified, both audio and video, before the sponsor's advertising material is first used, and should be signed off, both audio and video, after the sponsor's advertising material is last used.

9. Since advertising by television is a dynamic technique, a television broadcaster should keep under surveillance new advertising devices so that the spirit and purpose of these standards are fulfilled.

10. A charge for television time to churches and religious bodies is not recommended.

11. Reference to the results of bona fide research, surveys or tests relating to the product to be advertised shall not be presented in a manner so as to create an impression of fact beyond that established by the work that has been conducted.

XI. Advertising of medical products

1. The advertising of medical products presents considerations of intimate and far-reaching importance to the consumer because of the direct bearing on his health.

2. Because of the personal nature of the advertising of medical products, claims that a product will effect a cure and the indiscriminate use of such words as "safe," "without risk," "harmless," or terms of similar meaning should not be accepted in the advertising of medical products on television stations.

3. A television broadcaster should not accept advertising material which in his opinion offensively describes or dramatizes distress or morbid situations involving ailments, by spoken word, sound or visual effects.

XII. Contests

1. Contests shall be conducted with fairness to all entrants, and shall comply with all pertinent laws and regulations. Care should be taken to avoid the concurrent use of the three elements which together constitute a lottery—prize, chance and consideration.

2. All contest details, including rules, eligibility requirements, opening and termination dates should be clearly and completely announced and/or shown, or easily accessible to the viewing public, and the winners' names should be released and prizes awarded as soon as possible after the close of the contest.

3. When advertising is accepted which requests contestants to submit items of product identification or other evidence of purchase of products, reasonable facsimiles thereof should be made acceptable unless the award is based upon skill and not upon chance.

4. All copy pertaining to any contest (except that which is required by law) associated with the exploitation or sale of the sponsor's product or service, and all references to prizes or gifts offered in such connection should be considered a part of and included in the total time allowances as herein provided. (*See Television Code, XIV*)

XIII. Premiums and offers

1. Full details of proposed offers should be required by the television broadcaster for investigation and approved before the first announcement of the offer is made to the public.

2. A final date for the termination of an offer should be announced as far in advance as possible.

3. Before accepting for telecast offers involving a monetary consideration, a television broadcaster should satisfy himself as to the integrity of the advertiser and the advertiser's willingness to honor complaints indicating dissatisfaction with the premium by returning the monetary consideration.

4. There should be no misleading descriptions or visual representations of any premiums or gifts which would distort or enlarge their value in the minds of the viewers.

5. Assurances should be obtained from the advertiser that premiums offered are not harmful to person or property.

6. Premiums should not be approved which appeal to superstition on the basis of "luck-bearing" powers or otherwise.

XIV. Time standards for non-program material *

In order that the time for non-program material and its placement shall best serve the viewer, the following standards are set forth in accordance with sound television practice:

1. Non-Program Material Definition:

Non-program material, in both prime time and all other time, includes billboards, commercials, promotional announcements and

* See Time Standards for Independent Stations, p. 196.

all credits in excess of 30 seconds per program, except in feature films. In no event should credits exceed 40 seconds per program. The 40-second limitation on credits shall not apply, however, in any situation governed by a contract entered into before October 1, 1971. Public service announcements and promotional announcements for the same program are excluded from this definition.

2. Allowable Time for Non-Program Material:

a. In prime time on network affiliated stations, non-program material shall not exceed nine minutes 30 seconds in any 60-minute period.

In the event that news programming is included within the three and one-half hour prime time period, not more than one 30-minute segment of news programming may be governed by time standards applicable to all other time.

Prime time is a continuous period of not less than three and one-half consecutive hours per broadcast day as designated by the station between the hours of 6:00 PM and Midnight.

b. In all other time, non-program material shall not exceed 16 minutes in any 60-minute period.

c. Children's Programming Time—Defined as those hours other than prime time in which programs initially designed primarily for children under 12 years of age are scheduled.

Within this time period on Saturday and Sunday, non-program material shall not exceed 10 minutes in any 60-minute period after December 31, 1974 and nine minutes 30 seconds in any 60-minute period after December 31, 1975.

Within this time period on Monday through Friday, non-program material shall not exceed 14 minutes in any 60-minute period after December 31, 1974 and 12 minutes in any 60-minute period after December 31, 1975.

3. Program Interruptions:

a. Definition: A program interruption is any occurrence of non-program material within the main body of the program.

b. In prime time, the number of program interruptions shall not exceed two within any 30-minute program, or four within any 60-minute program.

Programs longer than 60 minutes shall be prorated at two interruptions per half-hour.

The number of interruptions in 60-minute variety shows shall not exceed five.

c. In all other time, the number of interruptions shall not exceed four within any 30-minute program period.

d. In children's weekend programming time, as above defined in 2c, the number of program interruptions shall not exceed two within any 30-minute program or four within any 60-minute program.

e. In both prime time and all other time, the following interruption standard shall apply within programs of 15 minutes or less in length:

  5-minute program—1 interruption;

  10-minute program—2 interruptions;

  15-minute program—2 interruptions.

f. News, weather, sports and special events programs are exempt from the interruption standard because of the nature of such programs.

4. No more than four non-program material announcements shall be scheduled consecutively within programs, and no more than three non-program material announcements shall be scheduled consecutively during station breaks. The consecutive non-program material limitation shall not apply to a single sponsor who wishes to further reduce the number of interruptions in the program.

5. A multiple product announcement is one in which two or more products or services are presented within the framework of a single announcement. A multiple product announcement shall not be scheduled in a unit of time less than 60 seconds, except where integrated so as to appear to the viewer as a single message. A multiple product announcement shall be considered integrated and counted as a single announcement if:

a. the products or services are related and interwoven within the framework of the announcement (related products or services shall be defined as those having a common character, purpose and use); and

b. the voice(s), setting, background and continuity are used consistently throughout so as to appear to the viewer as a single message.

   Multiple product announcements of 60 seconds in length or longer not meeting this definition of integration shall be counted as two or more announcements under this section of the Code. This provision shall not apply to retail or service establishments.

6. The use of billboards, in prime time and all other time, shall be confined to programs sponsored by a single or alternate week advertiser and shall be limited to the products advertised in the program.

7. Reasonable and limited identification of prizes and donors' names where the presentation of contest awards or prizes is a necessary part of program content shall not be included as non-program material as defined above.

8. Programs presenting women's service features, shopping guides, fashion shows, demonstrations and similar material provide a special service to the public in which certain material normally classified as non-program is an informative and necessary part of the program content. Because of this, the time standards may be waived by the Code Authority to a reasonable extent on a case-by-case basis.

9. Gratuitous references in a program to a non-sponsor's product or service should be avoided except for normal guest identification.

10. Stationary backdrops or properties in television presentations showing the sponsor's name or product, the name of his product, his trade-mark or slogan should be used only incidentally and should not obtrude on program interest or entertainment.

Time Standards for Independent Stations

1. Non-program elements shall be considered as all-inclusive, with the exception of required credits, legally required station identifications, and "bumpers." Promotion spots and public service announcements, as well as commercials, are to be considered non-program elements.

2. The allowed time for non-program elements, as defined above, shall not exceed seven minutes in a 30-minute period or multiples thereof in prime time (prime time is defined as any three contiguous hours between 6:00 PM and midnight, local time), or eight minutes in a 30-minute period or multiples thereof during all other times.

3. Where a station does not carry a commercial in a station break between programs, the number of program interruptions shall not exceed four within any 30-minute program, or seven within any 60-minute program, or 10 within any 90-minute program, or 13 in any 120-minute program. Stations which do carry commercials in station breaks between programs shall limit the number of program interruptions to three within any 30-minute program, or six within any 60-minute program, or nine within any 90-minute program, or 12 in any 120-minute program. News, weather, sports, and special events are exempted because of format.

4. Not more than four non-program material announcements as defined above shall be scheduled consecutively. An exception may be made only in the case of a program 60 minutes or more in length, when no more than seven

non-program elements may be scheduled consecutively by stations who wish to reduce the number of program interruptions.

5. The conditions of paragraphs three and four shall not apply to live sports programs where the program format dictates and limits the number of program interruptions.

Advertising Guidelines

The NAB's Radio Code, although a shorter document, is similar in content to the Code governing television. In addition to the Codes, the NAB's Code Authority issues advertising guidelines and clarifications expanding on provisions of the Code. Among areas that have been covered are acne products, alcoholic beverages, arthritis and rheumatism remedies, bronchitis, comparative advertising, children's premiums and offers, children's TV advertising, disparagement, hallucinogens, hypnosis, lotteries, men-in-white, non-prescription medications, personal products, testimonials, time standards, toys, vegetable oils and margarines, and weight reducing products and services. For example, paragraph 7, section IX of the Code's General Advertising Standards, states that the "advertising of beer and wine is acceptable only when presented in the best of good taste and discretion." The Code Authority has determined that this provision requires that commercials involving beer and wine avoid any representation of on-camera drinking.

Not all broadcast stations subscribe to the NAB's Code of self-regulation, and even subscribers sometimes violate its tenents. The primary, if unspoken, function of the NAB's Code is to keep official regulation at bay. In the opinion of many critics, the NAB has consistently manifested a dedication to the maintenance of the status-quo. A large part of the organization's activities involve the coordination of industry pressures against government or public threats to broadcasting's prevailing power structure. In over a half-century of operation, the NAB has proven itself to be an effective standardbearer for the broadcast industry. But its purpose and function is no different from that of any trade and professional association—which is to protect and to enhance the "image" of the industry it represents.

11

Noncommercial Television

AS THE READER WILL RECALL, the Federal Communications Commission instituted a "freeze" in September 1948 on new television channel allocations, so that the Commission could study the whole question of allocating spectrum space. During the almost four-year hiatus that followed, a movement toward the establishment of educational television stations gained momentum. An ad hoc Joint Committee (later changed to "Council") on Educational Television (JCET) was formed in October 1950, sponsored by the American Council on Education, the Association of Education by Radio-TV, the National Association of Educational Broadcasters, and others. Supplementary briefs in support of reserving a number of television channels for the exclusive use of education were offered in a series of hearings before the Federal Communications Commission. Numerous interested parties, in American political and educational circles, urged the FCC to set aside channels which would be operated exclusively as both nonprofit and noncommercial undertakings. The JCET assisted over 800 schools and colleges in the preparation of statements submitted to the FCC, indicating how they would inaugurate educational programming if channels were reserved. Educators were strongly supported by Commissioner Frieda B. Hennock, who had been appointed to the FCC in 1948 by President Truman. Prior to her appointment to the Commission, Ms. Hennock had worked in criminal law and as a corporation lawyer. At the age of 23, she received a fee of $55,000 in a single case involving a company merger. She was the first woman to serve as a commissioner on the FCC. Commissioner Hennock's vigorous, animated advocacy in favor of reserving television channels for educational use attracted nation-wide attention.

Sixth Report and Order

The FCC's hearings on the television channel allocations continued intermittently until the latter part of 1951. The Commission's April 1952 "Sixth Report and Order" provided for the establishment of 242 noncommercial television stations—80 channels in the VHF band, and 162 channels in the UHF band. (By 1966 these allocations had been increased to 116 VHF and 516 UHF channels). Noncommercial television licenses were to be issued only to bona fide, nonprofit educational organizations and to be used "primarily to serve the educational needs of the community." They were to transmit cultural, instructional, and entertainment programs on a purely noncommercial, nonprofit basis. The first television station to go on the air exclusively for educational broadcasting was KUHT in Houston, Texas, on May 12, 1953. Others followed, but even a decade later relatively few educational stations, out of the total number of channels reserved, had actually been activated. Noncommercial licenses were issued to local and state educational systems, colleges and universities, and to community organizations.

There were no provisions in the Sixth Report and Order for the funding of noncommercial television. On December 5, 1952, the Fund for Adult Education of the Ford Foundation announced the formation of an Educational Television and Radio Center (ETRC), funded with over a million dollars to aid in the development and exchange of quality films and kinescopes to be broadcast by educational television stations. The Center established headquarters in Ann Arbor, Michigan and in May of 1954, inaugurated a modest weekly program service to the four noncommercial stations then on the air. Only continued support from the Ford Foundation prevented the whole system from collapsing. There were nine stations on the air in 1954 and double that amount in 1956. The number of stations climbed to 27 the following year. In 1959, the ETRC moved its headquarters to New York City, maintaining its technical and distribution facilities in Ann Arbor. Its name changed to National Educational Television and Radio Center (NETRC) and later simply to National Educational Television (NET).

Programs were distributed to each member station individually, since the cost of AT&T interconnection was prohibitive.

Despite the efforts of the Ford Foundation, noncommercial television was virtually invisible to most Americans during the 1950s. In many large cities such as New York, Washington, D.C., and Los Angeles, all the VHF stations were licensed to commercial broadcasters. Most TV sets manufactured prior to 1964 required a converter in order to receive the UHF band, and the quality of reception was poor.

Educational Television Comes to the City

During the early 1960s noncommercial television began to receive increased support. In February 1961, National Telefilm Associates, licensee of WNTA-TV operating on Channel 13 in Newark, New Jersey, announced that the station was up for sale. A committee of prominent citizens organized under the name of Educational Television for the Metropolitan Area (ETMA) bid $4 million to acquire the license and facilities of WNTA-TV. Various commercial groups also bid on the station. One group, headed by Ely Landau, submitted a bid of $7 million. David Susskind, with the support of Paramount Pictures, offered $6 million. The educational group increased its bid to $5.5 million. Frances Langford and her husband, Ralph Evinrude, the head of Outboard Marine Inc., expressed interest in the station.

The Federal Communications Commission, exercising its prerogative under Section 403 of the Communications Act, issued a "Notice of Inquiry" and scheduled hearings to determine the desirability of securing noncommercial television outlets in New York and Los Angeles. Newton Minow, then FCC chairman, strongly favored sale to the educational group. The prospect of lengthy hearings caused Susskind and Landau to withdraw their bids. The New York City commercial stations, in an obvious effort to eliminate a potential competitor, each contributed to the educational group. The Department of Justice assured the stations that the contributions would not be construed as restraint of trade. National Telefilm Associates asked the FCC to approve transfer to the educational group. Governor Robert Meyner of New Jersey attempted to block the transfer because ETMA planned to center production in New York City, but his efforts were unsuccessful. Several concessions were made to the Governor, however, including pledges of service to New Jersey viewers and the addition of New Jersey representatives to Channel 13's board, including the Honorable Robert Meyner who is still on the board.

Congress passed the ETV Facilities Act of 1962, which sought to encourage the construction of noncommercial television stations by authorizing the Department of Health, Education and Welfare to provide $32 million over a five-year period on a matching basis. The following year, the Ford Foundation announced the first of its annual $6 million grants to finance the program service of NET. By 1963 there were 75 noncommercial television stations on the air. Congress also passed a law requiring that all television sets sold in interstate commerce after April 30, 1964 be equipped to receive UHF channels.

Carnegie Commission on Educational Television

In 1965, the Carnegie Corporation, at the urging of the National Association of Educational Broadcasters (NAEB), established a distinguished 15-member committee under the direction of Dr. James R. Killian Jr. of the Massachusetts Institute of Technology, to devise viable proposals which would "extend and strengthen educational television." The Commission grappled assiduously with the problems of semantics and nomenclature. A careful distinction was to be made between "public television" and "instructional television," even though this distinction was, essentially, psychological. Questions of what could be accomplished with, as well as without, a network were considered. Other problems were concerned with the need for audiences, and the goal of providing a service *not* provided by commercial television. Finally, there was the fundamental and crucial question of how public television could receive government financing and still remain free and independent of official control, censorship, and political pressures and interference.

In January 1967, the Carnegie Commission on Educational Television issued its report entitled "Public Television: A Program for Action." The Carnegie Report, written primarily by Stephen White, television critic for *Horizon,* was the result of eight major meetings and was based on information culled from more than 200 individual specialists and educational organizations. The Report made haste to distinguish between two kinds of noncommercial television services. *Instructional* television was to be designed for systematic instructional purpose in the classroom. *Public* television was to be specifically directed to the community at large. While it was stated that all television can be both instructional and entertaining, commercial television's objective is primarily to entertain large, heterogeneous audiences. Instructional television is based on theories of learning, and imposes a responsibility and an obligation on the viewer to participate. Public television, however, "includes all that is of human interest and importance" which is neither for instructional purposes nor supported by advertising. The Commission concluded that the existing educational service was not sufficiently well-financed to serve the variegated needs of the American public.

Public television, as envisaged by the Commission, was to be structured along a well-defined plan of procedure. Primarily, the Congress was urged to establish a federally chartered nongovernmental, nonprofit corporation to be called the Corporation for Public Television. Government and private sources would contribute necessary funds in order for the Corporation to become operative. The Corporation was specifically enjoined from "operations"—it was to distribute money and give leadership. Funding would be provided through some form of graduated tax revenues. The Commission recommended the passage by Congress of a manufacturers excise tax on receivers, beginning at 2 per cent and graduating to 5 per cent, thus providing increasing amounts from $40 million to a maximum of $100 million annually, plus support from private sources. In two final recommendations, the Carnegie Report urged legislation to permit the Department of Health, Education and Welfare to provide facilities for station operation, the Corporation for Public Broadcasting was to provide program service. The report further urged that federal, state and local agencies undertake studies to improve instructional uses of the television medium.

The Commission placed tremendous emphasis on the importance of the local station. The major strength of a public television service was thought to inhere in the local station which would be able to broadcast a full week, instead of going out of business over weekends, as was sometimes the case. It was basically to further local programming that the Commission urged the chartering of a Corporation for Public Television which would also make it possible to weld stations together into a nationally interconnected service. Still, the fear of federal control loomed large in the plan, and the Report insisted that the institution which disbursed funds be nongovernmental in character, free of political interference and totally devoid of control over local programming.

National production centers would outline an annual schedule which would secure the approval and support of the Corporation. The schedule would call for theatre and muscal production, children's programming, and documentaries on national and local problems. Structured into the plan would be 10 hours of national, and 20 hours of local programming each week, with the stations serving as a major source of program material. AT&T would provide station interconnection. Stations could use the national programs immediately or tape them for future broadcast. The "network" of stations would not be operated with a planned nationwide schedule of programs. The Commission considered the advisibility of a fourth network and rejected it as a solution. Congress was urged to take action which would give public television special preferred rates on interconnection facilities.

Public Broadcast Laboratory

The Ford Foundation apparently took issue with the Carnegie Commission's rejection of a centralized network service. Ford earmarked $10 million for the creation of a Public Broadcasting Laboratory to provide a two-hour live, regularly scheduled interconnected program titled "PBL" every Sunday evening, beginning in the fall of 1967, to most of the nation's 100-odd noncommercial stations. The prime mover in the development of PBL was Fred Friendly, former president of the CBS News Division and now Edward R. Murrow Professor of Broadcast Journalism at Columbia University's School of Journalism and advisor on Television Affairs to McGeorge Bundy, the president of the Ford Foundation. Friendly resigned from CBS on February 15, 1966, ostensibly to protest the network's refusal to pre-empt reruns of "I Love Lucy" and "The Real McCoys," in order to carry former Ambassador George Kennan's testimony on Vietnam before Senator Fulbright's Foreign Relations Committee. Friendly's disillusionment with CBS may have been attributable, in part, to a change in management which denied him direct access to chairman William S. Paley and then president Dr. Frank Stanton. Av Westin, then on leave from CBS News, was engaged as executive producer of PBL.

The topic for PBL's November 5, 1967 premiere broadcast was

"race relations." Part of the show consisted of a sometimes vitupera-
tive confrontation between blacks and whites, staged in a theatre-in-
the-round format. The program also included a play by Douglas
Turner Ward entitled "Day of Absence." The play concerns a southern town in which all of the black residents have suddenly disappeared. The town's people, unable to function, beg the black people to
return. What made the play especially controversial was that the white
townspeople were played by blacks in "whiteface." Some stations,
apparently informed in advance of the show's content, refused to carry
the program.

The new network got off to an inauspicious start. Friendly met
tremendous opposition from noncommercial station managers around
the country. Many stations seemed to feel that they were being relegated to the status of carriers. Other PBL programs included two
hours of the Polish National Theatre, with neither subtitles nor translation. Later programs were more professionally executed and sophisticated in content, but the experiment was doomed to failure. PBL, for
the most part, failed to deliver its overblown promises ("innovative,
experimental," etc.). Also, Friendly's alleged tactical errors earned
him the animosity of local station managers and he was never able to
consolidate the affiliates into a viable fourth network. PBL expired
after two seasons. It was an unmourned death.

Corporation for Public Broadcasting

On November 7, 1967, two days after PBL's debut, President
Johnson signed into law the Public Broadcasting Act. The Act, which
was an outgrowth of the Carnegie Commission proposal, established a
nonprofit, private organization, the Corporation for Public Broadcasting (CPB). The CPB would have a board of directors of 15 members
appointed by the President with the advice and consent of the Senate.
The Act also called for a three-year extension of the ETV Facilities
Act of 1962, authorizing $38 million and extending the grants to edu-
cational radio as well as television. In addition, the Act provided a
half million dollars for the Secretary of Health, Education and Welfare
to conduct a comprehensive study of instructional television and radio.
Since its inception, noncommercial television's most serious problem
had been funding. Congress rejected the Carnegie Commission's recommendation for an excise tax and allocated money on an annual

basis. A budget of $9 million was authorized for fiscal 1967–68. A million dollar contribution from CBS helped to sustain the CPB in its infancy.

The members of the CPB's board of directors were to be pillars of the cultural, intellectual and artistic communities. President Johnson's choice for CPB board chairman was Frank Pace Jr., a former Secretary of the Army and for many years the chief executive officer of General Dynamics, one of the largest defense contractors in the nation. Other appointees to the CPB board included John Macy, former special assistant to the Under Secretary of the Army, and Joseph D. Hughes, an aide to the Secretary of the Army from 1955–63. Female representation on the CPB board was provided by Oveta C. Hobby, director of the Women's Army Corps during World War II. The roster of names on CPB's board of directors read disturbingly like a who's who in the "military-industrial complex." The board's token concession to the arts was Erich Leinsdorf, former conductor of the Boston Symphony Orchestra.

Public Broadcast Service

Within its first year of operation the CPB embarked on its mandate to effect a workable system of station interconnection as prescribed by the Public Broadcasting Act of 1967, and as recommended by the Carnegie Commission. In May of 1969, 58 noncommercial stations were linked for two hours, five days a week. The CPB established the Public Broadcast Service (PBS) as a national distribution arm for noncommercial television programs. PBS's charter called for 11 board members, six of whom had to be managers of local stations. In addition, the governing board was to be comprised of the presidents of PBS, CPB, and NET (the latter two were ex-officio members) and two representatives from the general public. Later the number of station representatives was increased to give broader representation to the stations, and the two ex-officio members were removed. With money provided by CPB and the Ford Foundation, PBS arranged for the production of programs for national distribution. Prior to the creation of PBS, National Educational Television (NET) had been the primary source of programming material for educational television. Most NET programs were "bicycled"—that is, mailed from station to station. In the Summer of 1970, NET and Channel 13 in New York reluctantly merged. James Day, who came from KQED, San Francisco to become president of NET in 1969, recently noted that the merger resulted primarily from Ford Foundation pressure. Ford said it would no longer support two competing organizations in New York City. The Foundation's money had kept NET alive throughout most of its existence. At the present time, the Ford Foundation has announced plans to phase out its television support program.

With FCC encouragement, AT&T provided station interconnection for noncommercial stations at a reduced rate. By the end of 1972, 181 of the then 223 stations were interconnected. PBS gradually evolved into a fourth network, exercising authority over program selection, scheduling, promotion and distribution. In June 1972, President Nixon vetoed a two-year $155 million funding plan for public television on the grounds that PBS was acquiring too much centralized power and control over public television. Clay Whitehead, then director of the Office of Telecommunications Policy, called for a de-emphasis of national programming and a return to "grassroots localism." Conflict developed between CPB and PBS, and the two organizations attempted to delineate their respective functions and responsibilities. The "old" PBS was restructured and a "new" Public Broadcasting Service was established on March 30, 1973. Policy in the new organization rests with the station licensees, who elect a board of governors made up of *station board chairmen* instead of *station managers*. The board of managers remains, but is subservient to the board of chairmen. This change was precipitated by the crisis within the Nixon administration. It was realized that the "community leaders" represented by the local board chairmen would have more "clout" than the professionals represented by the managers.

On May 31, 1973, CPB and PBS approved an agreement to end their dispute over program decision making and overall control of public television. PBS won assurance that programs not funded by CPB would have access to station interconnection. Both parties reaffirmed the importance of public-affairs programs on public broadcasting and pledged to work jointly for long-range financing. A plan was devised by which local stations would be guaranteed a percentage of all future federal funds. Under the agreement, CPB would pay the Public Broadcast Service only for its operation of the interconnection of stations. Soon after the agreement was consummated, Congress approved, and the President signed, a two-year authorization bill which provided $55 million in support funds for CPB for fiscal 1974 and $65 million for fiscal 1975.

In July 1974, a "marketplace cooperative" plan went into effect whereby local stations bid on the national programs they wish to have produced and distributed. A catalogue of proposed programs is presented to the 252 noncommercial stations. A station indicates by negative or affirmative vote whether it is willing to pay for a portion of a particular program. If enough money is pledged to cover the production cost of a show or a series, then the project is incorporated into the PBS schedule. Only stations that contribute to the cost of a show are permitted to carry it. The Public Broadcast Service acts as a distribution service with little control over program content. PBS still exercises *some* control over programs—though, as a membership organization, that control is largely exercised through committees of station people. The public broadcasting system has never known unity and the member stations have frequently manifested seemingly irreconcilable differences as to the direction and priorities of public broadcasting. There has been particular friction between the major city' stations and those in smaller communities concerning the scope and mission of the noncommercial system. Also, there is no doubt that the CPB-PBS dispute, along with antagonism from some legislators and from the Nixon Administration, has hindered the development of a strong, economically viable and nationally interconnected system of public broadcasting.

The advent of a new year brought renewed hope to public broadcasting when early in January 1976, President Gerald Ford signed into law a bill which authorizes funding totalling a potential $634 million to the CPB over a five-year period. The new law provides for funding ceilings ranging from $88 million in the first year to $160 million by fiscal 1980.

Funding, of course, is not enough. Noncommercial stations will have to reconcile their differences and recognize that it is in their interest to have an effective national organization, perhaps, even one that functions as a "fourth network." Only then can the enormous potential of public broadcasting be fully realized.

12

Mass Communication
and the Supreme Court

THE CRUCIAL AND PERPLEXING problem of freedom, control and responsibility in the mass media looms ever larger in the context of a radically changing society. At the core of the matter is the concept of the fundamental role of mass communication in a democratic, pluralistic society, the delicate balance between freedom to communicate and responsibility for what is communicated.

Although the First Amendment to the U.S. Constitution states in unequivocal and unyielding terms that "Congress shall make *no* law . . . abridging the freedom of speech or of the press . . . ," the doctrine has never been interpreted to permit totally unbridled expression. The necessity for certain restraints on speech and press has always been assumed. The First Amendment to the Constitution was ratified by Congress in 1791. As early as 1798, Congress approved the Sedition Act which made it a crime to utter "any false, scandalous and malicious" statements against the government of the United States, the President or members of the Congress or "to incite against them the hatred of the good people of the United States." The law called for violators to be punished by a fine "not exceeding two thousand dollars, and by imprisonment not exceeding two years." At the time the Sedition law was enacted, war with France seemed imminent and rumors of French espionage and seditious activities were rampant. The law was used, however, in an attempt to suppress all criticism against those in power. Approximately 10 people were convicted under the Sedition Act, and they were all pardoned when Thomas Jefferson ascended to the Presidency in 1801.

The Sedition Act was not totally without merit, since it was the first national law which permitted truth as a defense and allowed the jury to determine the seditious character of the utterances. The impassioned plea of Andrew Hamilton made 63 years earlier in the *Zenger* case was finally recognized in law.

Freedom of expression always suffers its greatest abuses during times of national peril and emergency. In 1919, Justice Oliver Wendell Holmes, writing for a unanimous Court, enunciated the ''clear and present danger'' test, which would eventually become a guiding principle in determining the distinction between permissible and prohibited expression in cases involving national security and law and order [*Schenck* v. *United States* 249 U.S. 47 (1919)].

Charles T. Schenck, General Secretary of the Socialist party, had been convicted on a charge of conspiracy to obstruct the recruiting and training of draftees in World War I. He had distributed to men of draft age, in direct violation of the Espionage Act of 1917, circulars which were intended to obstruct conscription. The counsel for Schenck raised the defense of constitutionality, claiming that the First Amendment to the Constitution forbids Congress to make any law abridging the freedom of speech or press. The conviction was upheld by the Supreme Court. The Court, after conceding that the circular in question would have been protected by the provisions of the First Amendment in ordinary times, said that the conviction was justified because of the war conditions which brought about the legislation and conviction. In delivering the unanimous opinion, Justice Oliver Wendell Holmes set forth the ''clear and present danger'' test: ''The question in every case is whether the words used are in such circumstances and are of such a nature as to create a clear and present danger that they will bring about the substantive evils that Congress has the right to prevent.'' Although Holmes did not actually define ''substantive evils,'' he obviously meant that such an evil in this particular case was interference with the war power of Congress. The Court found that there was ''clear and present danger'' of such interference and this meant that the individual interest in free expression would have to give way to the national interest in successfully raising an army in order to win the war.

The meaning of the rule is plain: the danger involved must be both clear and present. And the rule is all pervasive—it applies to "every case." Yet it has been argued that this rule does not apply to cases where the legislature itself has made certain speech or writing a crime. This contention is clearly untenable. When stated as broadly as that, it would simply abolish the constitutional protection of free speech and free press. If that contention were the law, Congress could make any set of words criminal. Clearly all that the legislature can do is to say that, when circumstances are such that the utterance does create a clear and present danger, the prohibition could apply and its violation be punished.

The First Amendment prohibits only "Congress" from curtailing basic freedoms, it does not limit the state governments. Throughout the early history of the United States the quality of freedom lacked uniformity and the rights of free expression sometimes were flagrantly abused. In 1925, after long agitation, the Supreme Court made the First Amendment applicable to the states via the Fourteenth Amendment in *Gitlow* v. *New York* [268 U.S. 652 (1925)]. Benjamin Gitlow was convicted under New York State's Criminal Anarchy Law of 1902 for publishing a pamphlet entitled "The Revolutionary Age," which pleaded for the destruction of the bourgeois state. The Court, although it upheld Gitlow's conviction, ruled that freedom of speech and press are among those unspecified "privileges" and "immunities" protected by the due process clause of the Fourteenth Amendment from impairment by the states. In this way the First and Fourteenth Amendments complement each other.

Prior Restraint

Most freedom of expression cases involve government action after the fact. The concept of prior restraint of the press is so philosophically incompatible with the First Amendment that only two significant cases have been adjudicated by the Supreme Court. The issue of prior restraint of the press first came before the Court in *Near* v. *Minnesota* [283 U.S. 697 (1931)]. A small Minneapolis newspaper called the *Saturday Press* charged, among other things, that the city had fallen under the evil spell of a clique of Jewish gangsters. An injunction against the newspaper was granted to local officials under a Minnesota "gag law" which permitted the suppression of malicious, scandalous, defamatory or obscene publications. Robert McCormick, the conservative publisher of the *Chicago Tribune* and chairman of the American Newspaper Publishers Association's Committee on Freedom of the Press, retained counsel to challenge the constitutionality of the Minnesota law in the courts. The Supreme Court, in a 5-to-4 decision, held the law to be an unconstitutional infringement of freedom of the press. The Court, however, held out the possibility that prior restraint might be justified under extreme circumstances. The point was that suppression of a publication, however evil that paper might be, could set a precedent for the extension of "gag" laws to respectable publications which might print polemical viewpoints.

Forty years passed before the Supreme Court was again confronted with the issue of prior restraint of the press in *New York Times Company* v. *United States* and *United States* v. *Washington Post Company* [403 U.S. 713 (1971)]. The *New York Times* came into possession of a "Top Secret" 47-volume study entitled "History of the U.S. Decision-Making Process on Vietnam Policy" in March, 1971. The document is popularly known as "The Pentagon Papers." After three months of careful study and debate, the *Times* published the first of a series of major exerpts from the document. The federal government, in an unprecedented action, obtained a temporary injunction against the *Times,* and publication ceased after the third installment. Several days later, the *Washington Post* started a series of its own, and the government again attempted to halt publication. The District Court of the Southern District of New York refused to grant a permanent restraining order against the *Times* but the U.S. Court of Appeals in New York reversed the lower court's decision. The District Court for the District of Columbia ruled in favor of the *Post* and the U.S. Court of Appeals for the District of Columbia upheld the *Post's* right to continue full publication. On June 25, the Supreme Court in 5-to-4 decision voted to hear testimony and to continue the temporary order of prior restraint against both newspapers. Historically, this was an action virtually without precedent since the establishment of the Bill of Rights.

The attorneys for the two newspapers, apparently wary as a result of the high Court's decision to continue the restraining order, decided to argue the case on the narrower issue of the government's inability to prove jeopardy to national security rather than to oppose all prior restraint against the press as being unconstitutional. In a 6-to-3 *per curiam* decision, the Court rejected the Federal Government's claim that the national security would be imperiled by publication of the documents. Each justice expressed his views separately, though several concurred with each other's opinion. Justices Black and Douglas argued for absolute freedom of the press. Justice Brennan declared that the government failed to prove its case, but reserved the possibility of a prior restraint in extreme circumstances. Justices Marshall and Stewart agreed that the government had not proved its case, but left open the possibility of legislative authorization of certain forms of prior restraint. Justice White joined the majority, but stated that punishment after the fact might present an entirely different situation. The three dissenters—Chief Justice Burger and Justices Blackmun and Harlan—objected to the haste shown in the case and felt that they did not have adequate time to make a decision properly. Since the Court did not deal squarely with the issue of prior restraint, the case is more significant for its political implications than for its legal precedent.

Motion Picture Censorship

Motion pictures have never enjoyed the same constitutional rights as the press. The issue of prior restraint of motion pictures first came before the Supreme Court in *Mutual Film Corp.* v. *Ohio* [236 U.S. 230 (1915)]. Ohio had established a commission authorized to approve for public showing only those films determined to be of "a moral, educational or amusing and harmless character." Mutual sought to enjoin enforcement of the law because it violated the free speech guarantees of the Ohio Constitution, as well as the First Amendment.

A unanimous Supreme Court upheld the Ohio law, ruling that the exhibition of motion pictures is a "business pure and simple, originated and conducted for profit like other spectacles," and that movies should not be regarded as "part of the press of the country or as organs of public opinion." In its broadly worded opinion the Court excluded motion pictures from that class of communication media entitled to First Amendment freedoms. The classification of motion pictures as "spectacles," encouraged censorship by state and local municipalities. By the middle 1920s, the practice of licensing films had become widespread.

The *Mutual* decision was the only movie censorship case heard by the Supreme Court for 37 years. Then, in 1952, the Court brought film within the protection of the First and Fourteenth Amendments in *Burstyn* v. *Wilson* [343 U.S. 230 (1952)]. The case involved the film "The Miracle" in which a peasant woman, played by Anna Magnani, is seduced by a bearded stranger she believes to be St. Joseph. Later she conceives a male child, whom she imagines is Jesus Christ. The movie, which was produced by Roberto Rossellini, was presented with two French films as a trilogy entitled "The Ways of Love."

The motion picture division of the New York Education Department, headed by the New York State Board of Regents, originally licensed the film. Members of the Catholic War Veterans picketed the Paris Theatre in New York City where the movie was being shown. The theatre also received bomb threats. Cardinal Spellman, head of the Roman Catholic Archdiocese of New York, publicly denounced the film and enjoined Catholics throughout the country to boycott any theatre showing "The Miracle."

After receiving protests from various religious and other pressure groups, the New York Board of Regents requested the film's distributor, Joseph Burstyn, to show cause why his license should not be rescinded. After a hearing, at which Burstyn testified, the film's license was revoked on the basis that the film was sacrilegious. Burstyn appealed the Board's ruling in the courts. The New York Court of Appeals upheld "sacrilegious" as a valid standard for censorship, but a unanimous Supreme Court, in reversing the lower court decision, ruled that the New York motion picture licensing act was a state abridgment of freedom of speech and press in that it established as a prerequisite to exhibition censorial approval determined by a standard as vague as the "sacrilegious" test. The Court further held that the state has no legitimate interest in protecting the various religions from distasteful views which justifies prior restraint. The Supreme Court, however, did not deal with the broader issue of whether all prior licensing of motion pictures is in itself unconstitutional.

Throughout the 1950s the Supreme Court, in case after case, ruled against the censors. Finally, the Court in 1961 ruled on the constitutional status of film licensing per se in *Times Film Corp.* v. *Chicago* [365 U.S. 43 (1961)]. The Times Corporation paid a license fee but refused to submit the film "Don Juan," based on Mozart's opera Don Giovanni, to Chicago's board of censors. The city's censors denied permission for the film to be shown even though its content undoubtedly would have merited a license. The Times Corporation challenged Chicago's licensing system and the constitutionality of all prior restraints on motion pictures. In a 5-to-4 decision, the Supreme Court voted to uphold the constitutionality of prior censorship of motion pictures and the city's power to license films. The Court determined, as in the past, that freedom was *not* an absolute right and that each medium of communication "tends to present its own peculiar problem." Taking care to limit the scope of the ruling, the Court said that no "unreasonable strictures on individual liberty" should result from prior restraint.

In a heated dissent, Chief Justice Warren, supported by Justices Black, Douglas and Brennan, enumerated the historical abuses of prior restraint and concluded that the majority's decision "officially unleashes the censor and permits him to roam at will" limited only by standards that "are patently imprecise."

The Supreme Court attempted to clarify its position on prior restraint of motion pictures in *Freedman* v. *Maryland* [380 U.S. 51 (1965)]. The case involved the conviction and $25 fine of a Baltimore theatre manager who, with the backing of the Times Film Corporation, exhibited the movie "Revenge of Daybreak" without first obtaining a permit from the Maryland Board of Censors. The film concerned the Irish Revolution and was not considered objectionable. A unanimous Supreme Court decided for Freedman, but did not rule that criminal punishment for exhibiting an unlicensed film was unconstitutional. Rather, the Court held that Maryland did not provide adequate procedural safeguards "against undue inhibition of expression." The Court shifted the burden of proof to the censors and required swift review of the licensing process in future cases.

The U.S. Supreme Court faced the question of the constitutionality of motion picture classification in *Interstate Circuit, Inc.* v. *Dallas* [390 U.S. 676 (1968)]. In 1965, Dallas adopted an ordinance which established a Motion Picture Classification Board. The Board classified films as "suitable for young persons" or as "not suitable for young persons." A "young person" was defined as anyone who had not attained his 16th birthday. Interstate Circuit, a major theatre chain in the southwest, challenged the ordinance as being unconstitutionally vague. Interstate deliberately ignored the Board's ruling that the

United Artists release, "Viva Maria," starring Brigitte Bardot and Jeanne Moreau, was "not suitable for young persons," and showed the film without imposing age restrictions on its audience. A county court upheld the Board's determination and enjoined exhibition of the film. The Texas Court of Civil Appeals affirmed the county court decision.

The U.S. Supreme Court reversed the decision, stating that where expression is subjected to licensing there must be rigorous insistence upon procedural safeguards and judicial superintendence of the censor's action. The Court agreed with Interstate that the standards imposed by the Dallas Motion Picture Classification Board were unconstitutionally vague. The Court noted cautiously, however, that its ruling would not preclude a more carefully drafted age classification scheme proscribing minors from viewing certain films.

Corruption of the Public Morality

With most forms of prior restraint in a state of doubtful legality, guardians of the public welfare increasingly rely upon obscenity statutes to curtail the free flow of information. Federal laws ban obscenity from the mails, telephone, radio and television. Both state and federal jurisdictions have consistently maintained that obscenity is beyond the pale of constitutional protection. However, the Supreme Court's attempts to define obscenity and set standards for applying its definition have been vague and inconsistent. Consequently, the erudite Justices spend a disproportionate amount of their time examining alleged smut, and attempting to arrive at definitive standards.

The U.S. Supreme Court handed down its first major decision on obscenity in *Roth* v. *United States* [354 U.S. 476 (1957)]. Samuel Roth, who conducted a business in New York in the publication and sale of books, photographs and magazines, used circulars and advertising matter to solicit sales. He was convicted by a jury in the District Court for the Southern District of New York for mailing obscene circulars and advertising, and an obscene book in violation of the federal obscenity statute. He received a five-year prison sentence and a $5,000 fine. The U.S. Court of Appeals affirmed his conviction.

The U.S. Supreme Court, in a 5-to-4 decision affirming the conviction, ruled that "obscenity is not within the area of constitutionally protected speech and press," but that "sex and obscenity are not synonymous.'' Obscene material, said the Court, deals with sex in a manner "appealing to the prurient interest." The Court rejected the British *Hicklin* test of obscenity which allowed material to be judged merely by the effect of an isolated excerpt upon particularly susceptible persons, and sanctioned the test which had been evolving in the federal and state courts: "whether to the average person, applying contemporary community standards, the dominant theme of the material taken as a whole appeals to the prurient interest." The Court included under the protection of the Constitution "all ideas having even the slightest redeeming social importance."

Although the *Roth* decision did not specifically state what community was to furnish the contemporary standards, it did indicate approval of the trial court's instruction stating that standards of local jurors were to be used.

Five years later, the Supreme Court, in a 6-to-1 decision, found three magazines—*Manuel, Trim,* and *Grecian Guild Pictorial*—not to be obscene in *Manuel Enterprises, Inc.* v. *Day* [370 U.S. 478 (1962)]. The magazines were designed primarily for homosexuals and consisted largely of photographs of nude or nearly nude male models in various provocative poses. Despite the sizable majority, the Court could not reach a consensus as to the reasons for its decision. Justice Harlan, joined by Justice Stewart, announced the judgment of the Court, stating that the magazines were not so "patently offensive" as to affront contemporary community standards.

In *Jacobellis* v. *Ohio* [378 U.S. 184 (1964)], the Supreme Court again experienced difficulty in achieving consensus. The case involved Nico Jacobellis, a Cleveland Heights theatre owner who was convicted for possessing and exhibiting an obscene film, "The Lovers." The film, which contained a short, but explicit, love scene, had already been shown in a number of cities in the United States including Columbus and Toledo, Ohio. At least two critics of major importance rated it among the 10 best films of the year in which it was produced.

The U.S. Supreme Court, in a 6-to-3 decision, concluded that the film was not obscene within the standards enunciated in the *Roth* case since it was not *utterly* without redeeming social value. Justice Brennan, writing the judgment for the Court, held without qualification that a national standard should be used in applying the test for obscenity. He saw particular danger in a local standard's potential for inhibiting expression, since publishers might be reluctant to submit their work to the variations in tastes among different locales. Justice Brennan's opinion was joined only by Justice Goldberg. The other four prevailing Justices concurred separately and did not address themselves to the issue of national versus local standards.

The U.S. Supreme Court attempted to refine the test for obscenity in *Memoirs* v. *Massachusetts* [383 U.S. 413 (1966)]. The case involved a book entitled *Memoirs of a Woman of Pleasure,* better known as "Fanny Hill." The book, which was written in 1749, tells the story of an Eighteenth Century prostitute with vivid descriptions of her many sexual experiences. The Superior Court of Suffolk County, Massachusetts, found the book obscene, and the decision was affirmed by the Supreme Court of Massachusetts.

The U.S. Supreme Court ruled that the Massachusetts court had failed to weigh the "redeeming social importance" of the work. Justice Brennan, joined by Chief Justice Warren and Justice Fortas, announced the judgment of the Court. The Court stated that the test for obscenity requires the coalescence of three elements: (1) the dominant theme of the work taken as a whole must appeal to the prurient interest in sex; (2) the material must be patently offensive in that it affronts contemporary community standards relating to the description or representation of sexual matters; and (3) the material must be utterly without redeeming social value. Each of the three criteria must be applied independently. One cannot be weighed against or cancelled by another. Since the Massachusetts court had attributed to "Fanny Hill" a modicum of literary and historical value, its judgment was reversed by the U.S. Supreme Court. Although the *Memoirs* decision provided a significant refinement of the Roth definition, the flood of obscenity litigation continued.

On the same day as *Memoirs,* the Court handed down two other pronouncements on obscenity. In *Ginzburg* v. *United States* [383 U.S. 463 (1966)], the U.S. Supreme Court confronted the issue of pandering—"the business of purveying textual or graphic material openly advertised to appeal to the erotic interest. . . ." Ralph Ginzburg was convicted of violating the federal obscenity statute which makes it a crime to send obscene material through the mails. The publications involved were: *Eros,* hard cover magazine, *Liaison,* a bi-weekly newsletter, and *The Housewife's Handbook on Selective Promiscuity,* a short book. Ginzburg sought mailing privileges from various towns with suggestive names. He obtained mailing privileges from the postmaster of Middlesex, New Jersey. Several million circulars were mailed soliciting subscriptions for *Eros* and *Liaison;* and over 5,500 copies of the *Handbook* were mailed.

The U.S. Supreme Court, in a 5-to-4 decision, upheld Ginzburg's conviction, noting that his sole emphasis was on the sexually provocative aspects of his publications. The Court held that although the publications might not themselves be intrinsically obscene, the conviction could be sustained in view of Ginzburg's *pandering* in production, sale and publicity with respect to the publications. Ginzburg, after exhausting all other appeals, went to prison to serve a three-year sentence on February 17, 1972. While in prison he worked as a sexton in the prison church. He was released for good behavior after serving eight months of his sentence.

In *Mishkin* v. *New York* [383 U.S. 502 (1966)], the U.S. Supreme Court added another dimension to the test for obscenity. Edward Mishkin was convicted for his dominant role in several enterprises engaged in producing and selling books which depicted, among other things, sado-masochism, fetishism, and homosexuality. Mishkin claimed on appeal to the U.S. Supreme Court that since the books dealt with sexual deviancy they did not appeal to the prurient interest of the average person. The Court held, in a 6-to-3 decision, that when material is designed for and privately disseminated to a clearly defined sexual group, rather than to the public at large, the prurient appeal requirement of the obscenity test is satisfied if the dominant theme of the material taken as a whole appeals to the prurient interest in sex of the members of that deviant group.

In 1968, the U.S. Supreme Court upheld the constitutionality of a New York criminal obscenity statute which prohibits the sale of obscene material to minors under 17 years of age in *Ginsberg* v. *New York* [390 U.S. 629 (1968)]. Sam Ginsberg, who operated "Sam's Stationary and Luncheonette" in Bellmore, Long Island, was convicted under the New York Statute for selling to a 16-year old-boy two magazines which depicted female nudity. The U.S. Supreme Court upheld the conviction even though the magazines in question would not be deemed obscene for adults. Justice Brennan, writing for the 6-to-3 majority, affirmed that the authority of the state over the conduct of minors is broader than its authority over adults. This general philosophy, incidentally, also seems to apply in another context, to the recent imposition by the TV networks of a so-called "family viewing" hour in which adult themes are not shown between 7–9 p.m. EST.

The following year, the U.S. Supreme Court ruled on the constitutionality of possessing obscene materials in the home [*Stanley* v. *Georgia* 394 U.S. 557 (1969)]. Federal and state agents obtained a warrant to search the home of Robert Eli Stanley for alleged bookmaking activities. While looking through a desk drawer in an upstairs bedroom they found three reels of 8mm film. After viewing the films, the state officer concluded that they were obscene. Stanley was sentenced to one year in prison for possession of obscene material, a violation of Georgia law. Justice Marshall, delivering the opinion of the Court, ruled that the state may not prohibit mere possession of obscene material within the privacy of one's home. The state has no business, said Justice Marshall, telling a man what books he may read or what films he may watch in his own home.

Justices Stewart, Brennan and White concurred with the majority in the result, but based their reversal of Stanley's conviction on the indiscriminate nature of the search rather than on the question of private possession of obscenity.

On June 21, 1973, the U.S. Supreme Court adjudicated five cases that established new guidelines for obscenity legislation and control. The key case was *Miller* v. *California* [413 U.S. 15 (1973)]. Marvin Miller was convicted of violating a California obscenity law by mailing to unwilling recipients unsolicited, sexually explicit advertisements deemed obscene by a jury applying contemporary California standards. The advertisements primarily consisted of pictures and drawings of men and women engaging in a variety of sexual activities which left little to the imagination. On appeal, Miller contended that application of state rather than national standards violated the First and Fourteenth Amendments.

The U.S. Supreme Court, in a historic pronouncement, ruled that, in interpreting state statutes, obscenity is to be determined by applying contemporary community standards rather than uniform national standards. The Court's decision, which dramatically expands legislative prerogative in dealing with offensive material, leaves open the possibility of interpreting "community" as the locality trying a particular case. Chief Justice Burger, delivering the opinion of the 5-to-4 majority, formulated new standards for determining obscenity. The new criteria allow for curtailment of material that: (1) the average person, applying contemporary community standards, would find, taken as a whole, appeals to the prurient interest; (2) depicts or describes in a patently offensive way sexual conduct that is specifically defined by state law; (3) taken as a whole, lacks serious literary, artistic, political, or scientific value.

In the first of the four related cases the Court ruled that the exhibition of obscene films in an "adult theatre" is not protected by the First Amendment, even when the theatre effectively restricts viewing to consenting adults and does not engage in "pandering or obtrusive advertising." Expert testimony, said the Court, is not necessary for determining obscenity [*Paris Adult Theatre* v. *Slaton* 413 U.S. 49 (1973)]. In the second case, the Court held that the constitutional protection provided by the *Stanley* case does not extend to the possession of obscene material on common carriers, even if it is intended for private use [*United States* v. *Orito* 413 U.S. 139 (1973)]. The third case held that books without pictorial content may be judged obscene under the First Amendment [*Kaplan* v. *California* 413 U.S. 115 (1973)]. In the final case, the Court ruled that the commerce clause empowers Congress to ban importation of obscene material even if it is intended for private use in the home [*United States* v. *12,200 Foot Reels of Super 8mm Film* 413 U.S. 123 (1973)]. The same five-Justice majority prevailed in all five cases.

Laws of Defamation

Freedom of speech and press often come into conflict with the individual's right to protect his good name or reputation. Concern about protection of reputation is reflected in American society under the laws of defamation. Defamation is divided into two categories, slander and libel. Historically, slander involved spoken communication, whereas libel entailed written messages. The advent of mass communications has somewhat diminished the importance of these distinctions. Many states, for example, treat defamatory remarks made on the broadcast and film media under the laws governing libel.

There are 51 different defamation laws representative of each of the 50 states and the District of Columbia. In most states, damages are easier to collect for libel since it is considered a more serious offense than slander. In libel, the defamatory statements have greater potential for harm because they may be accessible for years. In addition, libel is more likely to be premeditated, whereas slander is generally thought to occur in the heat and emotion of the moment.

A libel suit is actionable merely by demonstrating that defamation has occurred. In several jurisdictions slander requires additional proof of pecuniary loss, unless there have been imputations of crime involving moral turpitude, or attribution of some loathsome disease, or accusations of incompetency or lack of integrity in business, trade or profession, or in some states, imputations of unchastity to a woman.

Defenses in a defamation suit are generally the same in most states. Truth in many states is an absolute defense. However, in 26 jurisdictions truth may be used as defense only if the remarks were made with good motives and for justifiable ends. In all jurisdictions, the defendant has the burden of proving the truth of his imputation. Statements by judges, jurors and witnesses in a court of law enjoy an absolute privilege and are not actionable. Absolute privilege is also given to remarks made by Congressmen on the floor of Congress as well as to communications between husband and wife.

Defamation is most often a civil action—a contest in which one party attempts to collect damages for alleged harm done to him by the accusations of another. Three types of damages may be awarded in a defamation suit. Compensatory damages are given for harm done to one's good name. Special or actual damages are awarded for actual money lost as a result of what was said. Punitive or exemplary damages are awarded in an effort to punish the defamer for actual malice. In most states, the statute of limitations for a defamatory action is two years. In Arkansas, Delaware, New Mexico and Vermont the limitation is three years; in Hawaii it is six years.

Beginning in 1964, the U.S. Supreme Court began to erect a constitutional bulwark against actions for defamation with its decision in *New York Times Co.* v. *Sullivan* [(376 U.S. 254 (1964)]. The case concerned a full-page advertisement carried in the *Times* by a civil rights organization which charged the Montgomery, Alabama police with improper conduct in responding to non-violent student demonstrations at the Alabama State College. L. B. Sullivan, Commissioner of Public Affairs of the City of Montgomery, Alabama, a job which entailed supervision of the Police Department, claimed the advertisement defamed him, even though his name or title was not mentioned. He sued the *New York Times* for libel and was awarded $500,000 by an Alabama jury. The Supreme Court of Alabama affirmed the judgment, but the U.S. Supreme Court unanimously reversed, enunciating a doctrine of far-reaching protection never before known by the press. The High Court said the First Amendment compelled a ruling that public officials be denied damages for defamatory falsehoods relating to official conduct unless a statement was made with actual malice, that is, with "knowledge that it was false or with reckless disregard of whether it was false or not."

In the ensuing years, the Supreme Court expanded the scope of First Amendment privilege to include "public figures," "newsworthy persons" and "candidates for public office."

The *New York Times* doctrine was expanded in *Rosenbloom* v. *Metromedia, Inc.* [403 U.S. 29 (1971)] to include an individual who was neither a public official nor a public figure. George Rosenbloom, magazine distributor, was arrested during a police raid on a Philadelphia newsstand as he arrived with a delivery of nudist magazines. He was charged with selling obscene material. Police obtained a warrant to search Rosenbloom's home and a barn he used as a warehouse. They confiscated hundreds of allegedly obscene books and magazines.

The police notified two radio stations, a wire service, and a local newspaper of the arrests. Rosenbloom alleged that radio station WIP, owned and operated by Metromedia, characterized him and his business associates as "smut distributors" and "girlie book peddlers."

Rosenbloom was subsequently acquitted of the criminal obscenity charges and filed a libel action against WIP. A jury awarded him $25,000 in compensatory damages and $725,000 in punitive damages. The trial judge reduced the punitive damages to $250,000. The U.S. Court of Appeals reversed the decision, holding that the *Times* doctrine was applicable. The U.S. Supreme Court in a 5-to-3 decision upheld the Court of Appeals reversal and extended First Amendment protection to all discussion and communication involving matters of public and general concern, "without regard to whether the persons involved are famous or anonymous." In determining the applicability of the *New York Times* test in a given case, the Court implied that the focus should be on the *event* in which the individual was involved, rather than his status. Justice Brennan delivered the judgment of the Court, in which Justices Black and White concurred in the result, but not the reasoning behind the plurality opinion. Although the Rosenbloom decision significantly broadened the scope of constitutional privilege, it left undefined those events that are of sufficient public concern to be encompassed by the privilege.

Three years later, the Supreme Court retreated from its trend of expanding First Amendment protection in *Gertz* v. *Robert Welch Inc.* [418 U.S. 323 (1974)]. The case involved Elmer Gertz, a prominent attorney who was retained by the Nelson family to represent them in a civil litigation against a Chicago policeman named Richard Nuccio who shot and killed young Ronald Nelson in 1968. In April of 1969, an article entitled "Frame-Up" with the subtitle "Richard Nuccio and The War on Police" appeared in *American Monthly,* a magazine published by Robert Welch Inc. The article falsely implied that Elmer Gertz had a criminal record and was the architect of a nationwide conspiracy to discredit the police. The article also falsely accused Gertz of being an official of the "Marxist League for Industrial Democracy" as well as a "Leninist" and a "Communist-fronter."

Gertz filed a libel action against Robert Welch Inc. in the U.S. District Court for the Northern District of Illinois. The jury initially awarded Gertz damages of $50,000. Upon reconsideration the District Court extended First Amendment privilege to include matters of public interest. Finding insufficient evidence of actual malice, the court ruled in favor of Robert Welch Inc. The Court of Appeals affirmed the decision of the District Court.

The U.S. Supreme Court, in a 5-to-4 decision, held that Robert Welch Inc. could not invoke the *New York Times* privilege by claiming that the false and defamatory statements regarding Gertz involved a matter of public or general interest. The Court, in effect, repudiated the extension of the *Times* test, proposed by the *Rosenbloom* plurality, to private individuals involved in matters of public concern. Since private individuals come to the public's attention through circumstances not of their own making, the Court reasoned that they cannot be considered to have waived any protection the state might afford them from irresponsible publicity. Since public officials and public figures usually enjoy significantly greater access to the channels of effective communication, they are not afforded the same protection as private individuals.

Fairness Doctrine

In 1969, the U.S. Supreme Court adjudicated two cases simultaneously which involved the FCC's fairness rules, the *RTNDA* and *Red Lion* [*Red Lion Broadcasting Co.* v. *FCC* 395 U.S. 367 (1969)]. The Radio Television News Directors Association (RTNDA) challenged the FCC's 1967 special fairness rules on personal attack and candidate endorsement as unconstitutional. The Court of Appeals upheld the RTNDA, but the U.S. Supreme Court unanimously reversed.

The *Red Lion* case concerned the refusal of WGCB-AM-FM, of Red Lion, Pennsylvania, to give time to Fred J. Cook for reply to a personal attack. Cook, the author of a book entitled *Goldwater—Extremist on the Right,* which was very critical of Barry Goldwater, had been charged with having Communist affiliations by the Reverend Billy Hargis in a syndicated radio program series, "The Christian Crusade." When Cook requested time to reply, the station demanded that he either pay for the time or offer proof that he could neither find a sponsor nor afford to pay for the time himself. The Commission stated that the Fairness Doctrine required a station to make time available for reply to a personal attack, free if necessary.

The Court of Appeals in the District of Columbia upheld the validity of the Fairness Doctrine in June 1967. (Three weeks later the FCC adopted the personal attack rules.) The Supreme Court unanimously supported the lower court, thus providing judicial affirmation of the FCC's Fairness Doctrine.

Right of Access

The Fairness Doctrine is not applicable to demands for access to the broadcast media. Under the Fairness Doctrine, determination of program format and selection of opposition speakers are retained by the broadcaster. In 1970, the Business Executives' Move for Vietnam Peace (BEM) filed a complaint with the FCC alleging that a Washington, D.C. radio station, WTOP, refused to sell the organization broadcast time to present a series of one-minute spot announcements urging the immediate withdrawal of American forces from Vietnam. WTOP explained that its station presented full and fair coverage of important public issues and was justified in refusing to air the editorial advertisements.

A few months later, the Democratic National Committee (DNC) requested that the FCC issue an order prohibiting broadcast stations from refusing to sell air time to responsible organizations for comment on public issues. The DNC claimed a limited *right of access* to the broadcast media. The FCC, considering the two cases together, rejected the arguments of BEM and DNC, ruling that it was permissible for broadcasters to impose a ban on all editorial advertisements. On appeal, the U.S. Court of Appeals reversed the Commission's ruling, stating that a flat ban on paid editorial announcements is in violation of the First Amendment, at least where a station accepts other sorts of paid announcements. The court concluded that the broadcasters' retention of total initiative and editorial control would be inimical to the protection of free speech and press.

The U.S. Supreme Court, reversing the Court of Appeals decision, ruled that First Amendment principles do not require a broadcaster to accept editorial advertisements nor do they assure the public a right to access to the broadcast media [*Columbia Broadcasting System, Inc.* v. *Democratic National Committee* 412 U.S. 94 (1973)].

Reporter's Privilege

In *United States* v. *Caldwell* [408 U.S. 665 (1972)] the U.S. Supreme Court ruled, in a 5-to-4 decision, that the First Amendment does not provide reporters with a privilege to refuse to disclose confidential facts and sources to federal and state grand juries engaged in the investigation of crime. This decision has been hotly protested by the press, which sees its privileges challenged and its rights jeopardized.

Earl Caldwell, a *New York Times* reporter, was subpoenaed by a federal grand jury to relinquish notes and tape recordings of interviews with officers and spokesmen of the Black Panther Party concerning the party's aims, purposes, and activities. Caldwell sought to quash the subpoena or, alternatively, to limit the scope of the inquiry in order to protect his sources. He argued that disclosure of confidential sources would jeopardize his ability to gather news from informants and thus violate his First Amendment rights. The District Court refused to excuse Caldwell from testifying, but granted a restrictive injunction prohibiting questions about sources. Caldwell did not comply with the court order and was cited for contempt. The U.S. Court of Appeals overturned the contempt citation and held that he had a qualified privilege under the First Amendment not to testify, since the government did not show a compelling need for the information sufficient to override the claimed invasion of free press interests.

The U.S. Supreme Court reversed, ruling that journalists did not have a First Amendment privilege, qualified or unqualified, to refuse to appear or answer relevant and material questions posed by a legitimate grand jury investigation. This decision, many journalists contend, was a stunning blow to a free and responsibile press and to a reporter's right to protect his news source's confidentiality.

The Supreme Court indicated that under certain circumstances refusal to appear or reveal confidential information or sources could be justified under the First Amendment. These circumstances include harassment of newsmen, grand jury investigations not held in good faith, and subpoenaing newsmen where there is only a remote and tenuous relationship between the information sought and the subject of the investigation. The Court in balancing the right of freedom of press against the obligation of citizens to provide relevant information about criminal conduct ruled for the latter on the basis of the facts in this particular case.

Since the *Caldwell* decision, dozens of reporters have been held in contempt for declining to reveal sources and information to grand juries and other governmental bodies. Peter Bridge, a reporter for the *Newark News,* was imprisoned for three weeks because he refused to give a New Jersey grand jury information about attempted bribes to public officials. The Supreme Court refused to hear his case. John Lawrence, *Los Angeles Times'* Washington bureau chief, was held in contempt for refusing to surrender confidential tapes of an interview with a principal in the ''Watergate'' break-in. The U.S. Court of Appeals upheld his contempt citation. William Farr, a *Los Angeles Herald-Examiner* reporter, was incarcerated for 46 days for refusing to disclose to the trial judge in the Manson-Tate murder case the source of a transcript of a key witness's confession. Justice Douglas ordered Farr released, but the Supreme Court ultimately refused to hear the case.

Freedom and Control

Although caution must be exercised in abridging speech and press, one must remember that the continued existence of freedom of expression depends upon an ordered society, which, in turn, demands that the freedoms given in the Constitution not be absolute. The safeguarding and fructification of free constitutional institutions is the very basis and mainstay upon which freedom of expression rests, and that freedom cannot be held to include the right to destroy such institutions. Some justices, however, have held that freedom is absolute and inviolate, notably Justices Hugo Black and William O. Douglas. While philosophically sound, their argument for an absolute interpretation of the First Amendment is pragmatically untenable. The problem is one of balancing the fundamental freedom of unimpaired expression against the danger to society that is sometimes likely to result from that expression.

13

The United States
and Global Communication

THE UNITED STATES holds a pivotal position in the arena of international communications. This is not to imply that the American system of broadcasting is necessarily the best. Many critics are convinced that other systems are superior, particularly from the standpoint of educational service and recognition of cultural minorities. But broadcasting in the United States is unique. Commercial broadcasting, based on networking and station affiliation, is entirely supported by advertising. Economically, it is a successful and powerful medium of mass communication. More homes have radio and television receivers than in any other country in the world. Despite the fact that broadcasting is a regulated industry, the philosophical basis for a free press, enunciated in the First Amendment, also applies to the broadcast media. The ultimate judge, at least theoretically, of the efficacy of the American system is the power of public opinion. The media are accountable to the viewer, the listener, the reader—the public. Thus, the press' Canons of Journalism and the Code of the National Association of Broadcasters stress service to the public and the FCC speaks of "the public interest, convenience and necessity."

In terms of the so-called "four theories of the press," the system of mass communications in the United States is predicated on the theory of social responsibility—which has been taken to mean that the media, both print and broadcast, function freely but with a sense of responsibility to the needs of the viewer, listener and reader. Restriction by government of this operating philosophy is considered censorship or prior restraint. Thus, a second theory, that of libertarianism—a *laissez-faire* concept which evolved over the last three centuries and insists that the media should function with total freedom from any restraint—is also implicit in the American system to some degree. Under a third method, that of authoritarianism, the media function under private or semi-private ownership, but are subject to strict government censorship and control, as in Nazi Germany and in Fascist Spain. Under the fourth theory, the system extant in Russia and Communist China prevails—that is, the government supports the media directly, because it owns and operates the press and broadcasting as a propaganda appendage of the totalitarian state.

The media managers in the United States are convinced of the superiority of the American system because, out of a healthy pluralism of viewpoints, out of the "multitude of tongues," a democratic consensus prevails. But there are still those who remain convinced that British "paternalism," as practiced by the British Broadcasting Corporation, is a unique phenomenon, where broadcasting, but not the print media, operates as a public corporation under state charter and is more responsive—and responsible—to the cultural needs of the public than any system in the world. Yet, British laws concerning the press are more stringent than in the United States. It is doubtful whether British newspaper reporters could enjoy the freedom of press prevailing in this country, despite recent efforts to erode press freedom by subpoenas and jailing of newsmen for refusing to reveal news sources to legislative and judicial authorities.

Media systems around the world, then, are revealing illustrations of national philosophies, of social, economic, religious, political and even geographic phenomena. Different countries have various ways of financing the press and broadcast systems, different modes of regulation and control. And since audience tastes differ because of social conditions, programming tends to differ—although the importation of American "westerns," such as "Bonanza," is sufficiently popular on an almost universal basis to override even the most serious effort at local programming. And, finally, methods of evaluating audience feedback differ. Most countries are interested in how many viewers watch what programs, but in no country is the reliance on ratings as pervasive as in the United States, where advertiser-supported television make large audiences a necessity for program survival. Only in Spain is the broadcast system as totally commercial as it is in this country, although several other countries support their system of broadcasting partially from commercial advertising. In no country, however, is there the direct identification of advertiser with program that prevails in the United States. Those countries which do accept advertising tend to control its times very stringently and to use a "magazine" format where commercials are employed at given intervals and are totally separated from program identification.

International News Services

Although there are many local and regional news agencies throughout the world, only five major worldwide wire service organizations are structured to reach virtually every country that is equipped to receive global communication. These powerful international press and wire services are: the Associated Press and United Press International in the United States; Tass in the Union of Socialist Soviet Republics; Reuters in Great Britain (with cooperative arrangements with Australia and New Zealand); and Agence France Presse in France. These "big five" are responsible fundamentally for the flow of daily news that originates in, and is also distributed to, the entire civilized world. And, with the increasing sophistication of communications technology on a worldwide basis, the wire services are in a position to gather and disseminate news speedily, accurately and pervasively. In general, the flow of world news by way of the wire services is unimpeded—but not entirely so. There are news controls by the government in many areas, but with the persistent talk of *"detente,"* both the Soviet Union and its satellite countries are finding it increasingly difficult to shut out news from the rest of the world and particularly from the United States. At the Helsinki meetings in 1975, the Russians may have enjoyed the process whereby their conquests and suppression of Czechoslovakia and Hungary were legitimized, but at the same time they spoke with seeming conviction of the need for unimpeded transmission of news to all countries. The major test, however, is still to come. In the light of Helsinki, how will Eastern Europe and Russia react to news which may be at variance with their own controlled communications over their own news agency, Tass?

Most, if not all, of the significant international news each day is disseminated by AP, UPI, Reuters, Tass, and Agence France Presse, but these services are supplemented by smaller agencies. Indeed as long as three decades ago, there were a variety of news services established in countries around the world. By the 1970s, more than 100 such organizations were in operation. Most involve exchange and liaison with neighboring countries. But the basic reliance for world news must necessarily fall on the five large news organizations. In the developing countries the economic problem is acute. There are simply insufficient funds available to take advantage of the burgeoning communications technology. In addition, there is considerable concern over the content that may accrue from too literal an interpretation of the concept of free information flow.

Fundamental reliance, therefore, is on the major wire service organizations. The Associated Press has bureaus throughout the United States and in more than 50 areas abroad. News travels around the world via AP in as many languages as there are operating bureaus, and it is now transmitted with incredible speed and accuracy because of sophisticated facilities for typesetting, transmission of facsimile and telephotos, and use of the Atlantic, Pacific and Indian Ocean satellites which, along with co-axial cable and microwave, play a new and vital role in world communications. At the present time, almost all non-TV originated news is transmitted by satellite from the five news organizations. But any of the worldwide communications technologies—cable, microwave or satellite—is equipped to convey a variety of messages including telephony, telex, and data processing. It is this unusual versatility and technical proficiency which makes these expensive systems economically viable. Unfortunately, "cultural lag" operates in this area as in so many others. Despite advanced technological achievement, political, social, cultural and economic patterns change slowly and are not transformed overnight by the dramatic proficiency of communications hardware.

International Broadcasting

The development of the International Telecommunications Satellite Consortium (Intelsat) and Communications Satellite Corporation (Comsat) (a public corporation in the United States for satellite development) is noted later in a discussion of satellite communications. At this time, the Intelsat Consortium consists of 80 member states and, since 1964, has launched four international satellite programs. Perhaps unfortunately for the development of international telecommunications, particularly in both the news and educational areas, this technology has been used overwhelmingly for international telephony, mostly by countries with advanced economic development and particularly by the United States. Powerful ground stations are expensive and this has precluded use of satellite communication by developing nations and, to some extent, by broadcast news organizations. In the main, satellites have transmitted content of a singularly timely and newsworthy nature to world TV audiences—a moon shot, a major international sports event, a world-shattering piece of "hard" news. But this exciting development in international telecommunications is still pretty much restricted to those who can afford to pay the expensive freight involved—economically affluent countries, major broadcast news organizations, and international wire and press service agencies. A democratic pluralism does not prevail as yet in international communications. Yet, innumerable meetings under the aegis of UNESCO and other organizations have emphasized the enormous potential of satellite communications in bringing the developing countries abreast of the Twentieth Century, in creating a free flow of international news, and in bringing a variety of educational experiences to peoples throughout the world.

Economics, however, is not the only obstacle to a free world news flow. Local and regional political problems create barriers. Propaganda efforts stand in the way of unfettered information and news. Russia is accused of total news control and the United States is criticized for using the available technology for multinational corporate purposes, rather than for educational and informational goals. In the arena of international information, each country has its own admitted informational nexus and the United States is no exception. The establishment of the United States Information Agency (USIA) in 1953 was no international secret. The purpose of USIA is clearly to bring information about American policies and philosophy to other countries around the world. Through every available communications instrumentality— books, films, telecasts, pamphlets and exhibits, this agency has done a generally creditable job on behalf of the United States—and a necessary one. The climate in which USIA has operated, however, has depended in good part on the point of view of the director who usually, but not invariably, reflects the philosophy of the President (and Administration) under whom he functions. Hence, there was considerable difference in outlook on the function and purpose of USIA under Edward R. Murrow as compared, for example, with Frank Shakespeare.

The USIA issues an annual report to the President which is available to the public. In general, the organization distributes material to its various overseas "posts" which then distribute to the foreign newspapers and magazines. Many magazines are also published and distributed by USIA. One of the most important functions is the operation of the Voice of America which reaches millions throughout the world through radio transmitting stations abroad. Neither the radio nor television efforts of USIA, incidentally, are broadcast in this country, but are used exclusively for foreign distribution. An interesting sidelight to the USIA broadcast program is the apparent conflict that some critics see in the juxtaposition of documentaries, designed to reveal the most affirmative aspects of this country, with some of the westerns and the police and crime dramas which are so widely distributed and viewed abroad.

European Broadcasting

Unlike the United States, European countries—because of their geographic proximity among other reasons—have formed a cooperative organization called Eurovision which functions under the auspices of the European Broadcasting Union (EBU). The Soviets have a similar system in the East which is known as Intervision. The Eurovision nerve center is in Brussels, the central location of a daily exchange of television film which links 22 countries together each day. Through the exchange, news and other events are offered and accepted or rejected by the countries involved. The strongest feature of EBU is its unusual independence and its non-political, as well as non-commercial, structure. Its function is to serve as an exchange center, using Brussels as the focal point. But this independence, of course, does not prevent participating countries from restricting the data offered, obviously for political reasons.

There are distinct differences in philosophy and practice between most foreign broadcasting systems and that of the United States. The base of American broadcasting is commercial. It is supported exclusively by advertising. European broadcasting, with the exception of Spain, is financed largely by license fees on television receivers. In Russia, it is paid for and controlled by the government. Some foreign countries mandate a given amount of time for educational, religious or public service programming. In the United States, the FCC offers guidelines for license renewal, but has no control over programming. Where commercials are permitted in foreign broadcasting, they are not identified with the program, are restricted to certain stated times, and are shown in blocks or clusters. They do not interfere with the program continuity. A brief summary of broadcasting in such countries as Great Britain, France, Japan and Russia will illustrate the salient differences between these countries and the United States.

Great Britain

Some American skeptics may scoff at British television, particularly the BBC, as overrated and stuffy, but other more positive evaluations look upon it as the quintessence of what excellence in television should be. Over the past few years, one thing is certain: the British have exported some enormously successful fare to the United States— "The Forsyte Saga" (turned down by commercial networks), "All In the Family" (the American version of "Till Death Do Us Part"), "Upstairs-Downstairs" (the inspiration for CBS' "Beacon Hill"), among others.

Ask a resident of London why their "telly" is deemed to be so fine and an American will be told, perhaps with unctuous pride, that it is not encumbered by endless commercials, that it is totally free of political pressure, and that the British have a long literary tradition and an unswerving commitment to excellence. To this, might be added the comment that there is less reliance on imports of American situation-comedies and crime shows than prevails in other countries. Great Britain boasts two BBC channels (BBC I and BBI II), as well as a more recently established and popular commercial network kown as ITV. In general, the establishment of BBC II shook the BBC channel out of its complacency, as did competition from ITV. Some complain about the commercialism of ITV, but others see in the three enterprises a healthy diversity and a complementary and competitive service. Perhaps the unique quality of broadcasting in Great Britain is its unusual ability to withstand political pressure. Appointments are based on sound ethical and cultural qualifications, not on political favoritism or party affiliation. The documentaries offered are frequently superb, and there is a wholehearted effort to give the news with impartiality. Unlike the FCC, where members are appointed by the President along political party lines, the governors of the BBC come from various fields and represent a diversity of viewpoints and backgrounds.

The British have shown constant concern over the quality of their so-called official broadcasting system. In 1962 there was issued the Pilkington Report, a series of recommendations for improvement that ensued from a lengthy study. The Report was not flattering to ITV, and urged the establishment of a second BBC channel. Perhaps as a result of this study, there was instituted a more careful scrutiny of ITV programming and, in 1964, a television act was promulgated which called for a 25 per cent tax on commercials. But the pull of entertainment is strong, as American TV reveals consistently, and the BBC has had strong and serious competition from ITV. BBC I and BBC II may be said to be complementary, rather than overtly competitive. Programs tend to vary, so that duplication is avoided and both channels cross-promote each other's offerings.

ITV is analogous to the commercial system as it functions in the United States but with important controls on commercials. It is, in effect, not one unit but a number of companies each of which must earn its keep, since there are no license fees to support this system as in the case of the BBC. Programming is decentralized, unlike the BBC, into a series of regional networks and there is keen competition for a place on the major network from both the larger city companies and the smaller regional networks. Commercials are carefully selected and comprise about 40 per cent less time per hour than in the United States. Certainly the leading entrepreneur in commercial television in Great Britain is Sir Lew Grade, an international showman who has developed ties with American TV, and particularly with the American Broadcasting Companies. In this hands-across-the-sea arrangement, however, the direction in recent years has been pretty much from East to West. Our country has imported some of its most successful programs—both on the commercial and public broadcasting networks—from England.

France

Unlike Agence France-Presse, (the news service), broadcasting in France suffered virtually total domination by Charles De Gaulle who appropriated radio and television as his own. While the print media in France traditionally have been outspoken, forthright and certainly polemical, the broadcast media have not enjoyed comparative freedom. During his stormy tenure, De Gaulle saw to it that television news gave his political philosophy top priority, and few evening news programs excluded at least one item of positive coverage on the activities of the head of state. Unfortunately, the electronic media were simply powerless to speak with the acerbic criticism of the French press. The broadcast system, Office de Radiodiffusion Television Français (ORTF) was controlled rigidly by the De Gaulle government, to the extent that cooperation was refused to the United States when satellite-transmitted programs carried content that De Gaulle felt was inimical to his interests. Since De Gaulle's death and the change in government, however, ORTF has had more freedom and latitude, carrying a sizeable number of public affairs and documentary programs over the one black-and-white and the two color networks, as well as over the three radio networks. The French, incidentally, persuaded the Russians to adopt their color television system, known as SECAM, while most of the other Western European nations use PAL, the West German color system.

France has approximately 14 million television receivers, and the operating funds for ORTF accrue from the license fee which is slightly under the equivalent of $22 per year. Other funding comes from the very limited amount of time—which is in great demand—given to commercials. The French permit fewer than 10 minutes during the entire day to commercial messages—quite a comparison with the United States where almost 10 minutes of commercials are scheduled in each hour of prime-time. Thus, French television is a national (i.e. government) institution in a very real sense, despite its liberalization after the austere De Gaulle regime. The governing board, or Administrative Council, consists of a variety of personalities drawn from political life, the press, the audience, and distinguished figures in public and cultural life. Because of the popularity of the language, ORTF cooperates readily with other French-speaking countries, such as Switzerland and

Belgium. And, for propaganda reasons as well as because language ties still exist, the French work arduously to project their programming in the former French colonies of Asia and Africa.

Even under Pompidou, however, French television, while given greater freedom, was reminded constantly that it had an obligation to serve the government. Recently, there has been a more aggressive push toward independence and a greater degree of healthy competitive spirit between the black-and-white and color networks in the area of news coverage. But the French, as a long-standing habit, are suspicious of their media and still do not quite agree that television and radio purvey the news as credibly as they might. But there are positive aspects, as well. Commercial television is frowned upon. Fine programs are presented as a result of cooperative arrangements with other countries for the showing of excellent documentaries and historical programs. These seem to be preferred to the importation of popular American series, although ''Ironside,'' a hardy perennial, prospers in France and in other countries as well.

ORTF, apart from its problems with the political structure, has taken its mandate seriously: to produce first-rate cultural programs. As a result, the French viewer has ample opportunity to watch ballet, symphonies, opera and some significant documentaries in the news area. Nor is the question of children and violence neglected—an interesting aspect since the television industry in the United States has set aside the hours between 7 and 9 p.m. (Eastern Time) as family viewing time. The French are somewhat more pragmatic. They simply insert a white dot in the corner of the screen as a warning signal that the program may not be suitable for children and that parental discretion is advised. As a further warranty of fairness, ORTF also has a policy of offering an alternative program, presumably suitable for children, on the second channel—a practice hardly likely to be emulated in the United States.

Russia

The mass media in the Soviet Union are simple to describe from an operational standpoint, but more complicated when looked at as an expression of national political philosophy. The press and broadcast media function as organs of the state, are an integral part of the state, express the official position of the state. They are thoroughly controlled. Yet, the Russians claim the media are quite free to be critical—provided that criticism does not concern itself with the philosophical base of Communism. Put as graphically as possible, the media in America can be critical of the President and the Congress. The media in Russia do not criticize the Premier or the Politburo members—unless *officially* authorized to do so. Thus, Tass, *Pravda, Izvestia* and Russian broadcasting speak for the official political apparatus in Moscow.

The Soviets arrived at a philosophy of mass communication by a singular route. After the Revolution of 1917, much was said of the formation of a press for the people, for the masses. The media were urged by Lenin to express the deepest and most patriotic feelings of the great hordes of peasants. Representing the people—the masses—was the press. In Lenin's words, the press functioned "to fertilize the proletarian revolutionary movement." At first blush, these words might have been used by Tom Paine or Sam Adams during the American Revolution. But events of 1917 in Russia scarcely followed the pattern of the American Founding Fathers in 1776. The Soviet Union recognizes no Bill of Rights and no First Amendment. And neither print journalists nor television newsmen have any independence. The media in Russia are a conduit, a transmission belt for propaganda, both internally and externally. The people see, hear and read what the government decrees. Tass may never distribute a story which, however newsworthy to the rest of the world, is considered inimical to the interests of the Soviet Union.

The press in the United States, operating on the theory of freedom and social responsibility, is constantly mindful of the fact that it is a surrogate of the people. Hence, investigative reporting will turn up political scandal, such as Watergate. Such enterprising reportage would neither be understood nor permitted in Russia. For in that regime, the media and the government are not adversarial but united. How do the Russians rationalize this position? Simply by pointing out that media in the United States are bourgeois and decadent, because media managers represent capitalist control. In the Soviet Union, on the other hand, the claim is that the media are owned by the people and represent their interests only, not those of private enterprise. Unfortunately, however, the people do not have the benefit of independent news analysis, of investigative documentaries or of any semblance of criticism of the party leadership.

Television transmission in the Soviet Union, apart from political content, presents formidable technical problems. Transmission is an awesome task because of the sheer size of the terrain to be covered, and the many and various cultures and language differences that prevail. The Russian winter is also no boon to broadcasting. Finally, the governing body has the almost insurmountable task of bringing together under one basic political philosophy a vast, heterogeneous series of Republics with more than 50 different language patterns. How is unity managed in this diverse geographical and cultural structure? Under the Soviet system of mass communications, *Pravda* is the official newspaper. But throughout the country there are small regional papers, mostly of tabloid size. All journalistic functions are appendages of the Communist party apparatus and all purvey the identical party lines. The media function virtually as a series of company publications, or house organs, to convey the official viewpoint to the people. The media, therefore, are adjuncts of the political order, the state.

In recent years, with the constant talk of detente and the participation in the Helsinki Conference in 1975, the Soviets have been in rather a defensive position. There is considerable concern about opening the television screen to satellite transmission from the United States. There is an implicit challenge for Tass to cover the world news scene, particularly in the West, with less selectivity. While television is growing in the Soviet Union, the basic thinking is still in "linear" terms, with print receiving major government support. The broadcast media follow the pattern of the press. News is never analyzed. Entertainment is plentiful, but always with an educational or political patina. Programs are oriented toward the achievement of youth, of workers. Literature and drama, as well as news, stress heroic effort on behalf of the people.

Yet, interestingly enough, the Russians were pioneers in the electronic media. As previously noted, it was a Russian, Vladimir Zworykin, who made a significant contribution to the development of television, and the Russians were experimenting with radio as early as the period of Guglielmo Marconi. Lenin wrote that radio was a most powerful purveyor of propaganda and "agitation," and the present party leaders continue to agree. There are about 50 million radio receivers in the country and virtually all of Russia is accessible to radio transmission by means of both long and short wave. The country boasts about 30 million television receivers, but because of the Soviet adamancy about admitting news from the outside world, there is strict control over what is broadcast. But there is keen recognition of the educational propaganda potential of television. The Soviets are using cable, as well as satellites, to reach the widely dispersed regions of the country with homogenized news and information. Networking, which emanates primarily from the Ostankino headquarters near Moscow, is under strict government supervision. A national committee, supplemented by more than a hundred smaller regional councils work together to assure uniformity and control. The major programs come from Moscow, supplemented by more than a hundred additional regional program centers located in various parts of the country.

In short, Soviet press and broadcast media are an integral part of the government. But the Russians face a challenge and a dilemma. Satellite communications poses a serious threat to their traditional insularity. If the Soviet Union is to follow its declaration of working harmoniously toward detente with the West, sooner or later it will have to open its doors to unrestricted communication from the rest of the world.

Japan

Television has scarcely gained a foothold in the developing countries of Asia where economic and political problems make a viable system impossible at this early stage. But Japan is a remarkable phenomenon. It has one of the most successful and most popular television systems in the world, and one which in many ways rivals the expertise of the United States. In technology, it may even threaten to surpass the formidable achievement of this country. The Japanese public broadcasting system, known as NHK, is probably the most technically advanced in the world. A highly computerized arrangement makes it possible, with remarkable technical proficiency, to air several hundred programs each week—and every program controlled by an expertly programmed computer. It is also possible to employ the computer to find film sequences on virtually any subject at a moment's notice. Japanese broadcasters have reason, indeed, to be proud of their technical prowess.

But Japanese television relies on more than technology. Software is also important, and NHK is considered by many critics to present the most proficient public television to be found in any country in the world. There are two main channels, and each is on the air for 18 hours daily. One channel concentrates on public or educational television; the other presents programming of a varied general nature. As in the United States, almost all of the country is within reach of Japanese television and, again like America, color TV is dominant. In addition to operating television channels, NHK also operates radio networks—both AM and FM.

Typical of the ETV offerings are varied programs for in-school use, as well as public TV offerings in the afternoon for home viewing. On the general channel (channel I) there are innumerable popular entertainment productions. Historical drama, presented with a flourish, gains a large audience, as do the enormously popular "samurai" plays. But in the area of news and public affairs, NHK predominates. This organization has correspondents in major countries all over the globe and is literally an international, as well as national, news gathering phenomenon. The correspondents and newsmen, however, are not personalities as in this country and the recent trend in the United States toward "happy news" on many stations would be rejected by the utterly sober Japanese presentation.

Unlike many other countries, both in Europe and Asia, Japanese television offers a number of discussion programs and includes at least one segment weekly of presentations by representatives of the political parties. Access for viewers is also made available, where public viewpoints can be aired. And, most significant, particularly in view of the fact that the Congress in Washington is considering permission for television coverage, the debates of the Japanese Parliament are carried in their entirety. The one interesting aspect of NHK news is its persistence in avoiding controversial issues. News "analysis" means a simple, sober, balanced presentation, without advocacy and without commentary. There is no need, apparently, for a Japanese version of the FCC Fairness Doctrine.

Funding for the system comes primarily from license fees, although the commercial programs charge for advertising time which runs to 10 minutes per hour in Japanese "golden time"—which is analogous to primetime in the United States. Indeed, one of the major reasons for the success of NHK is the enormous income from license fees, running to almost $300 million. Viewers in Tokyo have a choice of seven channels—identical to New York—and the other cities of Japan each boasts six channels. Commercial television, from the start, was closely aligned with newspaper interests—another interesting comparative feature at a time when the FCC is trying to eliminate cross-ownership of newspapers and broadcast properties. And more than four-fifths of Japanese programming is not imported, but originates in Japan. Program content is rarely, if ever, interfered with by the government, which may account for the sexual permissiveness of many of the dramas and soap operas shown on the commercial channels. The pride of Japanese television is the NHK News, an organization overtly dedicated to fine public service and fiercely protective of its journalistic independence and integrity.

Evaluation

It is impossible to make a one-to-one comparison between foreign systems and broadcasting in the United States. The economics are radically different. Methods of control and operation also vary. Yet, despite the criticism leveled at the United States for overcommercialization and for "cultural imperialism," the fact remains that American programs enjoy enormous popularity throughout the world, which means that viewers everywhere still want to be entertained. The question remains, however, whether the popular programs being sent abroad offer the best or the "real" image of this country. Many vouchsafe that they do not. On the other hand, despite the excellence of public affairs broadcasting abroad, there is no disputing the fact that television—and indeed all mass media—in the United States enjoy an unparalleled and enviable freedom. Where, it may be asked, would a program like "The Selling of the Pentagon" be permitted to be aired freely? In what country would the Watergate scandal be so clearly and relentlessly exposed as it was in the United States? It is this freedom, along with the development of cable and public broadcasting—and the elevation of viewer taste for commercial TV as audiences demand higher standards—that gives American television its still unrealized potential.

14

Media and Minorities

THE TERM "MINORITY" is one of those connotative expressions that is both meaningful and confusing at the same time. We speak of a multiplicity of minorities in the American scene: cultural minorities, culturally deprived minorities, religious minorities. Minority frequently means roughly what those who use it intend it to mean. Furthermore, minorities are not cemented in hard and fixed stratified areas. There is considerable crossing of lines. An individual may be considered a minority group-member in one classification and not in another. Generally, however, minorities are those groups which do not enjoy the same privileges, do not have the same opportunities and are not accorded the same degree of power or, in the vernacular, "clout" as so-called majority groups. In the broadcasting media, for example, cultural minorities are those whose tastes are not given the same consideration by the program-makers as those majority audiences who are significant factors in the ratings and, therefore, in the economic success of the program.

The concern in this context is with media that are largely structured toward reaching minority publics, and particularly with what has been called "the black press." There are those who will resist this kind of classification as cultural stereotyping. From an empirical point of view, however, it is possible to establish distinct entities in the communications media, and to show that very real differences exist between majority and minority media. Magazines reach specific target audiences. Many books are not published for the vast majority of readers, but for particular groups. And the newspaper, too, is not always intended to reach all readers on all levels of society. In addition to general circulation newspapers, there are many daily papers, available in large cities with heterogeneous populations, which offer news and comment for a variety of special audiences—Greek, Jewish, Hispanic-American, Irish and German, among others. The black press directs most of its coverage and orientation to the concerns of black readers. A comparison with the white-oriented newspaper reveals quite graphically how each treats hard news, analyses and investigative reporting in terms of the interest of the readers. There are areas, of course, where both majority and minority coalesce in terms of coverage, but on most topics it is possible to show a distinct difference in the way news is covered and processed by the media "gatekeepers" who decide ultimately how a subject will be approached and presented. This is true equally of the broadest media as it is of the print media, but less so of film.

Historical Perspective

The black press was once believed to be "the greatest single power in the Negro race." That evaluation was made some years ago when the blacks were almost totally disenfranchised. In the 1960s—and continuing inexorably, despite some regressive steps taken since the Supreme Court decision on "equal rights" in 1954—the influence of black Americans increased, and this tendency to break down false barriers and distinctions has been clearly evidenced in the mass media, particularly in television commercials and in many television programs where blacks no longer are relegated to shameful stereotypes.

The first black newspaper in this country, published in 1827—some 30 years before the Civil War—was printed, as might be expected, in protest against minority restrictions. It was aptly called *Freedom's Journal* and its appearance was largely of historical significance, since it certainly did not have the dramatic effect on public opinion of a special-interest paper like William Lloyd Garrison's *The Abolitionist,* a vigorously anti-slavery publication. Another publication, *The Ram's Horn,* which succeeded *Freedom's Journal* was instigated largely by a comment attributed to the editor of *The Sun*—that *"The Sun* shines for all white men, but never for the black man."* The early black newspapers were devoted more to specific grievances and less to news than the more professionally edited papers of today. Understandably, the crying need was for publicity to be given to acute social issues, such as the germination of the anti-slavery movement and to general opposition to the tendency toward what might be called "malign neglect" of the black people and their needs and aspirations for themselves as an integral part of American society.

Since the publication of *Freedom's Journal,* about 3,000 black newspapers have been printed. Few survived. Many went out of business because of lack of advertising, lack of facilities, circulation and readership. But some did survive and, with notable additions from the more "radical" or "black power" groups, are still in evidence in the Twentieth Century—*The Courier, The Defender, The Afro-American.* These, and others, may be called "black newspapers" because they are owned, published and edited specifically by and for blacks, and they are oriented and directed toward the continuing struggle for equal rights and opportunities for blacks in a majoritarian white society. The black papers, too, are based on a particular perception of the majoritarian white newspapers. This perception yields the conclusion that the white press had discriminated against blacks in its coverage of black America, both overtly and indirectly or implicitly, and that the white-dominated media—broadcast and print—have largely ignored the positive contributions of blacks to society, have concentrated on traditional negative stereotypes and have emphasized the involvement of blacks in crime and violence.

Black Papers in the 1970s

Criticism of the white press by blacks has been accompanied, since the 1960s, by equally excoriating condemnation of the so-called traditional black press. The "black power" movement has been impatient with the black newspapers, blaming their editors and publishers particularly for taking too placid a stand on crucial issues. The result has been the publication of a group of newspapers which are devoted less to hard news than to militant discussion of the necessary goals yet to be achieved by black citizens. These newspapers might be compared roughly to many of the "underground" white publications. They represent more of an ideological viewpoint than the conventional paper and they are patently partisan in purpose and content. Although economics plays a role in their publication, influencing opinion and galvanizing readers to action is their major thrust. Examples of these more militant publications are *Muhammad Speaks,* a weekly with a circulation of 100,000, and *Black Panther.* Conservative black leaders deplore many of these publications, but readership and circulation reveal that they have a formidable following.

The more conventional black press faces a number of serious dilemmas. Despite fairly large readership, problems are acute. Some of these problems extend from the rise of the broadcast media and have an effect parallel to the impact of television on many white publications. Other problems involve higher cost of printing, dearth of trained black journalists—certainly a challenge to schools and departments of journalism—and the continuing struggle to obtain advertising. The last poses a formidable problem, in view of the essential correlation among the news content of a paper, its circulation and its ability to obtain advertising. For a good many years, not only did white papers refuse black-oriented advertising, but the black press itself had difficulty securing ads from black business and industry. Few black editors will deny that they face discrimination by advertisers—white and, unfortunately, black as well. It was only in 1965 that a major department store finally ordered an ad in the *Amsterdam News* and, following this breakthrough, other advertisers hardly have broken down the doors to advertise in the black press. There is also a very real concern by the black press over competition offered on the part of white media for black journalists.

Thus, the black press, even in this period of black consciousness, is not a totally viable institution, although from a social standpoint it is a productive one. According to statistics from *Editor and Publisher,* the mid-1970s shows about 175 newspapers published by and for blacks, with a combined circulation of between three and four million. Major black newspapers include such publications as the *Amsterdam News* (New York), the *Afro-American* (Baltimore), the *Pittsburgh Courier* (Pittsburgh), *Chicago's Defender* (Chicago), and the *Sentinel* (Los Angeles). Several black newspaper chain-ownership arrangements are in operation, notably the Afro-American Newspapers, the Post group, and the largest and most powerful black press organization, the Robert S. Sengstacke papers. This group is comprised of such papers as the *Defender* and *Courier* chains, with publications in the large cities around the country.

The difficulties noted have made it impossible for black newspapers to sustain daily publication. In 1975, there were only two regularly printed dailies, the *Defender* and the *Daily World* (Atlanta) the latter, in fact, appears only four times a week. Most of the black press—traditional as well as the more politically oriented—is published weekly. Some papers are published regionally whereas they once had national circulation. But the magazine for black audiences has a large, if not spectacular, circulation and readership. Where such formidable national magazines as *Life* and *Look* were forced to discontinue publication, a magazine for black readers such as *Ebony* has a steady and loyal following.

A major criticism directed against black journalism concerns newspaper content. The purpose of much of the black press is to offer the black reader substance that the white majoritarian papers either cannot, or will not, cover: local news, society news, human-interest happenings germane to the interest of the black community. Yet, much of the traditional black press carries sensational headlines and stories and, because of a paucity of reporters and facilities, tends to use press releases uncritically. Thus, it is inevitable that many black readers, while still maintaining pride in black newspapers, also turn to white publications for news and opinion. The unfortunate fact is, however, that the white majoritarian newspaper ignores perfectly legitimate news about blacks and tends to perpetuate negative stereotypes by an emphasis on crime and violence. And the broadcast media have been scored for engaging in the same practice in their coverage of the black community.

Direction of Black Newspapers

The black newspaper faces a paradoxical situation. With black pride and consciousness at high levels, and blacks receiving belated recognition as community citizens, the traditional newspapers do not reflect sufficiently that new sense of identification. The reasons have been noted—economic problems, insufficient numbers of trained writers and editors, lack of advertising, competition from the more militant papers, and radio and television. The audience is also becoming fragmented by the broadcast media and by the more strident voices of the "black power" movement. The tendency, however, seems ultimately to be in the direction of a more news-oriented paper, largely because of the need to obtain advertising dollars. Profit motive may yet triumph over militancy and protest and, while the revolutionary movement may draw sympathizers, economic reality will tend to direct the black newspaper toward a more traditional approach to editorial and news content. But the competition is not over, by any means, and the "establishment" black press still faces a formidable challenge from the militant group. In the long run, it can be anticipated that the reader, along with the advertiser, will determine the direction of the black newspaper in America. For what the black newspaper contributes, and the way in which it serves society, is essentially determined by the receiving audience. There is growing evidence that black readers want coverage of phenomena not included in the white majoritarian newspapers, and that they respond to such coverage in terms of its emphasis and evaluation on the basis of the black experience.

Broadcasting Media

Network television in the 1970s shows increasingly greater recognition and acceptance of blacks, even in those areas of the country where anti-black bias was once intense. Black models appear in major commercials, and programs have evolved from token roles for blacks to successful full-time series. This is, of course, a belated and overdue development, for the broadcast media were not distinguished for an honest and forthright portrayal of blacks any more than was the Hollywood film industry. After 1965, however, blacks began to appear sporadically in commercials and in minor, but nonstereotyped roles, in regular series. Black correspondents also were assigned to cover news events. It is true that, in 1965, a very small percentage of blacks was used in commercials and those commercials were carefully selected, with some of the major prestige industries and institutions notable by their abstention. Several factors provided incentive for an increase in the employment of black performers in television. The Kerner Commission Report pointed up the size of the black audience—a fact which is constantly substantiated by demographic studies. Black leaders and organizations, such as The National Urban League, supplemented by the efforts of such groups as The United Church of Christ, presented irrefutable evidence of the disenfranchisement of the blacks in the broadcasting industry. The result of several years of pressure by civil rights groups also was being felt. Above all, however, was the factor most powerful with television producers—that audiences accepted and enjoyed the talent of black actors and actresses. There is some indication, too, that the various electronic unions, once accused of delaying tactics, have now recognized the right of blacks to full and equal employment.

By the mid-1970s, there were successful program series on the air on a continuing basis and starring or featuring black talent. Blacks in commercials were no longer an innovative social phenomenon. This, of course, was a delayed recognition of the millions of black citizens who watch television and buy the products advertised on this medium. But, from a sociological viewpoint, nagging questions remained and were being asked by thoughtful critics of the media. Both black and white critics have questioned the maintenance of stereotypes in many new television programs. Were programs with black performers and so-called black "themes" simply transplants of the white image of reality? Were blacks still being subtly stereotyped? Or, was the black experience finally being revealed in its own environment, on its own terms and in its fullest integrity? Thus, while there were more blacks on the screen, there were still problems of how they could be represented in a way that would preserve their identity. Some white critics still maintained, for example, that the "Amos 'n' Andy" syndrome was being subtly perpetuated. Others were concerned that television was still dealing with the black experience largely in terms of "bad news," covering not the positive aspects of the black community, but stressing militant activities, drugs, ghettos, crime and violence.

Blacks, in other words, were still being showcased on the media as just that—blacks—instead of as integrated personalities, no different except for color, from whites. Thus, this recognition of a black community, of a so-called black "sub-culture," was healthy in one aspect and deleterious in another. In a revolution of rising expectations, how would the black child react, for example, to programs, products, advertisements and ideas which stem basically from white perceptions of the world and which do not cohere with the black experience of reality? The problem still remained, therefore, to preserve black integrity and yet to stress the equal role of the blacks in terms of their unique contribution to a democratic and pluralistic society.

Florynce Kennedy, a black attorney, is quoted as claiming that the broadcast media still foster images of a world where white power is supreme, where the black participates vicariously and by sufferance: "Television feeds the frustrations and angers of the black masses by showing them a way of life that they may never enjoy, a world from which they are forever barred . . . TV, by excluding the Negro from most of its programs, helps to reinforce the image of rejection."

This was probably true five or ten years ago. It is less so today. The problem is not any longer one of simply offering greater opportunity to blacks, but of developing concepts and images with which both the white *and* black audiences can identify. For it is generally recognized that television, perhaps to a greater degree than the other media, can provide the catalytic agent for developing and cementing a genuinely fruitful communication between blacks, as well as between black and white. More black faces on television are productive from a social standpoint only to the extent that, by fostering understanding, they bring about a greater sensitivity of the problems of the inner-city, an amelioration of conflict and a greater degree of effective communication.

In the Fall of 1975, the first black UHF television station began operating in Detroit, and several major advertisers committed at least a quarter of a million dollars in advertising to the station. The establishment of a black television station on an Ultra High Frequency channel marked a major step forward in providing programming of relevance to black audiences.

National Urban League Study

Both radio and television have black broadcasting organizations. A subsidiary of the Mutual Broadcasting Corporation, for example, is The Mutual Black Network, with offices in Washington and New York. There is also a National Black Network, with headquarters in New York and an affiliation of more than 70 AM and FM stations. Black radio is becoming increasingly important as the blacks also find themselves positions in the white-oriented broadcast systems.

A study by the National Urban League research group in the late 1960s offers interesting insights and information, although it was necessarily limited in scope. This was a "pilot study" of "coverage of minority group affairs in the New York news media, and the black evaluation" of the the data available. Working together on the report were representatives of the Graduate School of Journalism, Columbia University Bureau of Applied Social Research, and the National Urban League.

Three New York City television stations, identified with ABC, CBS and NBC cooperated by producing film clips. The study, incidentally, involved both print and broadcast media. In the TV medium, four channels (2, 4, 5 and 7) were monitored for a four-week period, five days each week from Monday through Friday. Some of the findings were not unanticipated. For example, those channels carrying the greatest number of hard news stories also had more items which could be classified as "minority." The areas covered were coded as follows: Education, Employment, Crime, Militant and Protest groups, Poverty, Politics, Police Relations, Welfare, Drug Addiction, Positive Action of Whites, General Minority Problems, Housing, other Cultural Areas, Sports, and Black GIs.

By comparison to the print media, the researchers found a greater diversity of coverage among the television stations. And, in coding the findings, effort was made to determine the emphasis placed on racial and ethnic conflict as against racial cooperation and harmony. On what might be called a modified semantic differential scale, it was certainly plain that each of the four channels which was monitored placed greater emphasis on coverage of conflict than of harmony, again bringing to mind McLuhan's thesis that "bad" news tends to overwhelm the good.

As for exposure of blacks as compared with all persons in minority areas, it was clear from the findings that the black community had fewer opportunities to state its case than the nonblack groups. But the stations also made an effort, in covering minority affairs, to avoid specific reference to color in discussing the personalities involved. And, in general, the researchers found that there appeared to be greater "flexibility" in television coverage of minority events than in the print media.

Finally, an effort was made to ascertain the views of what the Report calls the "black influential" on both television and print as a source of news. The respondents watched television news regularly and rather extensively throughout the week, and also were heavy users of both black newspapers and magazines. It was significant, however, that they depended also on non-black media to "round out their picture of what's going on." Generally, the respondents indicated that most black influentials (64 per cent) felt that television was the best source of news, superior to radio and newspapers. But, while television may have been most interesting as a source of news, most of the respondents ultimately depended on the newspaper—a finding which seems to be at variance with nationwide media preference studies reported by the Roper organization which cites television as the most credible and the medium of choice. As in the Roper reports, this more modest study, however, also reported that respondents found television the most interesting and believable of four media choices— newspapers, television, radio and magazines.

Based on complaints recorded in the Kerner Commission report (National Advisory Commission on Civil Disorders), three questions were posed with respect to television coverage of the black community. The questions are implicit in these replies:

1. Four-fifths felt that television was not doing a fair job of showing the problems of life in the black community.
2. Three-fourths felt that television had not done a "fair job" of revealing the difficulty of being black in the United States.
3. Three-fourths also did not feel that television adequately showed an understanding of "black culture, thought or history."

Thus, the problem of the role of blacks in the media, as well as the coverage of blacks by the media, while improving constantly, is still in need of further organized effort. To tell the story of the black community requires more blacks as reporters and writers, as well as more blacks on camera in sequences that are non-violent and affirmative. There is still a perception of the black community and the black experience as phenomena which are out of the milieu of the white-dominated institutional power structure. But the portents are clearly positive—as the 1970s merge into the 1980s, it is possible to predict with confidence that the black community will receive more adequate and more honest coverage by all the media and that perceptions will change to an acceptance of the black community as an integral and creative entity in the social, political and economic life of this country.

Special Interest Publics

Minority pressures on the print and broadcasting media have extended, over the past decade, to embrace a larger—and still growing—number of special interest groups, each either demanding access or insisting that the media present, and be responsive to, their particular bias or objective. Consumerism, a necessary and healthy phenomenon, also has its negative aspects in that some special pressure publics have used this particular axe to grind as a way of forcing broadcast licensees to air frequently narrow and parochial points of view.

The basic problem, of course, is one of social frustration, a sense of being shut out by failing to gain access to media; or of anger because the media did not cover a particular position as a result of news judgment. A strong advocate of direct access, such as Professor Jerome Barron, has urged that access for special interests and for "have-not" groups be mandated by the Federal Courts, if necessary. This is a debatable question, but what is more acute is the growth of irresponsible consumerism. There is no doubt that the work of Ralph Nader and his organization and of John Gardner's "Common Cause" have been a powerful and exemplary influence in making the needs of the consumer articulate and in exposing social and economic abuses that have disenfranchised and exploited the consumer.

Considerable criticism has been leveled at the government regulatory agencies for failure to protect the consumer. Nader, for example, has accused the agencies of being "too cozy with the industries they oversee." Not omitted from these critiques were the Federal Trade Commission, concerned with truth in advertising, and the Federal Communications Commission which functions to regulate broadcasting. One commission chairman resigned because it was revealed that he had accepted favors from an independent broadcasting organization. But the FCC, like other agencies, is also subject to pressures from government, as well as from industry. It is a creature of the Congress, its appointees are political and it has no genuine legislative or judicial authority. Nor have its decisions been immune—perhaps fortunately—from review by the courts. One particularly significant example of consumer complaint was the case of minority discrimination practices at Station WLBT in Jackson, Mississippi. The complaint was that the station had totally neglected the sizeable black community in its programming. Nevertheless, despite ample documentation, the FCC renewed the station's license, but the Courts reproved the Commission and the decision was reversed.

This case was a valid one, symptomatic of too many other situations where minority interests are neglected. But the case ultimately had its negative feedback, as well. The stage was set, not only for legitimate license challenge, but also for the abuse of the right of challenge. The Fairness Doctrine was invoked by John Banzhaf III to convince the FCC that cigarette advertising ought to be offset by anticigarette "spots." And it certainly was not anticipated that another result of license challenge right would be a serious move toward "counteradvertising" which, in the opinion of former FCC Commissioner, Lee Loevinger, would not only be impossible to establish equitably, but which would also have formidable political implications. In addition, various minority groups seized upon the license challenge opportunity as both a threat and a wedge to coerce stations into meeting their demands—whether those demands were justified or not. And licensees, wishing to avoid expensive and time-consuming legislation, found it expedient to accede to many outrageous demands, in addition to legitimate ones.

Thus minority consumerism, excellent in principle, is not always so in fact. In some instances, for example, several minority groups presented *identical* 25-page agreements to radio and television stations throughout the country. The substance of many identical complaints was that the programming was not "relevant"—which was not defined, except in terms of the goals of the particular group involved, not of the broad spectrum of the public. In addition, the complaints exceeded even the hazy performance standards set by the FCC. In one case, a group insisted that 40 per cent of the total program "mix" be "relevant" to the needs of that group—and the judge of relevancy was to be the particular special interest public involved.

Thus, minority consumerism—necessary and affirmative in most cases—also raises certain fundamental questions about the obligation of the broadcaster and his service to the public, some of which still await answers. For example, is programming for ethnic minorities relevant only if it has "a direct ethnic connotation?" Should stations be mandated to communicate separately to various minorities in terms of their numbers in the population? Would the viewing public accept such programming fragmentation? Would radio and television still function as media of *mass* communications?

These and other questions are part of a continuing examination of the role of broadcasting in a pluralistic and democratic society—a role which has to achieve the difficult objective of dealing fairly with some while meeting with equal fairness the needs of all.

15

Public Relations
and Advertising

THIRTY OR 40 YEARS AGO, public relations was spoken of as the newest profession. In fact, persuasive communication—informational and propaganda messages purveyed for the express purpose of influencing public opinion and galvanizing people to action—is almost as old as human communication. Indeed, there are those who speak of public relations as the oldest profession, because man as communicator—as encoder of messages—has always tried to influence the behavior of other men, both individually and in groups.

The idea of public relations as a new phenomenon, however, probably stems from the process by which this informational and persuasive mode of communication has slowly become both ubiquitous and institutionalized. It is possible briefly to trace this development of public information activities through its historical evolution into the highly technical and sophisticated form in which public relations now functions in a world of immediate and instantaneous global communication. Man the communicator is also man the persuader, and the process of attempting to influence the attitudes, opinions and actions of others goes on all of the time, sometimes subtly or implicitly and more often explicitly. The Roman Empire had its Acta Diurna which the Caesars distributed throughout the length and breadth of the Empire as a rudimentary organ of propaganda. In the middle ages, the Church employed propaganda in its classic and original usages for the propagation of faith. Missionaries communicated persuasive messages to people of diverse languages, beliefs and backgrounds.

This communication was, of course, far more naïve and different, both in quality and quantity, from the persuasive communication which engulfs us for so many hours of our Twentieth Century day. But it was a kind of rudimentary public information, designed to create a consensus of thought and action. Public relations was brought to its present highly refined state by a number of factors, some of which pre-date this period but nevertheless were most significant. One factor was the development of national languages. Another most vital development was that of the printing press and of the newspaper which served as a spur to literacy and to political democratization, and which provided a medium for the mass distribution of informational and persuasive messages. The first major function of the press in America, for example, was to provide business and commercial information to the merchants of New England—hence, advertising very soon became one way of paying for the printing and distribution of the Colonial newspaper.

Above all, however, there was the inevitable growth of the power of public opinion—as significant a factor as the development of media and one which interacted with the rise of the media of mass communication. Public opinion functions best in democratic or libertarian states, but that it is also important to authoritarian governments is evidenced by the use of wall posters in Maoist China, and by the long-standing Soviet concept of the press originally articulated by Lenin—that the media are to function as the voice of the proletariat and are to "agitate" the peasantry to embrace the proletarian revolution. Thus it was the rise and importance of public opinion, paralleled by the invention of media both to reach and to express public opinion, which became vital factors in the growth of the public relations function. Media —the newspaper, magazine, radio and television—along with other modalities such as film, slides, videotape, posters, brochures and direct mail promotion—provided the necessary ingredients for the evolution of both public relations and advertising into highly specialized communicative arts. There was rudimentary coverage of the Civil War and even of the Spanish-American War (despite the hundreds of correspondents). But by World War I, this government, as well as both ally and enemy, was acutely aware of the importance of the psychological or propaganda aspects of warfare. The Germans, in particular, used the motion picture as a propaganda tool through their War Press Division. In the United States, President Wilson wisely appointed George Creel as chief government information officer, and Creel approached his problem with a sense of the needs of the press and public in mind, weighing each against the need to restrict information which might be of aid to the enemy. Creel's brilliant and ethical public information was watched with interest by such pioneers in public relations as Ivy Lee and Edward L. Bernays who saw clearly the possibilities inherent in public information as a tool in influencing public opinion.

In World War II which, largely because of the growth of radio, became a war in which propaganda was a vital instrument, President Franklin D. Roosevelt—also with great wisdom—established such agencies as the Office of War Information under the impeccably honest direction of Elmer Davis. Once again, the power of the media to persuade and to inform was established, along with additional knowledge about the process of communication as persuasion. By 1945, therefore, public relations activities began to flourish as a "new" profession, because practitioners set up independent offices, people who needed exposure to the public hired press agents, and the corporate institution found in public relations a valuable tool in a variety of areas—employee relations, government relations, stockholder relations and, above all, press relations. All these, and more, became subsumed under the concept of public relations.

It is probable that Edward L. Bernays was the first to use the term "public relations." Bernays was certainly one of the earliest professional practitioners. But the founder of modern public relations and publicity techniques was the late Ivy Lee who, like many of his successors and emulators, began as a newspaperman. Lee went into a business called publicity, but what he practiced was more than the mere attention-getting device of achieving a client's name in print. Lee, representing the Pennsylvania Railroad, set a pattern for direct, candid and full disclosure to the press. To that point, the attitude of many business executives had been one apocryphally attributed to Commodore Vanderbilt, head of the New York Central Railroad, "the public be damned." It was this arrogant disregard for the public's rights and opinions which is the antithesis of sound public relations, and it was Lee who transformed publicity and propaganda into that high level public relations which develops a healthy respect for public opinion. Subsequently, after the damaging disclosure of Ida Tarbell's history of the Standard Oil Company, Lee undertook to build a new "image" for one of the first of the great American tycoons, John D. Rockefeller. The significant aspect of Lee's contribution is that he did not attempt to whitewash or explain away deeds which were not in the public interest, but rather to confront a problem in a way that would earn public approval and a positive press. This is the essence of sound public relations. And Lee's pattern was followed, developed and refined by the most successful and eminent practitioners—Bernays, Pendleton Dudley, Carl Byoir, among many others.

A comment should be made, at this juncture, of a special breed of publicist known as the press agent. These individuals are less interested in concepts, images and ideas—less concerned about earning good will—than in getting the client's name mentioned in print. Their work is patterned on the brilliant exploitation tactics of P.T. Barnum who devised ingenious gimmickry in order to publicize those who retained his services. Press agents are specialists in concocting stunts and other varied exploitation devices that will intrigue editors to the point of covering and running a story and/or picture in the newspaper. Exposure is the important objective, and the press agent performs a valuable function to those who are in need of publicity—performers, authors, and even political figures. But public relations is not press agentry and, in some conservative institutions, is actually the antithesis of both press agentry and publicity. The objective is, rather, "good deeds in the public interest," earned by a record of service to the public.

Public Relations Today

By the 1970s it was estimated that more than 100,000 individuals practice public relations in this country. In addition, PR is growing abroad—in England, France, Japan and other countries where it is practiced internally and where many of the multi-national corporations have established overseas departments. PR men practice in various areas. Many are internal company executives, heading a staff of sub-specialists in publicity, advertising and promotion. Many operate as private, special counsel to clients and, of these, some specialize in specific aspects of the field, such as financial public relations. These practitioners come from many segments of the communications spectrum. Some are former newspapermen. Some go into PR directly from journalism schools. And others get their training in industry and gravitate toward the public relations department.

For a number of reasons, and despite its roots in history, public relations is very much a technique of the Twentieth Century. The reasons for this are clear. The practice of effective PR presupposes the availability of media capable of carrying messages to large audiences. Mass media, such as the newspaper, magazine, motion picture, radio and television have this capability. A second factor is a relatively free and competitive economy. Because many businesses and other institutions must compete for public support and approval, each finds it necessary to disseminate persuasive communication to those segments of the public upon whom their activities impinge and whose good will the company needs in order to function effectively in a competitive environment. Thus, presence of media and competition for public affirmation coalesce to make public relations a necessary and productive form of communication. Indeed, the media themselves engage in vast advertising and promotional campaigns because of the power and reach of public opinion. And this power is another reason for the practice of contemporary public relations. The past two decades have seen an enormous respect for the opinion of the public. Presidents avidly study public opinion polls, and many organizations now specialize in conducting surveys of various kinds for organizations—employee attitude studies, market testing of products, and, indeed, studies of public opinion on a wide variety of areas of interest to press and public, from school busing to women's lib and homosexuality. Never in history has public opinion been so carefully probed and dissected as in this period of mass persuasion.

Public relations, in fact, has become institutionalized by the establishment of a major national organization for practitioners, the Public Relations Society of America. This organization, along with the International Public Relations Association and The American College Public Relations Association, has done important work in raising standards, establishing ethical principles and weeding out the shady practitioners. The attaining of membership is a rigid process and requires both background and high recommendations, as well as an examination to be admitted. And, once admitted, members must adhere to the

Code of Professional Standards set up by PRSA. These include, in part:

1. Fair dealing towards clients and employers, members of PRSA and the public.
2. A regard for the public welfare.
3. Adhering to standards "of accuracy, truth, and good taste."
4. Safeguarding the confidences of clients and employers.
5. Manifesting a regard for "the integrity of channels of public communication."

It was Walter Lippmann, a journalist-philosopher with a profound understanding and respect for public opinion in a democracy, who stated with unusual prescience that the press could not be everywhere at all times. Therefore, Lippmann concluded, the ethical and reputable publicist is a useful source of news, even though much of the news purveyed by PR men may have a self-serving aspect on behalf of the client. And this observation by Lippmann has been substantiated over the past 50 years, by a mutual respect that has developed between the able public relations practitioners and the media. Alert and knowledgeable PR men seek more than space in print or time on the air. They develop a genuine reciprocal relationship with the press by providing a constant service in the way of useful information. As Lippmann also implied, the remoteness of institutions from the public which they serve, makes direct contact impossible and, therefore, the publicist serves a useful function as a kind of catalytic agent.

In his classic volume, *Public Opinion,* first published in 1922, Lippmann wrote: "The development of the publicity man is a clear sign that the facts of modern life do not spontaneously take a shape in which they can be known. They must be given a shape by somebody, and since in the daily routine reporters cannot give a shape and facts, and since there is little disinterested organization of intelligence, the need for some formulation is being met by individual parties."

Lippmann's analysis was both incisive and predictive at a time when contemporary public relations was in its formative stages. The PR practitioner is a catalyst, an intermediary between the institution and its public environment. The information specialist, of course, is motivated primarily by considerations of the institution which he or she represents. Out of this motivation has grown a considerable suspicion of public relations as Machiavellian propaganda. Questions of ethics have arisen as to the probity of the PR specialist and his identification with special interests. It is clear, of course, that those who are retained to purvey information must represent the basic interest of the client. But ethical considerations dictate that sound public relations demands a recognition of the need to identify the objectives of the client with the interest of the public. Good will is one objective of public relations. But good will, as contemporary PR conceives of it, must be buttressed by a sound regard for service to the public.

There is also pragmatic justification for ethical public relations. It works. The press and other media learn quickly to distinguish between the honest public information specialist—a genuine catalyst—and the charlatan. And, in the long run, the public also tends to reject shoddy service, no matter what effort is made to gloss it over with a patina of spurious claims of public interest. Ultimately, the best public relations men convince their management or clients that sincere identification with the needs of the publics involved is not only justified by good business, but very often by service to the media, it enhances the public's right to know.

Public Opinion

It is evident that public relations deals with an amorphous phenomenon called "public opinion." During the past two or three decades, this country has developed an almost uncanny mystique about opinion, so much so that few major decisions are made either by government or business without soundings of the climate of opinion. Public opinion studies have generated a corps of highly trained specialists, with specific background in economics and statistics, communications, psychology, sociology and political science. Advertising agencies employ research departments for various kinds of testing of products and ideas. Government officials, beginning with the President, keep a constant surveillance of the public opinion surveys of such organizations as Harris and Roper, among others. Corporations make studies of employee and stockholder opinion, by questionnaires and interviews and also may undertake content analysis of the mass media. Educational institutions, since the 1960s, have solicited student opinion before implementing projected policies.

Why this absorption in public opinion when even the most avid pollster will admit that surveys are not definitive and that very often they can be grossly misleading? The answer is that public opinion studies have been correct often enough to warrant taking them seriously. Furthermore, without some analysis of opinion, the public relations practitioner has virtually no guidance at all. Soundings of opinion provide, therefore, an important barometer and direction finder and enable the PR man to develop a viable "two-way street" relationship between the institution and the public upon which it depends for both sales and good will. In addition, public opinion research not only delineates various possibilities by revealing what the public thinks about various problems, but also reveals areas of ignorance—what the public does not know. Too often, PR and advertising campaigns are undertaken at a great outlay of time, effort and money only to reveal belatedly that the public did not react because of ignorance, rather than apathy. In other words, studies in public opinion often indicate where a need for public information exists, but has not been fulfilled. At other times, preliminary surveys will reveal negative opinions. A case in point is that of a major international corporation which blithely made plans to build oil refineries in a quiet New England area, only to be told—after considerable money had been spent—that the community did not want and would not countenance the environmental changes that would have resulted from the project. A study of community opinion would not only have indicated this position in advance, but of more importance, would have given the company information which might have helped to get the project approved.

Public opinion studies are, therefore, usually a necessary and productive first step in a public relations campaign. This may be called the phase of analysis. Once the information specialist has received the results of a preliminary survey, the findings must be evaluated in a second phase, that of interpretation. What the findings show suggests a third phase, that of implementation, or proceeding to develop plans in accordance with the expressed opinions of the public. And this leads to the final phase, that of action, in which measures are taken to develop an informative program by the skillful use of the media as conduits to the publics involved. Too often, unfortunately, difficulties result—as in the case of the oil company in New England—because management tends to demand immediate results via publicity and advertising without concern for the preliminary phases.

Most public relations research attempts to discover what people think and how they might act under certain circumstances. This information provides useful grist for internal implementation and external action and is, therefore, a foundation for a sound public relations campaign. As has been noted, many variables enter the process. Unexpected changes in the climate of opinion often occur. The data are not always accurate. Opinions are not firm and fixed. It is difficult to construct a so-called "objective" questionnaire and even more difficult to conduct a personal interview. Despite these problems, research is an invaluable tool. Internally, it reveals opinions by employees, management manpower, dealers and suppliers. Externally, it offers valuable information from such interests as the consumer and stockholder, as well as from the press itself. Research experts use various methods at costs ranging from a modest few hundred dollars to as much as $100,000. Companies maintain suggestion boxes for employees, or send questionnaires to employees which are answered anonymously. Letters from various publics are codified carefully. Media content is analyzed. Probability samples are prepared in which a demographically selected microcosm is studied to reveal the opinions of a larger universe—as in the case of the A. C. Nielsen studies on audience ratings.

Because public opinion studies have become sophisticated and complex, owing to techniques developed by social and behavioral scientists, they are best undertaken by organizations which are trained to engage in surveys. It is the findings—and their interpretation, implementation and action—which directly involve the public relations function. All of the information obtained from surveys contributes significantly to the necessary background of the public information specialist and prepare him to deal with a complicated communications environment in which the public and its opinions has become acutely significant.

Most effective public relations practitioners would agree that public opinion polling is both useful and necessary. Surveys reveal what people think and often why they think or choose as they do. They help to make latent opinions manifest. They may be used in creating consensus through the means of mass communication, especially where it is found that no genuine consensus exists. Frequently survey information is helpful in reconciling apparently irreconcilable differences, as in a capital-labor dispute. In terms of function, public relations practitioners must be aware of the fact that, in dealing with public opinion, they are confronting more often than not a highly volatile and competitive environment. The same public may be subjected to many surveys and its affirmative support and action are certainly solicited by many competing entities. How a public will act, in the long run, depends not only on how cogently the practitioner has interpreted the findings, but on how skillfully the PR program is promulgated by means of the press and the other mass media. Opinions are expressed on issues that are implicitly or explicitly controversial. Sound public relations functions by reconciling differences as well as by delineating clearly areas of competitive choice. Successful PR almost invariably suggests a direction to follow or a mode of action which should be taken, based on the results of public opinion studies.

The Pragmatism of Public Relations

The function of public relations in action is determined, in large part, by certain operational factors. The practitioner must understand very clearly the nature of the problem involved or the goal sought by the client. Second, the kind of client involved is of prime consideration. Public relations usually functions in four areas—institutions, products, individuals, and ideas. Institutions are of various kinds—educational, business, government, public service and professional, among others. Products are manufactured and distributed by business institutions and are brought to the attention of the public by a combination of advertising, promotion (such as direct mail) and publicity. Individuals retain PR counsel to develop a public "image" or to keep their name and/or picture before the public by engaging in activities that make news for the media. "Ideas" are those concepts that various organizations develop and for which they attempt to win public support—religious (Hari Krishna), public interest (Common Cause), political ("Democracy," "Communism").

Finally, public relations campaigns necessarily must be determined by the accessibility of media. In some cases, the objective is to avoid publicity. In others, every effort may be made to produce as many press clippings as possible, as well as coverage on radio and television. Unfortunately, publicists too often do not understand the nature of news and the result is that they put out releases or arrange press conferences or interviews which lack a sound "news peg" and are therefore rejected by editors. In the action area, as in research, the public relations man must understand and fulfill the needs of the editors with whom he must deal. Publicity will only be used if it is newsworthy. But a publicist who has achieved a record of constant and helpful year-round service to the editors will stand a better chance of succeeding than those who turn up only when they are in urgent need of coverage. Editors, like other publics, form value judgments and have opinions of the PR men with whom they deal.

Public relations executives usually are successful, too, when they have developed a clear idea of what it is they want to achieve on behalf of the institution, product, individual or idea which they represent. This grows out of the development of a sound management philosophy, a concept of what the institution represents, what it wants from press and public, how it proposes to go about earning support and good will. To make these determinations, the PR executive must find the answers to certain fundamental questions. What kind of public opinion prevails? How can it be improved? What are the internal roadblocks to effective communication? What "image" does the institution employ with the media?

Regardless of how these questions are answered in terms of individual situations, certain broad objectives may be postulated as maintaining in all good public relations. Sound public information campaigns seek to develop a reputation for integrity, for service. Competition is also accompanied by social responsibility. Relations with employees, stockholders, legislative bodies and the press are candid and helpful, rather than obstructive. Above all, institutions which practice effective public relations develop close communication between management and other company echelons, between the staff and line functions. All departments usually will defer to the public relations executive in decisions that involve the media. Short term "hypo" press-agent campaigns are usually relegated in favor of sound, long-range programs. In the last analysis, public relations is fundamentally an expression of company or management philosophy. It can be used, of course, to make the worse appear the better reason.

It is most effective, however, when all phases—analysis, interpretation, implementation and action are coordinated, and when the objective is to earn a reputation for both ethics and responsibility by the skillful promulgation of sound service in the public interest.

Advertising

One of the spectacular differences between media in almost any country abroad and in the United States is the phenomenon of commercial advertising. The almost total immersion of the press and broadcast media in an advertising-dominated economy spells out the one clear distinction between the function of media in this country and in such foreign countries as Great Britain or France. Television and radio are totally supported by advertising in the United States. Most of the space in the newspaper is taken up by advertising, which has also supported the national magazine. Indeed, the only mass medium not paid for by advertising revenue is the motion picture. This reliance on advertiser support has resulted in some excoriating criticism of the media by a number of eminent critics in various disciplines, the most articulate of whom have been John Kenneth Galbraith and Arnold Toynbee. Professor Toynbee implied that the media distribute large quantities of frivolous material because of advertiser domination. Professor Galbraith is even more direct and acerbic. The money spent on advertising products could be spent better by allocating it to various social and ecological needs in the public sector. At best, advertising may move goods, but in so doing it creates spurious needs and develops an unhealthy keeping-up-with-the-Jones' society. The public, Professor Galbraith insists, do not need to be prodded into an artificial demand for products they do not need and which, indeed, they might be better off without. The advertising industry is the cause of these false and unnecessary public needs, and the result is a value system that is unrealistic and that synthesizes wants through manipulation and socially harmful methods of persuasive communication. In short, people do not need what they purport to need. Their false needs are spurred by a production-consumption syndrome that must constantly sell goods in order to keep the economy on the move. Advertising is the medium which stimulates these fabricated needs.

Yet, while advertising came into its own in the Twentieth Century and is now considered a billion-dollar industry and essential to a healthy economy, its value was known almost from the beginning of media in America. As soon as a merchant class developed, the early press became a vehicle for marketing commodities, particularly on the Eastern seaboard. The establishment of special mailing privileges by the Post Office also acted as a stimulus to publication and subsequently to advertising. By the beginning of the Twentieth Century, media were completely dependent on advertising. The beginnings of advertising in this country, however, did not involve the large, complex multi-million-dollar advertising agencies that exist today. In the Nineteenth Century, the editor sold space directly to the client, or advertiser, without benefit of an agent as catalyst. As advertising communications proved its value as a stimulus to sales, companies sought space in the newspapers and magazines, and the media began to depend basically on advertising revenue in order to function in a viable way. Eventually, the manifest need was for a middleman, or agent, whose business consisted of securing space. Prior to the establishment of the advertising agency as it now functions, the newspaper publishers established their own agents. These middlemen frequently represented many publications and solicited ads from potential space buyers.

Among the pioneers in advertising in this country three individuals are of historical importance. They are Volney B. Palmer, who set up a rudimentary advertising business in Philadelphia—probably the first of its kind; John Hooper, who opened a similar agency in New York; and George Rowell, who established an agency in Boston. These early advertising men worked essentially for, and with, the newspapers and magazines. They solicited ads from clients and placed them in the media. Eventually, the agents sold space to advertisers and then used the funds to buy space in the press. Rowell went a step further by reserving space in the press and then selling it in blocks to advertisers. This was welcomed by publishers, for they had no problem of selling space to clients, having sold it directly to the agent whose concern was to parcel it out to advertisers.

In 1875, what was to become one of America's most famous agencies was established by F. Wayland Ayer. The company is now known as N. W. Ayer & Son. As the agency became accepted, the publishers organizations recognized its usefulness as a middleman and agreed that agencies were entitled to a commission—a system which obtains today. At the present time, advertising not only handles billions of dollars of client business, but is in its own right a major institution—so much so that those who defend the agency against its critics maintain that advertising is utterly essential to a successful economy. Almost 5,000 advertising agencies exist, from the largest which handles the most wealthy and prestigious of clients to smaller organizations with modest accounts. The agency no longer exists merely to buy space. It offers a multiplicity of services which include variously: researching data (market research) media buying, layout and preparation of copy, devising of radio and television commercials and producing them on film or videotape, preparing and placing billboard ads, and direct mail campaigns. There are several large agencies which also offer a public relations service to clients, mostly in the form of promotional and publicity material. Professional advertising is well represented in an organizational sense by the 4-A's, the American Association of Advertising Agencies.

The largest amount which agencies allocate from their client's monies has been earmarked for the broadcast media—well over a billion dollars on an annual basis. Despite the inroads of television, however, the newspaper still manages not only to survive but also, in most instances, to turn in a profit. But the magazine market has been badly damaged. Siphoning of funds to television, along with higher production costs and increased postal rates, have given many national magazines rough sledding and such once spectacularly successful publications as *Life, Look* and *The Saturday Evening Post* have had to go out of business. Surviving are specialized publications—magazines that are skillfully designed to reach specific target audiences and which still offer good advertising outlets for those particular audiences.

Advertising is so deeply rooted in the economic scheme of things that, despite critics like Galbraith, it is not likely to change—except for the better. The pervasive presence of media, the rise of consumer organizations, the possibility of greater vigilance by the Federal Trade Commission, and even the growth of responsibility in the advertising industry, all tend to improve advertising standards and to eliminate false and deceptive messages. Advertising itself is competitive, and competition forces a healthy regard and respect for public opinion. And the public itself, growing in literacy and sophistication, has tended to respond more effectively to well-planned, literate ad campaigns than to old-fashioned, blatant "hard sell." Critics of advertising often admit, albeit reluctantly, that some of the best popular writing and art have been developed in the advertising agencies.

What the advertiser seeks on behalf of the client is, of course, circulation. In the print media this is provided by the Audit Bureau of Circulation. The broadcasters offer the ratings system of the A. C. Nielsen Co. or the American Research Bureau. What the sponsor (advertiser) buys is a concept known as CPM, or cost-per-thousand, which is the cost to the client involved in reaching each unit of a thousand readers or viewers. Obviously, in television in particular, the larger the audience, the higher the cost per thousand. Professional football, along with successful primetime programs, command the highest rate-card figures for commercial minutes, the cost going as high as $100,000 when the audience reaches 60 or 70 million viewers. So-called "buys" in the various media depend on many factors—the product to be advertised, the company involved and the public to be reached by the message. One most important factor is now the demographic concept—the conclusion that it is not so much how many are reached, how much "tonnage," but the *kind* and quality of audience—its age, economic situation, educational background, among other variables. The print media offer one advantage that television and radio simply cannot meet competitively. Newspapers can expand or contract according to the amount of advertising received on a given day. But television is locked into a fixed time pattern, with only a limited number of commercial messages possible in a half hour or hour format. At that, however, the clustering of commercials at station breaks has engendered some irritation both from viewers and critics.

Television and newspapers, along with special magazines, receive the major part of national advertising, but these are by no means the only media used—nor, in every case, the most effective. While the development of television radically changed the character of radio, this medium has survived and is even flourishing. Radio draws advertising in the morning and evening when many automobiles are on the highways, but again—as in the case of magazines—radio has changed its programs to meet specialized audience needs. Stations now concentrate on all-news or all-rock formats, and it is unfortunate, from the standpoint of cultural minorities that there is not a larger audience demand, and therefore more advertising available, for classical music stations.

Supplementing the conventional mass media are such related advertising areas as billboards and special promotion campaigns. Billboard advertising has drawn criticism, however, for what might be called aesthetic ecology. There are highly articulate critics who believe that these signs which beckon along every major highway simply deface the national beauty of the American scene. Billboards and posters were widely used prior to the development of mass media and, despite the print and broadcast media, are still a powerful advertising device. Even the efforts of one First Lady and a distinguished Senator did not succeed in doing away with the billboard advertising business. Those who sell billboard space, in fact, claim that it is a practical, useful and informative method of communication that not only provides information but also varies the monotony of driving and is, therefore, helpful to the motorist. In addition to billboard advertising, many product manufacturers supplement media campaigns by offering premiums, contests in those states which permit them, and other promotional devices to arrest public attention.

Advertising will always have its detractors. There is certainly a considerable point made by John Kenneth Galbraith when he contends that advertising creates wants for products with which we are surfeited and that many of the millions spent on it might better be used for public services. Other critics also have a tenable case in their conviction that advertising dominates the media and forces standards of taste downward instead of elevating them. Cultural minorities believe they are deprived of better fare on television simply because this medium must meet the needs of the mass market, and this mass culture syndrome tends to cheapen and vulgarize quality.

From another perspective, however, advertising must also be viewed with equal candor as a significant factor in a healthy economy. Media have developed and prospered on advertising revenues and have also enjoyed a freedom of information unparalleled anywhere in the world. Advertising competition, it is claimed, also results in lower prices to the consumer and better products. And, like the school, the home and the religious institutions, advertising has become a potent educational force, as well as an agency of social control. It would appear that the problem of advertising in the mass media is not so much one of what to do about this phenomenon, but to devise ways of using the creativity of advertising as a positive and constructive social force. This means that the advertising industry must continue to develop high standards of social responsibility and ethics. It means that the media must accept only advertising that meets their own high standards of excellence and honesty. And finally, it means that the consumer—the public—must be alert and aware to false claims and must also demand that advertising perform the essential function of contributing to intelligent choice and an informed public opinion.

16

The Impact
of New Technology

SEVERAL RECENT ADVANCES in media technology will ultimately alter the character and structure of both domestic and international communication systems. The burgeoning field of cable television has become all things to all parties concerned with this new communications technology. To the commercial broadcaster—networks as well as stations—cable is anathema, particularly the growing menace of pay cable and its presumed effect on national programming. To the members of the National Cable Television Association, cable looms both with potential and with frustration, the latter a result of what NCTA believes is foot-dragging and favorable tilting toward the commercial broadcasting interests by the Federal Communications Commission. To the FCC, cable presents an embarrassment, as well as a dilemma, the first growing out of the oft-repeated position of the Commission that free commercial broadcasting must not be vitiated; the second out of an obligation to regulate cable (even though it is not over-the-air broadcasting) with the interest of the public—especially minority publics—in mind. To the Congress, cable poses challenging questions of protection of copyrighted material, while the legislators ponder the fine points of the pending first new copyright law since 1909. And to the public, all of these factitious factors—along with numerous academic studies of the potential of cable—present a communications puzzle which, while dimly understood, in reality offers confusion worse confounded.

The problem was not always that tenacious. Indeed, the origin and first uses of community antenna television (CATV) were simple, pragmatically useful and comprehensible. They were to bring television signals to areas which could not receive them because of geographic obstacles in the path of transmission over the air—as in mountainous regions and rugged terrain in such areas as Oregon and Pennsylvania, for example. It was *after* these early experiments had proved successful that the full potential of cable was recognized. Today, one speaks no longer of cable TV, but rather of "broadband communications networks," of a multiplicity of social and economic uses, of "wired cities" and "wired nations." The ramifications became sufficiently complicated to result in a special study and report on cable to the President of the United States in 1974, undertaken by a Cabinet Committee on Cable Communications, and directed and presented by Clay T. Whitehead who then headed the Office of Telecommunications Policy, on behalf of the White House.

Cable's Historical Perspective

A brief summation of the development of cable, however, is germane to an understanding of the complex task undertaken by the Whitehead Committee. In terms of origin and evolution, community antenna television developed to meet two fundamental objectives. The first was to surmount natural or artificial obstacles to clear reception. Subsequently, CATV was employed in situations where the scarcity of channels made it expedient to bring in signals from distant areas. This latter function, incidentally, created some resistance from the local broadcasting stations in operation, which felt that the importation of distant signals would mean erosion of audiences.

In effect, the term "broadband communications network" is, indeed, more explicit than cable television, co-axial cable being an integral part of a broadband communications technology. Originally, CATV grew out of technical necessity in the 1940s. Those homes situated over mountainous terrain received signals by means of the co-axial cable which emanated from high receiving antennas. These antennas literally picked up signals from distant areas and relayed the clear image to those homes which paid an original installation fee for the service they received. This relatively simple and plausible use of cable was benign enough and elicited little concern, either from the government or from the commercial broadcasting interests. In the 1950s, the modest applications of cable continued, with approximately 70 small systems in operation and about 15,000 subscribers.

Had cable been aborted or stabilized at that point, probably no problems would have accrued. But it did not stop there. In the decade between 1960–1970, the subscribers grew to almost one million and the extant systems in operation proliferated to about 800—miniscule compared to commercial broadcasting, but nevertheless a dramatic and formidable absolute augmentation of services.

By 1970, the potential of cable was clearly evident to the FCC, the broadcaster, the cable operator and to the communications community. No longer was CATV a modest spur to bettering inadequate reception. It was recognized that cable, because it is *not* over-the-air broadcasting and therefore does not take up crowded spectrum space, had a capacity of at least 20 and, ultimately, many more operating channels. Through these rich channel availabilities, cable could bring a variety of experience to the receiving audiences—education, facsimile reproduction of news wire reports, two-way communications, processed data, weather, health, banking and stock reports, and a host of other material. Furthermore, the cable can reach almost anywhere, including areas not ordinarily accessible by over-the-air broadcasting—homes, schools, business offices, commercial institutions, hospitals. And, because it can carry two-way messages, it provides message encoding and decoding, along with significant feedback mechanism between senders and receivers.

Cable television, then, is no longer a modest experiment. Although its full growth and potential are still to be realized and may not be achieved for perhaps a decade, this new technology has already revealed sufficient capability to arouse the concern of the broadcaster, the interest of the public, and the attention of the Congress and the FCC. The latter, at the request of the Congress which oversees its activities, has been mandated to regulate the burgeoning cable industry, even though broadband communications is not broadcasting because it does not use the publicly owned airwaves. Originally, the Commission claimed no jurisdiction over cable simply because it was not broadcasting and did not come within its official purview. But regulation was ultimately inevitable, particularly because cable did have to use microwave facilities and because it was necessary to use AT&T pole attachments from receiving antennas to the home. The telephone company, it will be recalled, is a common carrier and is regulated by the FCC. In 1966, therefore, the Federal Communications Commission assumed regulatory powers over cable, and the Supreme Court subsequently affirmed that CATV was, indeed, an adjunct communications service requiring government regulation.

Immediately, the FCC appeared to antagonize proponents of cable by placing restrictive rules on the growth of CATV in the 100 largest broadcast markets. By 1972, the Commission announced its regulatory power over all non-broadcast channels—which went a step beyond jurisdiction over the transmission of broadcast signals. The results have not been difficult to foresee. The broadcast industry perceives cable television—and particularly pay-cable—as a threat. This threat may not be immediate, but the industry's reaction is what might be expected—an effort to protect its interests against ''siphoning'' of its network programs, its equity in copyrighted program substance, its present virtual monopoly over motion pictures and major sports events. The growing cable industry, on the other hand, insists that the FCC has favored the commercial broadcaster by restrictions on cable in major markets, for example, and by ruling that cable may not present motion pictures which have been in existence between three and ten years.

Despite the conflict, however, and the confusion over whether—and how much—cable should pay for the use of copyrighted material, the looming importance of national broadband communications cannot be denied. For cable is no longer a technical extension of broadcasting signals. It is in every way a new and exciting communications medium, capable of bringing education and information, as well as a whole new cultural perspective, to the American people—and particularly because of its increased channel capacity—to cultural minorities who do not receive the service they would like to have from conventional over-the-air broadcasting.

In a very significant way, broadband communications can make a very important contribution to a democratic and pluralistic society. Indeed, there are those who already express concern that the channel capability of cable not only may overwhelm us with information overload which we are not able to absorb, but that the information storage capacity of cable may present formidable problems of the individual's right to privacy. This could lead to much information and little genuine learning. It could also enhance the danger of surreptitious surveillance. Finally, there are those who quite seriously argue that cable eventually will fragmentize audiences and prove deleterious to the viability of our system of free, competitive commercial broadcasting.

On the other hand, advocates envision a positive and exciting future for cable. This new technology, for example, has the channel capacity to enhance a healthy democratic pluralism. It will bring programs not available on commercial broadcast channels. It will serve the young, the old and the various cultural minorities which are now deprived of recognition by current broadcast capabilities. It can, in short, once again provide the facilities for access and involvement by the public in the political, cultural and social process.

One developing aspect of cable is of particular concern to the commercial broadcasting industry. That is the growing potential of pay-cable. In this system, in addition to cable installation, the receiving homes pay an additional monthly fee of about $7 over and above the regular monthly cable service fee of approximately the same amount. Eventually, it is anticipated that patrons will pay a fee for the "unscrambling" of individual programs, instead of a flat monthly amount. Like cable itself, pay-cable is growing modestly by commercial broadcasting standards, but nevertheless it is growing. On both East and West coasts, homes are receiving new and recent motion pictures for a monthly fee, while nationwide approximately 200,000 homes have opened subscriptions to the reception of cable for a fee. Still far from an imminent danger to the broadcaster, pay-cable appears to be sufficiently important in the future to have engendered a massive public relations campaign by the industry trade association, the National Association of Broadcasters.

In the middle of 1975, however, an event occurred which may be portentous for the future. That was the commitment of several million dollars by Home Box Office, a subsidiary of the Time, Inc. organization, for a satellite communications system which would be operated on a fee basis. The intent is to present pay-TV movies, sports and other events of interest to possible subscribers. That the move was well-timed was indicated by the alacrity with which the Teleprompter Corp. and other cable network systems responded by indicating a desire to become affiliated with Home Box Office services. The basic implication of this move for the broadcaster is that it will provide still another step far beyond the original purview of cable, from the rural hinterland to the large, populous urban areas.

This whole range of broadband communications development must be viewed against the formidable presence of the Congress and the FCC, as well as the White House. However placid the growth of cable as compared to broadcasting, the fact is that the new industry is growing, and this growth has made imperative the need for a broad policy by the government. In January of 1974, there was submitted a long-awaited Report to the President by the Cabinet Committee on Cable Communications, under the direction of Clay T. Whitehead who had headed the controversial Office of Telecommunications Policy for the White House.

In a published letter to the President, Whitehead introduced the Report by stating that the goal of the study was "to insure that Cable would develop as a communications medium open and available to all Americans free of private or governmental barriers to its use." The plan was presented not as a "master" program, but a prospectus for integrating cable within the framework of our communications nexus in a way that would continue to insure and enhance a free flow of information.

The heart of the Whitehead Committee recommendations may be distilled into one basic concept: the separation of control of cable as a communications medium or technology from control of the messages carried on that medium. Thus, separation of technology from content would not entangle cable either with private monopolistic interests or with government control of substance. Cable, the Report stated, should provide channels for a multiplicity of programs, along with advertising and information, with no more restriction than is imposed on the print or film medium. Broadcasting, a regulated industry by the FCC, is not mentioned. The only caveats are the need to assure individual privacy from incursion and for patently offensive material to be restricted from home reception.

The change in the political complexion in Washington in 1974 and 1975, as well as the election of 1976, have worked to hold implementation of the Whitehead plan in abeyance. But professional observers welcomed the Report as a sensible, viable and attainable goal. The need is clearly for the Congress to act affirmatively and, either unilaterally or through the FCC, finally to set a firm course for a broadband communications system that would serve the public but which, at the same time, would also recognize the virtually free television services which commercial broadcasting has provided to the American people.

Further Developments: Cassettes

The so-called "communications revolution" does not end with broadband communications. Even the field of cable is still yielding to fruitful technological research and development. Experiments have been made, for example, with the use of the laser beam in order to eliminate some of the more cumbersome devices for home reception. By the 1980s cable enthusiasts predict a capacity of from 40 to 80 channels which, in addition to providing the public access not available through the present commercial and public broadcasting systems, will also allow for the receiver to develop two-way communication, dial up films, receive banking information, supermarket information, facsimile of news and wire reports, medical data, and a variety of other material.

Meanwhile, an interesting development in playback facilities is to be found in the experimental work with video cassettes. This field had a sudden flurry of activity in the 1960s when a number of companies developed competing systems of video recording. Unfortunately, these systems were incompatible with each other, thus confusing the market and holding further progress in abeyance. CBS, for example, produced and illustrated a dramatic process called Electronic Video Recording, better known as EVR. But RCA and Sony were also working on cassette systems which were technically at variance with each other and with EVR. Theoretically at least, the public could accept one system only, since not all three could be attached equally to the television receiver. The principle in all three, however, was the same—a visual recording device which could be plugged into the TV set, which used a cassette to show films and other programs which were to be shown on unused channels. Eventually, it is expected that the technology will be stabilized and standardized. At the outset, because of cost factors, the cassette system will be useful primarily to schools and other institutions, but eventually it will be priced within a range which the public can afford. This development is not expected before the 1980s.

Satellite Communications

The most dramatic communications development of the 1960s was the orbiting of the satellite, a technological hardware achievement which has shown consistent promise of making Marshall McLuhan's "global village" a reality. Although the United States has moved forward to an extent with domestic satellites, such as Western Union's system, "Westar," the major impetus has been in the exciting areas of international communications. By the mid-1980s technical experts look with confidence to transmission from the "bird," 22,500 miles above the equator, *directly* to the home receiver, without the intermediate step of ground stations. The implications of this futuristic phenomenon for networking are certainly immense, as are the possibilities for the developing countries of Asia and Africa which cannot at present afford the expense of building ground stations.

The first experimentation in satellites in this country was by the Army Signal Corps which, in 1946, beamed radar signals to the moon and received a "reply" in the form of an echo, the moon being a satellite of the earth. In the 1950s the Soviet Union was also active in satellite studies. When the Russians launched their first space-ships, TV pictures were sent to both East and West European networks by means of Intervision (the Soviet system) and Eurovision (system of the European Broadcasting Union).

The primary interest by the United States in a satellite system has been in military and industrial technology, at least to this date. One major usefulness of the satellite is its capacity to handle a multiplicity of telephone calls over international areas. In 1962, the President proposed that there be established a private corporation to run the satellite program, and in 1963, COMSAT (Communications Satellite Corporation) was established, with 50 per cent of the stock held by common carriers by authorization of the FCC, and 50 per cent by private investors.

In 1964, an organization known as Intelsat (International Telecommunications Satellite Consortium) was created, and foreign governments thereby invested in global communications technology. The first orbited satellite in 1965 was known as "Early Bird," or Intelsat I. Since then, three additional Intelsat satellite series have been launched, each revealing the enormous range and power of this "hardware" for global communications.

Unfortunately, there has been some criticism of so-called "cultural imperialism" by the United States which has been scored for emphasis on telephones for industrial purposes and for neglecting the broader telecommunications and educational potential of satellite communications. Because of the advanced technology of this country, such criticism was perhaps inevitable, but there is evidence also that the United States is not unmindful of the television potential of the satellite. One major problem is a recurring one—the presence of "cultural lag" or the inability of society to keep pace with the rush of technology.

One hopes, with some optimism, that within the next decade technological advances in communications will not only serve multinational industrial interests, but will realize the potential of television as a superb instrument for expanding educational and cultural perspectives and for creating greater understanding among nations.

A Selective Bibliography

SOCIAL ASPECTS OF MASS COMMUNICATION

Bagdikian, Ben H. *The Information Machines: Their Impact on and the Media*. New York: Harper & Row, 1971.

Baker, Robert H., and Sandra J. Ball. *Mass Media and Violence*. Washington, D.C.: U.S. Government Printing Office, 1969.

Berlo, David K. *The Process of Communication*. New York: Holt, Rinehart, & Winston, 1960.

DeFleur, Melvin. *Theories of Mass Communication*. 2nd ed. New York: David McKay, 1970.

Dexter, Lewis, and David Manning White. *People, Society and Mass Communications*. New York: Free Press, 1964.

Doob, Leonard. *Public Opinion and Propaganda*. Hamden Conn.: Archon Books, 1966.

Gerbner, George, and others (eds.). *Communications Technology and Social Policy: Understanding the New "Cultural Revolution."* New York: Wiley, 1973.

Glessing, Robert J., and William P. White. *Mass Media: The Invisible Environment*. Palo Alto, California: Science Research Associates, Inc., 1973.

Halloran, J. *The Effects of Mass Communication*. Leicester, England: Leicester University Press, 1965.

Innis, Harold. *The Bias of Communication*. Toronto: University of Toronto Press, 1951.

———. *Empire and Communication*. Oxford: Oxford University Press, 1951.

282

Katz, Elihu, and Paul F. Lazarsfeld. *Personal Influence.* New York: The Free Press, 1955.

Klapper, Joseph T. *The Effects of Mass Communication.* New York: Free Press, 1960.

Larsen, Otto N. (ed.). *Violence and the Mass Media.* Harper and Row, 1968.

Maddox, Brenda. *Beyond Babel: New Directions in Communications.* New York: Simon and Schuster, 1972.

McLuhan, Marshall. *The Gutenberg Galaxy: The Making of Typographic Man.* Toronto: University of Toronto Press, 1962.

————. *Understanding Media: The Extension of Man.* New York: Signet Books, 1964.

————. *The Mechanical Bride.* Boston: Beacon Press, 1951.

————. *The Medium is the Message.* New York: Bantam Books, 1967.

————, and Quentin Fiore. *War and Peace in the Global Village.* New York: Bantam Books, 1968.

Rosenthal, Raymond, (ed.). *McLuhan: Pro and Con.* New York: Funk and Wagnalls, 1968.

Schiller, Herbert. *Mass Communications and American Empire.* New York: Augustus M. Kelley, 1970.

————. *The Mind Managers.* Boston: Beacon Press, 1973.

Shannon, Claude E. and Warren Weaver. *The Mathematical Theory of Communication.* Urbana: The University of Illinois Press, 1949.

Stearn, Gerald E., (ed.). *McLuhan: Hot and Cool.* New York: Signet Books, 1967.

Steinberg, Charles. *The Communicative Arts.* New York: Hastings House, 1970.

————, (ed.). *Mass Media and Communication.* New York: Hastings House, 1972.

Weiner Norbert. *Cybernetics: Or Control and Communication in the Animal and the Machine.* New York: John Wiley and Sons, 1948.

Wright, Charles R. *Mass Communication: A Sociological Perspective.* 2nd. edition. New York: Random House, 1975.

THE AMERICAN PRESS

Adler, Ruth. *A Day in the Life of The New York Times.* Philadelphia and New York: J. B. Lippincott, 1971.

Agee, Warren K. (ed.). *Mass Media in a Free Society.* Lawrence: University Press of Kansas, 1969.

Aronson, James. *The Press and the Cold War*. New York: The Bobbs-Merrill Co., Inc., 1970.

———. *Deadline for the Media: Today's Challenges to Press, TV and Radio*. Indianapolis: Bobbs-Merrill, 1973.

Bagdikian, Ben H. *The Effete Conspiracy: And Other Crimes by the Press*. New York: Harper and Row, 1972.

Barrett, James W. *Joseph Pulitzer and His World*. New York: Vanguard Press, Inc., 1941.

Berger, Mayer. *The Story of the New York Times, 1851–1951*. New York: Simon and Schuster, 1951.

Bernstein, Carl and Bob Woodward. *All the President's Men*. New York: Simon and Schuster, 1974.

Bruce, Robert V. *Bell: Alexander Graham Bell and the Conquest of Solitude*. Boston: Little, Brown and Co., 1973.

Brucker, Herbert. *Communication Is Power: Unchanging Values in a Changing Journalism*. New York: Oxford University Press, 1973.

Emery, Edwin. *The Press and America: An Interpretative History of the Mass Media*. 3rd. ed. Englewood Cliffs, N.J.: Prentice-Hall, Inc., 1972.

Gerald, J. Edward. *The Social Responsibility of the Press*. Minneapolis: University of Minnesota Press, 1963.

Gross, Gerald. *The Responsibility of the Press*. New York: Fleet Publishing, 1966.

Hohenberg, John. *The News Media: A Journalist Looks at his Profession*. New York: Holt, Rinehart and Winston, 1968.

Hynds, Ernest C. *American Newspapers in the 1970's*. New York: Hastings House, 1975.

Keogh, James. *President Nixon and the Press*. New York: Funk & Wagnalls, 1972.

Kobre, Sidney. *Development of American Journalism*. Dubuque, Iowa: Wm. C. Brown Company, 1969.

———. *Modern American Journalism*. Tallahassee, Florida: Florida State University, 1959.

———. *The Yellow Press and Gilded Age Journalism*. Tallahassee, Florida: Florida State University, 1964.

Lacy, Dan. *Freedom and Communications*. Urbana: University of Illinois Press. 1961.

Lindstrom, Carl E. *The Fading American Newspaper*. New York: Doubleday, 1960.

Merrill, John C. *The Elite Press: Great Newspapers of the World*. New York: Pitman Publishing Corp., 1968.

Minor, Dale. *The Information War*. New York: Hawthorne Books, Inc., 1970.

Mott, Frank L. *American Journalism, A History: 1690–1960*. 3rd. ed. New York: The Macmillan Company, 1962.

Neilson, Winthrop and Frances. *What's News-Dow Jones: Story of The Wall Street Journal*. Radnor, Pa.: Chilton Book Co., 1973.

Nixon, Raymond S. *Henry W. Grady: Spokesman of the New South*. New York: Alfred A. Knopf, Inc., 1943.

Pollard, James E. *The Presidents and the Press*. New York: Macmillan, 1947.

———. *The Presidents and the Press: Truman to Johnson*. Washington: Public Affairs Press, 1964.

Rivers, William. *The Opinionmakers*. Boston: Beacon Press, 1965.

Schapsmeier, Edward and Frederick. *Walter Lippmann: Philosopher-Journalist*. Washington, D.C.: Public Affairs Press, 1969.

Swanberg, W. A. *Pulitzer*. New York: Charles Scribner's Sons, 1967.

Talese, Gay. *The Kingdom and the Power*. New York: The World Publishing Company, 1969.

Tebbel, John. *The Compact History of the American Newspaper*. New York: Hawthorne Books, Inc., 1969.

———. *The Life and Good Times of William Randolph Hearst*. New York: Dutton, 1952.

The Wall Street Journal: The First Seventy-Five Years. New York: Dow Jones & Company, Inc., 1964.

MOTION PICTURES

Agee, James. *Agee On Film*. New York: McDowell, Obolensky, Inc., 1958.

Barsam, Richard. *Nonfiction Film*. New York: E. P. Dutton, 1973.

Behlmer, Rudy (ed.). *Memo from David O. Selznick*. New York: The Viking Press, 1972.

Bluem, A. William and Jason Squire, (eds.). *The Movie Business*. New York: Hastings House, 1972.

Bobker, Lee R. *Elements of Film*. New York: Harcourt, Brace & World, 1969.

Brownlow, Kevin. *The Parade's Gone By*. New York: Knopf, 1968.

Clarens, Carlos. *An Illustrated History of the Horror Film*. New York: G. P. Putnam's Sons, 1967.

Cogley, John. *Report on Blacklisting, Vol. I, The Movies*. New York: Fund for the Republic, 1956.

Conant, Michael. *Antitrust in the Motion Picture Industry*. Berkeley, Calif.: University of California Press, 1960.

Crowther, Bosley. *The Lion's Share*. New York: Dutton, 1957.

Dale, Edgar. *The Content of Motion Pictures*. New York: The Macmillan Company, 1935.

Day, Beth. *This Was Hollywood*. Garden City, New York: Doubleday and Co., Inc., 1960.

Farber, Steven. *The Movie Rating Game*. Washington, D.C.: Public Affairs Press, 1972.

Fielding, Raymond. *The American Newsreel, 1911–1967*. Norman: The University of Oklahoma Press, 1972.

French, Philip. *The Movie Moguls*. Chicago: Henry Regnery Company, 1969.

Goodman, Ezra. *The Fifty-Year Decline and Fall of Hollywood*. New York: Simon and Schuster, 1961.

Guback, Thomas H. *International Film Industry*. Bloomington: Indiana University Press, 1969.

Halliwell, Leslie (ed.). *The Filmgoer's Companion*, 4th ed. New York: Hill and Wang, 1974.

Hampton, Benjamin B. *History of the American Film Industry*. New York: Dover Publications, 1970.

Happé, L. Bernard. *Basic Motion Picture Technology*. 2nd ed. New York: Hastings House, 1975.

Haskell, Molly. *From Reverence to Rape: The Treatment of Women in the Movies*. New York: Holt, Rinehart and Winston, 1974.

Hendricks, Gordon. *Eadweard Muybridge: The Father of the Motion Picture*. New York: Viking Press, 1975.

Inglis, Ruth. *Freedom of the Movies*. Chicago: The University of Chicago Press, 1947.

Jacobs, Lewis. *The Emergence of Film Art*. New York: Hopkinson & Blake, 1969.

———. *The Rise of the American Film*. New York: Teachers College Press, 1967.

Jobes, Gertrude. *Motion Picture Empire*. Hampton, Conn.: Archon Books, 1966.

Kahn, Gordon. *Hollywood on Trial*. New York: Boni and Gaer, 1948.

Knight, Arthur. *The Liveliest Art*. New York: Macmillan, 1957.

Limbacher, James. *Four Aspects of the Film*. New York: Brussel and Brussel, 1968.

Lindgren, Ernest. *The Art of Film*. New York: Macmillan, 1963.

MacCann, Richard Dyer. *Hollywood in Transition*. Boston: Houghton, Mifflin, 1962.

MacGowan, Kenneth. *Behind the Screen*. New York: Delacorte Press, 1965.

Mapp, Edward. *Blacks in American Films: Today and Yesterday*. Metchen, N.J.: The Scarecrow Press, Inc., 1972.

Mast, Gerald. *A Short History of the Movies.* New York: Pegasus Books, 1971.

Michael, Paul. *The Academy Awards: A Pictorial History.* New York: Crown Publishers, Inc., 1972.

Noble, Peter. *The Negro in Films.* Port Washington, N.Y.: Kennikat Press, 1969.

Powdermaker, Hortense. *Hollywood: The Dream Factory.* London: Secker and Warburg, Ltd., 1951.

Ramsaye, Terry. *A Million and One Nights.* New York: Simon and Schuster, 1926; London, Frank Cass, 1964.

Randall, Richard. *Censorship of the Movies.* Madison: The University of Wisconsin Press, 1970.

Rosen, Marjorie. *Popcorn Venus: Women Movies and the American Dream.* New York: Coward, McCann and Geoghgan, 1973.

Rosten, Leo. *Hollywood: The Movie Colony, The Movie Makers.* New York: Harcourt, Brace and Co., 1941.

Schmach, Murray. *The Face on the Cutting Room Floor.* New York: William Morrow, and Co., 1964.

Stedman, Raymond W. *The Serials: Suspense and Drama by Installment.* Norman: The University of Oklahoma Press, 1971.

Thomas, Bob. *King Cohn: Life and Times of Harry Cohn.* New York: G. P. Putnam's Sons, 1967.

———. *Selznick.* Garden City, New York: Doubleday and Company, Inc., 1970.

———. *Thalberg: Life and Legend.* New York: Bantam Books, 1970.

Tyler, Parker. *Magic and Myth of the Movies.* New York: Henry Holt, 1947.

Walker, Alexander. *The Celluloid Sacrifice.* London: Michael Joseph, 1966; New York: Hawthorn Books, 1967.

Zierold, Norman. *The Moguls.* New York: Coward McCann, Inc., 1969.

Zinman, David. *Saturday Afternoon at the Bijou.* New Rochelle, N.Y.: Arlington House, 1973.

BROADCASTING

Abramson, Albert. *Electronic Motion Pictures: A History of the Television Camera.* Berkeley: University of California Press, 1955.

Agnew, C. M., and Neil O'Brien. *Television Advertising.* New York: McGraw-Hill, 1948.

Archer, Gleason L. *Big Business and Radio.* New York: American Historical Company, 1939.

———. *History of Radio to 1926*. New York: American Historical Society, Inc., 1938.

Arlen, Michael J. *Living-room War*. New York: Viking Press, 1969.

Banning, William. *Commercial Broadcasting Pioneer: The WEAF Experiment, 1922–1926*. Cambridge, Massachusetts: Harvard University Press, 1946.

Barnouw, Eric. *A Tower in Babel : A History of Broadcasting in the United States to 1933*. New York: Oxford, 1966.

———. *The Golden Web: A History of Broadcasting in the United States 1933–53*. New York: Oxford, 1968.

———. *The Image Empire*. New York: Oxford University Press, 1970.

Beck, A. H. W. *Words and Waves: An Introduction to Electrical Communications*. New York: McGraw-Hill World University Library, 1967.

Bluem, A. William. *Documentary in American Television: Form, Function, Method*. New York: Hastings House, 1965.

———. *Religious Television Programs: A Study of Relevance*. New York: Hastings House, 1969.

Blum, Daniel. *A Pictorial History of Television*. New York: Chilton, 1959.

Blumer, Jay and Denis McQuail. *Television in Politics*. Chicago: University of Chicago Press, 1969.

Bower, Robert T. *Television and the Public*. New York: Holt, Rinehart, and Winston, 1973.

Brown, Les. *Television: The Business Behind the Box*. New York: Harcourt, Brace, Jovanovich, Inc., 1971.

Buxton, F., and B. Owen. *Radio's Golden Age*. New York: Easton Valley Press, 1966.

Cantril, H. *The Invasion from Mars*. Princeton, N.J.: Princeton, 1940.

Carnegie Commission on Educational Television. *Public Television, a Program for Action*. New York: Bantam Books, 1967.

Chase, Francis. *Sound and Fury: An Informal History of Broadcasting*. New York: Harper, 1942.

Chester, Edward. *Radio, Television and American Politics*. New York: Sheed and Ward, 1969.

Chester, Giraud, *et al. Television and Radio* 4th ed. New York: Appleton-Century-Crofts, 1971.

Cirino, Robert. *Don't Blame the People: How the News Media Use Bias, Distortion and Censorship to Manipulate Public Opinion*. New York: Random House, 1971.

Cogley, John. *Report on Blacklisting*, Vol. II, Radio-Television. New York: The Fund for the Republic, 1956.

Cole, Barry G., (ed.). *Television*. New York: Free Press, 1970.

DeForest, L. *Father of Radio*. New York: Wilcox and Follett, 1950.

Dunlap, Orrin E. *The Story of Radio*. 2nd ed. New York: The Dial Press, 1935.

———. *Dunlap's Radio and Television Almanac*. New York: Harper, 1951.

Dryer, S. *Radio in Wartime*. New York: Greenberg, 1942.

Ellison, Harlan. *The Glass Teat*. New York: Ace Publishing Corporation, 1970.

Emery, Walter B. *Broadcasting and Government,* 2nd. ed. East Lansing: Michigan State University Press, 1971.

Epstein, Edward Jay. *News From Nowhere: Television and the News*. New York: Random House, 1973.

Fang, I. E. *Television News,* 2nd ed. New York: Hastings House, 1972.

Faulk, John Henry, *Fear on Trial* New York: Simon and Schuster, 1964.

Friendly Fred W. *Due to Circumstances Beyond Our Control . . .* New York: Random House, 1967.

Garnett, Bernard E. *How Soulful is "Soul" Radio?* Nashville, Tenn. 37212: Race Relations Information Center, 1970.

Gordon, G. N. *Educational Television*. New York: Center for Applied Research in Education, 1965.

Green, Maury. *TV News: Anatomy and Process*. Belmont Calif.: Wadsworth, 1969.

Gross, Ben. *I Looked and I Listened*. rev. ed. New York: Arlington House, 1970.

Harmon, Jim. *The Great Radio Heroes*. New York: Doubleday, 1967.

Head, Sydney, W. *Broadcasting In America: A Survey of Television and Radio*. 3rd ed. Boston: Houghton Mifflin, 1976.

Hill, H. E. *The National Association of Educational Broadcasters: A History*. Urbana, Ill.: National Association of Educational Broadcasters, 1954.

Himmelweit, Hilde T., et al. *Television and the Child*. London: Oxford University Press, 1958.

Hulteng, John L, and Roy Paul Nelson. *The Fourth Estate: An Informal Appraisal of the News and Opinion Media*. New York: Harper & Row, 1971.

Jaffe, Leonard. *Communications in Space*. New York: Holt, Rinehart & Winston, 1966.

Johnson, Nicholas. *How to Talk Back to Your Television Set*. Boston: Little, Brown, 1970.

Jolly, W. P. *Marconi* New York: Stein and Day, 1972.

Kahn, Frank J. (ed.). *Documents of American Broadcasting*. 2nd ed. New York: Appleton-Century-Crofts, 1973.

Kempner, Stanley. *Television Encyclopedia*. New York: Fairchild, 1948.

Kendrick, Alexander. *Prime Time*. Boston: Little, Brown, 1969.

Kuhns, William. *Why We Watch Them: Interpreting TV Shows*. New York: Benzinger, 1970.

Landry, Robert J. *This Fascinating Radio Business*. Indianapolis: Bobbs-Merrill, 1946.

Lang, Kurt, and Gladys Engle Lang. *Politics and Television*. Chicago: Quadrangle, 1968.

LeRoy, David J., and Christopher H. Sterling (eds.). *Mass News: Practices, Controversies, Alternatives*. Englewood Cliffs, N.J.: Prentice Hall, 1972.

Lessing, Lawrence. *Man of High Fidelity: Edwin Howard Armstrong* 2nd ed. New York: Bantam Books, 1969.

Lichty, Lawrence W., and Malachi C. Topping. *American Broadcasting: A Source Book on the History of Radio and Television*. New York: Hastings House, 1975.

Lyle, Jack. *The News in Megalopolis*. San Francisco: Chandler, 1967.

Lyons, Eugene. *David Sarnoff*. New York: Harper and Row, 1966.

MacLean, Roderick. *Television in Education*. New York: Barnes & Noble, 1968.

Macneil, Robert. *The People Machine: The Influence of Television on American Politics*. New York: Harper & Row, 1968.

Mayer, Martin. *About Television*. New York: Harper & Row, 1972.

McGinniss, Joe. *The Selling of the President*. New York: Trident, 1969.

McNicol, Donald. *Radio's Conquest of Space*. New York: Murray Hill Books, Inc., 1946.

Metz, Robert. *CBS: Reflections in a Bloodshot Eye*. Chicago: Playboy Press, 1975.

Mickelson, Sig. *The Electric Mirror: Politics in an Age of Television*. New York: Dodd, Mead, 1972.

Miller, Merle, and Evan Rhodes. *Only You, Dick Daring!* New York: Sloane, 1964.

Noll, Roger G., Merton J. Peck and John J. McGowan. *Economic Aspects of Television Regulation*. Washington, D.C.: The Brookings Institute, 1973.

Owen, Bill and Frank Buxton. *Radio's Golden Age: The Programs and the Personalities*. New York: Easton Valley Press, 1966.

Quaal, Ward L., and James A. Brown. *Broadcast Management: Radio and Television*. 2nd ed. New York: Hastings House, 1976.

Rubin, B. *Political Television*. Belmont, Calif.: Wadsworth, 1967.

Sampson, Anthony. *The Sovereign State of ITT*. New York: Stein and Day, 1973.

Sanger, Elliott M. *Rebel in Radio: The Story of WQXR*. New York: Hastings House, 1973.

Schulman, Arthur, and Roger Youman. *How Sweet It Was—Television: A Pictorial Commentary*. New York: Chorecrest, 1966.

Schurick, E. P. J. *The First Quarter Century of American Broadcasting*. Kansas City: Midland Publishing Co., 1946.

Siepmann, Charles A. *Radio, Television and Society*. New York: Oxford University Press, 1950.

———. *Radio's Second Chance*. Boston: Little, Brown, 1946.

Skornia, Harry J. *Television and the News*. Palo Alto, Calif.: Pacific Books, 1968.

———. *Television and Society: An Inquest and Agenda for Improvement*. New York: McGraw-Hill, 1965.

——— and J. Kitson (eds.). *Problems and Controversies in Television and Radio*. Palo Alto, Calif.: Pacific Books, 1968.

Small, William. *To Kill a Messenger: Television News and the Real World*. New York: Hastings House, 1970.

Stanley, Robert H. *The Broadcast Industry: An Examination of Major Issues*. New York: Hastings House, 1975.

Steinberg, Charles (ed.). *Broadcasting: The Critical Challenges*. New York: Hastings House, 1974.

Summers, Harrison B. *A Thirty Year History of Programs Carried on National Radio Networks in the United States: 1926–1956*. Columbus: Ohio State University Department of Speech, 1958.

Taylor, Sherrill (ed.). *Radio Programming in Action*. New York: Hastings House, 1967.

Thomey, Tedd. *The Glorious Decade*. New York: Ace Books, 1971.

Tuchman, Gayle (ed.). *The TV Establishment: Programming for Power and Profit*. Englewood Cliffs, N.J.: Prentice Hall, Inc., 1974.

Upton, Monroe. *Inside Electronics: The How and Why of Radio, TV, Stereo and Hi-fi*. New York: Signet Books, 1965.

Vaughn, Robert. *Only Victims: A Study of Show Business Blacklisting*. New York: G. P. Putnam's Sons, 1972.

Weinberg, M. *Television in America: The Morality of Hard Cash*. New York: Ballantine Books, 1962.

White, Llewellyn. *The American Radio: A Report on the Broadcasting Industry in the United States from the Commission on Freedom of the Press*. Chicago: University of Chicago Press, 1947.

Whitfield, Stephen E., and Gene Roddenberry. *The Making of Startrek*. New York: Ballentine, 1968.

Wyckoff, G. *The Image Candidates*. New York: Macmillan, 1968.

MASS COMMUNICATIONS AND THE LAW

Ashley, Paul P. *Say It Safely: Legal Limits in Publishing, Radio, and Television*. 4th ed. Seattle: University of Washington Press, 1969.

Borchardt, Kurt. *Structure and Performance of the U.S. Communications In-*

dustry: Government Regulation and Company Planning. Boston: Harvard University Graduate School of Business Administration, Division of Research, 1970.

Bowers, Claude. *Jefferson in Power*. Boston: Houghton Mifflin Company, 1967.

Chafee, Zechariah. *Government and Mass Communications*. [two vols.] Chicago: University of Chicago Press, 1947.

Chenery, William I. *Freedom of the Press*. New York: Harcourt, Brace & World, 1955.

Cherington, Paul W., Leon Hirsch and Robert Brandwein (eds.). *Television Station Ownership: A Case Study of Federal Agency Regulation*. New York: Hastings House, 1971.

Clark, David G., and Earl R. Hutchinson (eds.). *Mass Media and the Law: Freedom and Restraint*. New York: Wiley/Interscience, 1970.

Commission on Freedom of the Press. *A Free and Responsible Press*. Chicago: University of Chicago Press, 1947.

Devol, Kenneth (ed.) *Mass Media and the Supreme Court: The Legacy of the Warren Years*. 2nd ed. New York: Hastings House, 1976.

Edelman, Jacob Murray. *The Licensing of Radio Services in the United States: 1927 to 1947*. Urbana: University of Illinois Press, 1950.

Emery, Walter P. *Broadcasting and Government: Regulations and Responsibilities*. rev. ed. East Lansing: Michigan State University Press, 1971.

Gillmor, Donald M. *Free Press and Fair Trial*. Washington, D.C.: Public Affairs Press, 1966.

Gilmor, Donald M., and Jerome A. Barron. *Mass Communication Law: Cases and Comment*. 2nd ed. St. Paul: West Publishing Company, 1974.

Hachten, William A. *The Supreme Court on Freedom of the Press: Decisions and Dissents*. Ames: Iowa State University Press, 1968.

Kahn, Frank J. (ed.). *Documents of American Broadcasting*. 2nd. ed. New York: Appleton-Century-Crofts, 1973.

Kittross, John M. and Kenneth Harwood (eds.) *Free & Fair: Courtroom Access and the Fairness Doctrine*. Philadelphia: APBE, 1970.

Koenig, Allen E. (ed.) *Broadcasting and Bargaining: Labor Relations in Radio and Television*. Madison: University of Wisconsin Press, 1970.

Kohlmeier, Louis M., Jr. *The Regulators: Watchdog Agencies and the Public Interest*. New York: Harper and Row, 1969.

Krasnow, Erwin G., and Lawrence D Longley. *The Politics of Regulation*. New York: St. Martin's Press, 1973.

Levin, Harvey J. *The Invisible Resource: Use and Regulation of the Radio Spectrum*. Baltimore: Johns Hopkins University Press, 1971.

———. *Broadcast Regulation and Joint Ownership of Media*. New York: New York University Press, 1960.

Lichty, Lawrence W., and Malachi C. Topping. *American Broadcasting: A Source Book on the History of Radio and Television.* New York: Hastings House, 1975.

Minow, Newton M. *Equal Time: The Private Broadcaster and the Public Interest.* New York: Atheneum, 1969.

Mitau, G. Theodore. *Decade of Decision.* New York: Charles Scribner's Sons, 1967.

Nelson, Harold L, and Dwight L. Teeter, Jr. *Law of Mass Communications: Freedom and Control of Print and Broadcast Media.* 2nd ed. Mineola, N.Y.: Foundation Press, 1973.

Pember, Don. *Privacy and the Press: The Law, the Mass Media, and the First Amendment.* Seattle: University of Washington Press, 1972.

Pennybacker, John H., and Waldo W. Braden. *Broadcasting and the Public Interest.* New York: Random House, Inc., 1969.

Phelan, John (ed.). *Communications Control: Readings in the Motives and Structures of Censorship.* New York: Sheed & Ward, 1969.

Phelps, Robert and Douglas Hamilton. *Libel: A Guide to Rights, Risks, Responsibilities.* London: Collier Macmillan Ltd., 1966.

Rucker, Bryce. *The First Freedom.* Carbondale: Southern Illinois University Press, 1968.

GLOBAL COMMUNICATIONS

Bauer, Raymond A., Alex Inkeles and Clyde Kluckhohn. *How the Soviet System Works.* Cambridge, Massachusetts: Harvard University Press, 1957.

Briggs, Asa. *The History of Broadcasting in the United Kingdom.* Vol. 1, *The Birth of Broadcasting;* Vol. 2, *The Golden Age of Wireless.* London: Oxford University Press, 1965.

British Broadcasting Corporation: BBC Handbook (Published Annually)

Buzek, Antony. *How the Communist Press Works.* New York: Frederick A. Praeger, 1964.

Cherry, Colin. *World Communication: Threat or Promise.* New York: Wiley Interscience, 1971.

Coase, R. H. *British Broadcasting: A Study in Monopoly.* Cambridge, Massachusetts: Harvard University Press, 1950.

Cohen, Bernard C. *The Press and Foreign Policy.* Princeton, New Jersey: Princeton University Press, 1963.

Columbia Broadcasting System. *Communications by Satellite.* New York: Twentieth Century Fund, 1969.

Davidson, W. Phillips. *International Political Communication.* New York: Frederick A. Praeger, 1965.

Deutschmann, Paul *et al. Communication and Social Change in Latin America*. New York: Praeger, 1968.

Durham, F. Gayle. *News Broadcasting on Soviet Radio and Television*. Cambridge: Center for International Studies, Massachusetts Institute of Technology, 1965.

Emery, Walter. *National and International Systems of Broadcasting*. East Lansing: Michigan State University Press, 1969.

Fischer, Heinz-Dietrich and John C. Merrill (eds.). *International Communication: Media-Channels-Functions*. New York: Hastings House, 1970.

Green, Timothy. *The Universal Eye*. New York: Stein and Day, 1972.

Harris, Robert D. G. *A Report from Spain: The Press in an Authoritarian State*. Los Angeles: University of California Press, 1964.

Hopkins, Mark W. *Mass Media in the Soviet Union*. New York: Pegasus Books, 1970.

Inkeles, A. *Public Opinion in Soviet Russia*. Cambridge: Harvard University Press, 1950.

King, Vincent S. *A General Study of the Channels of Communications Between Communist China and the Western World*. Cambridge: Center for International Studies, Massachusetts Institute of Technology, 1964.

Kruglak, Theodore. *The Foreign Correspondents*. Geneva: E. Droz, 1955.

———. *The Two Faces of Tass*. Minneapolis: University of Minnesota Press, 1962.

Lerner, David, and Wilbur Schramm. *Communications and Change in Developing Countries*. Honolulu: East-West Center Press, 1967.

Maddison, John. *Radio and Television in Literacy*. Paris: UNESCO, 1971.

Markel, Lester, (ed.). *Public Opinion and Foreign Policy*. New York: Harper, 1949.

Merrill, John C. *The Elite Press: Great Newspapers of the World*. New York: Pitman Publishing Corp., 1968.

———, Carter R. Bryan and Marvin Alisky. *The Foreign Press*. Baton Rouge, La.: State University Press, 1970.

NHK. *The History of Broadcasting in Japan*. Tokyo: NHK Press, 1967.

Paulu, Burton. *British Broadcasting in Transition*. Minneapolis: University of Minnesota Press, 1961.

———. *Radio and Television Broadcasting on the European Continent*. Minneapolis: University of Minnesota Press, 1967.

Reston, James. *The Press and World Affairs*. Minneapolis, 1949.

Schiller, Herbert. *Mass Communications and American Empire*. New York: Augustus M. Kelly, 1969.

Schramm, Wilbur. *Mass Media and National Development*. Stanford, Calif.: Stanford University Press and Paris: UNESCO, 1964.

Siebert, Fred, Theodore Peterson and Wilbur Schramm. *Four Theories of the Press*. Evanston, Ill.: University of Illinois Press, 1956.

Sommerland, E. Lloyd. *The Press in Developing Countries*. Sydney: Sydney University Press, 1966.

UNESCO. *Communication in the Space Age: The Use of Satellites by the Mass Media*. Paris: UNESCO, 1968.

Wells, Alan. *Picture-tube Imperialism? The Impact of U.S. Television on Latin America*. Maryknoll, N.Y.: Orbis Books, 1972.

—— (ed.). *Mass Communication: A World View*. Palo Alto, Calif.: National Press Book, 1974.

World Radio TV Handbook 1975, 29th ed. Soliljeve, Denmark: Billboard, A. G., 1975.

PUBLIC RELATIONS AND ADVERTISING

Agnew, Clark M. and Neil O'Brien. *Television Advertising*. New York: Mc-Graw-Hill, 1958.

Backman, Jules. *Advertising and Competition*. New York: New York University Press, 1967.

Bernays, Edward I. *Biography of an Idea: Memoirs of a Public Relations Counsel*. New York: Simon & Schuster, 1965.

Bettinghaus, Erwin P. *Persuasive Communication*. New York: Holt, Rinehart and Winston, 1968.

Brown, J. A. C. *Techniques of Persuasion*. Baltimore: Penguin Books, 1963.

Canfield, Bertrand R. and Frazier Moore. *Public Relations: Principles and Problems*. 5th ed. Homewood, Ill.: Richard D. Irwin, 1973.

Center, Allen H. *Public Relations Practices: Case Studies*. Englewood Cliffs, N.J.: Prentice-Hall, 1975.

Clark, David G., and Earl R. Hutchinson. *Media and the Law*. New York: John Wiley & Sons, 1970.

Cutlip, Scott M. *A Public Relations Bibliography*. Madison: University of Wisconsin Press, 1965.

——, and Allen H. Center. *Effective Public Relations*. 4th ed. Englewood Cliffs, N.J.: Prentice-Hall, 1971.

Dichter, Ernest. *The Strategy of Desire*. Garden City, N.Y.: Doubleday, 1960.

Dunn, S. Watson. *Advertising: Its Role in Modern Marketing*. New York: Holt, Rinehart & Winston, 1969.

Galbraith, John K. *The Affluent Society*. New York: Houghton Mifflin, 1958.

Lesly Philip, (ed.). *Public Relations Handbook*. 6th ed. New York: Prentice-Hall, 1971.

Lucas, D. B., and S. H. Britt. *Advertising Psychology and Research*. New York: McGraw-Hill, 1950.

Machiavelli, Nicolo. *The Prince*. W. K. Marriott, trans. New York: E. P. Dutton, 1958.

Mayer, Martin. *Madison Avenue, U.S.A.* New York: Harper and Brothers, 1958.

Pearce, Michael, Scott M. Cunningham and Avon Miller. *Appraising the Economic and Social Effects of Advertising: A Review of Issues and Evidence*. Cambridge, Mass.: Marketing Science Institute, 1971.

Steinberg, Charles. *The Creation of Consent: Public Relations in Practice*. New York: Hastings House, 1975.

Stevenson, Howard (ed.), *Handbook of Public Relations*. 2nd ed. New York: McGraw Hill, 1971.

Turner, E. S. *The Shocking History of Advertising*. New York: Ballantine Books, 1953.

Wood, James Playsted. *The Story of Advertising*. New York: Ronald Press, 1958.

INDEX

"Queen Elizabeth" (film), 49
"Queen Kelly" (film), 58
Quigley, Martin, 80
Quiz programs, TV, 163-64

Radio, 101, 107; advertising on, 120, 197, 267, 270; black, 250; FM, 147; as "hot" medium, 7; news on, 116-17; and number of sets, 101; pioneers of, 101-05; rating services for, 120-22; shows on, 114-16; and *War of the Worlds* broadcast, 10-11; during wartime, 105, 118-20; *see also* Broadcasting; Networks
Radio Act, 123, 124, 125, 126
Radio City Music Hall, 51
Radio Code, NAB, 179, 180, 197
Radio Corporation of America (RCA), 58, 106, 107, 109, 110, 119, 125, 131, 146, 147, 148, 150, 151, 279
Radio Keith Orpheum (RKO), 56, 58, 59, 63, 67, 68, 72, 94, 110, 152
Radio Manufacturers Association, 147
Radio-Television News Directors Assocation (RTNDA), 224
Radulovich, Milo, 155
Ram's Horn, The, 244
Random House, 110
Rappe, Virginia, 78
Rating services, 120-22, 170-73, 264, 270
Raymond, Henry J., 26, 28, 30
Reader's Digest, The, 43
"Real McCoys, The" (TV program), 203
"Red Channels" reports, 157-58, 160
Red Lion Broadcasting Company v. *FCC*, 136, 224
Reeves, Steve, 70
Reid, Wallace, 78
Renaissance, 16, 17
Renoir, Jean, 53
Reporter's privilege, 224-26
Republic Pictures Corporation, 162
Reston, James, 29
Reuters news service, 230, 231

"Revenge of Daybreak" (film), 214
Revue Productions, 61, 128
Ridder Publications, Inc., 39
Rise and Fall of the Third Reich, The (Shirer), 117
"Rise and Shine" (radio program), 141
River, Charles, 138, 139
Rivington, James "Jemmy," 23
Rivoli Theatre, 51, 55
RKO Teleradio Pictures, Inc., 113, 162, 163
Robinson, Edward G., 59, 63
Robinson, Edward G., Jr., 141
Rockefeller, John D., 259
Rogers, Ginger, 66
Rogers, Lela, 66
Rogers, Roy, 162
Rogers, William P., 39, 138
Roget, Peter Mark, 45
Roland, Gilbert, 60
Rolle, Esther, 167
Roosevelt, Franklin D., 147, 258
Roper organization, 252, 262
Rosenbloom, George, 222
Rosenbloom v. *Metromedia, Inc.*, 222, 223
Rossellini, Roberto, 213
Roth, Samuel, 215
Roth v. *United States*, 215, 216, 217
Rothafel, Samuel, 51
Rowan, Dan, 165
Rowell, George, 268
Roxy Theatre, 51, 52
"Royal Gelatine Hour" (radio program), 115
Rule, Janice, 160
Russell, Jane, 94, 95
Russia, *see* Soviet Union
Ryan, J. Harold, 118
"Ryan's Daughter" (film), 99

Safire, William, 29
St. Louis Chronicle, 38
St. Louis Globe-Democrat, 38
St. Louis Post-Dispatch, 35, 40
Salisbury, Harrison, 29
San Francisco Call-Bulletin, 32
San Francisco Chronicle, 32

San Francisco Examiner, 32, 36, 39
"Sanford and Son" (TV program), 167, 168
Sarnoff, David, 58, 104, 106, 110, 119, 125, 147, 150
Sarnoff, Robert, 110
Satellite communications, 231, 232, 239, 240, 277, 280-81
Saturday Evening Post, 269
Saturday Review, 156, 165
Schary, Dore, 72, 73
Schechter, A. A., 116
Schenck, Charles T., 209
Schenck, Joseph, 57, 58, 62
Schenck, Nicholas, 57, 72, 73
Schenck v. *United States*, 209
Schneider, John A., 112
Schulberg, Benjamin, 59
Screen Actors Guild, 76
Screen Gems, Inc., 62, 72, 75, 162, 163
Scripps newspapers, 25, 30, 38
Scripps-Howard newspapers, 38
Sedition Act (1798), 208, 209
"See It Now" (CBS news documentary), 155-57
Seeger, Pete, 161
Seldes, Gilbert, 156
"Selling of the Pentagon, The" (TV program), 242
Selznick, David O., 58, 62, 64
Selznick, Lewis J., 79
Sengstacke, Robert S., 246
Sennett, Mack, 49, 50
"Sergeant York" (film), 59
Sevareid, Eric, 117
Shakespeare, Frank, 233
Shannon, Claude, 5
Shayon, Robert Lewis, 165
Sheen, Fulton, 151
Sheridan, Ann, 59
Sherman Anti-Trust Act, 67, 163
Sherwood, Robert, 118
Shirer, William L., 117
Shockley, William, 148
Shurlock, Geoffrey, 95
Silverman, Fred, 166 and *n.*
Skelton, Red, 120, 173
Skouras, George, 59, 68
Skouras, Spyros, 57, 59
Slaby, Adolphus, 102
Slander, 220, 221
Smith, Kate, 119
"Smothers Brothers" (TV program), 161, 176-78